D1806794

Multimodal Transport Security

COMPARATIVE PERSPECTIVES ON TRANSPORTATION
SECURITY

Series Editors: Joseph S. Szyliowicz, *University of Denver, USA* and Luca Zamparini, *University of Salento, Italy*

Focus on security has dramatically sharpened at all levels of government following the terrorist attacks experienced in several regions of the world in the last decade. Improvement in transport security now represents one of the key topics on the agendas of counter terrorist agencies worldwide. The Comparative Perspectives on Transportation Security series provides a much-needed platform for international and comparative analysis of transport security policies and practices. Looking at different modes of transport in turn, each book in the series offers a comprehensive and multidisciplinary analysis of security issues for a particular transport mode, incorporating case studies of several key countries.

Titles in the series include:

Maritime Transport Security
Issues, Challenges and National Policies
Edited by Khalid Bichou, Joseph S. Szyliowicz and Luca Zamparini

Multimodal Transport Security
Frameworks and Policy Applications in Freight and Passenger Transport
Edited by Joseph S. Szyliowicz, Luca Zamparini, Genserik L. L. Reniers and Dawna L. Rhoades

Multimodal Transport Security

Frameworks and Policy Applications in Freight and Passenger Transport

Edited by

Joseph S. Szyliowicz

University of Denver, USA

Luca Zamparini

University of Salento, Italy

Genserik L. L. Reniers

Delft University of Technology, the Netherlands

Dawna L. Rhoades

Embry-Riddle Aeronautical University, Florida, USA

COMPARATIVE PERSPECTIVES ON TRANSPORTATION SECURITY

Edward Elgar
PUBLISHING

Cheltenham, UK • Northampton, MA, USA

© Joseph S. Szyliowicz, Luca Zamparini, Genserik L. L. Reniers and
Dawna L. Rhoades 2016

All rights reserved. No part of this publication may be reproduced, stored
in a retrieval system or transmitted in any form or by any means, electronic,
mechanical or photocopying, recording, or otherwise without the prior
permission of the publisher.

Published by
Edward Elgar Publishing Limited
The Lypiatts
15 Lansdown Road
Cheltenham
Glos GL50 2JA
UK

Edward Elgar Publishing, Inc.
William Pratt House
9 Dewey Court
Northampton
Massachusetts 01060
USA

A catalogue record for this book
is available from the British Library

Library of Congress Control Number: 2015950294

This book is available electronically in the Elgaronline
Social and Political Science subject collection
DOI 10.4337/9781783474820

MIX
Paper from
responsible sources
FSC
www.fsc.org   FSC® C013056

ISBN 978 1 78347 481 3 (cased)
ISBN 978 1 78347 482 0 (eBook)

Typeset by Servis Filmsetting Ltd, Stockport, Cheshire
Printed and bound in Great Britain by TJ International Ltd, Padstow

Contents

Figures

Tables

Contributors

Megan Anderson, University of Leiden, the Netherlands

Monika Bak, University of Gdansk, Poland

Jan Burnewicz, University of Gdansk, Poland

Eric Depré, EDConsulting, Belgium

Yahel Giat, Jerusalem College of Technology, Israel

Jukka Hallikas, Lappeenranta University of Technology, Finland

Olli-Pekka Hilmola, Lappeenranta University of Technology, Finland

Evaristus Irandu, University of Nairobi, Kenya

Jay B. Kshirsagar, Ministry of Urban Development, India

Pawan Kumar, Ministry of Urban Development, India

Lauri Lättilä, Lappeenranta University of Technology, Finland

Gerrit Nieuwenhuis, University for Applied Sciences, Rotterdam, the Netherlands

Genserik L. L. Reniers, Delft University of Technology, the Netherlands

Dawna L. Rhoades, Embry-Riddle Aeronautical University, USA

Yihong Ru, Beijing Jiaotong University, China

Brent Shapiro, University of Southern Illinois, USA

Joseph S. Szyliowicz, University of Denver, USA

Luca Talarico, University of Antwerp, Belgium

Coen van Gulijk, Delft University of Technology, the Netherlands

Jyri Vilko, Lappeenranta University of Technology, Finland

Michael J. Williams, Embry-Riddle Aeronautical University, USA

Yair Wiseman, Bar-Ilan University, Israel

Chunyan Yu, Embry-Riddle Aeronautical University, USA

Luca Zamparini, University of Salento, Italy

1. Introduction

Genserik L. L. Reniers, Dawna L. Rhoades, Joseph S. Szyliowicz and Luca Zamparini

Recent decades have witnessed the emergence and implementation of a new vision of transportation across the globe. That vision, known as intermodalism or multimodal transport grew out of technological innovations and a realization that the traditional modal approach to moving people and goods by road, rail, water or air no longer sufficed. This modal approach, whereby each mode is administered and operated in isolation from the other modes, had created a situation characterized by numerous problems including urban congestion, environmental pollution and bottlenecks that prevented the smooth flow of goods and people thus imposing ever-heavier costs upon communities and governments everywhere. Accordingly, it became increasingly obvious that it was essential to view transportation in a new way, one that recognized transportation as a system, that the modes, though possessing individual characteristics, were interrelated. Technological changes in transportation and communication have been a powerful driver that unleashed these forces. Indeed it has been argued that intermodalism emerged from a box in 1956 when a ship called the *Ideal X* sailed from New Jersey to Texas carrying freight packed in containers. Until then, ships were loaded and offloaded much as they had been for centuries; now goods could be shipped across the globe at greatly reduced costs since the freight needed to be packed only once. Thus ships could be loaded and unloaded more quickly. Malcom McLean had created a new technology that transformed international trade and investment patterns.

Since the container could easily be transported not only by sea but by road or rail, those modes also began to change to accommodate the new technology, and imaginative entrepreneurs who recognized the economic advantages of shipping freight in an integrated way through different modes were able to seize market opportunities. Concomitantly, important technological innovations, such as double stack trains, further spurred the revolution whereby air, ship, rail and truck became intertwined so that intermodal systems began to be created.

1

Passenger traffic was also transformed since populations were growing everywhere and increasing numbers of people were traveling domestically and internationally. To meet this ever-growing demand for faster, reliable, convenient travel services, linkages among passenger road, air and rail services began to be created, a process that continues to the present. This is particularly important in the case of international and/or intercontinental trips that rely on air transport in order to reach virtually every possible destination in a reasonable amount of time. It is then evident that the air transport network has to be connected with the networks/infrastructures of the other transport modes. Moreover, as people everywhere became increasingly concerned with issues such as congestion, air, water and noise pollution and climate change, the social costs of existing transportation systems became increasingly apparent and the need to view transportation not merely in traditional economic terms but in terms of its sustainability became ever more apparent.

Thus, as the 20th century came to a close, it became increasingly obvious that the traditional modal approaches no longer sufficed and that new policies and practices were required to deal with the new demands and challenges. In the US, for example, Congress enacted, in 1991, the landmark Intermodal Surface Transportation Efficiency Act (ISTEA) that moved policy away from the age old emphasis on specific modes, notably the highways, towards intermodalism. For the first time, federal legislation recognized the constraints and negative consequences imposed by traditional modal policies and the need for a new approach that emphasized flexibility, innovation and greater public involvement. One of the most notable effects of this new approach and of concurrent technological innovations (i.e. containers, intermodal hubs and so on) has been a drastic contraction of overall transportation costs. This rationalization of costs has been one of the main determinants of the large increases in international trade.

Though the concept of an integrated transportation network quickly gained widespread acceptance among transportation professionals, it has proven difficult to define. Indeed many – including contributors to this volume – continue to prefer the term 'multimodal'. In our view, however the term 'multimodal' which is widely used throughout the world is not adequate because it can be used to refer simply to the obvious fact that goods and people may use more than one mode of transportation from origin to destination. This term ignores the obvious fact that people have traveled and shipped goods in this way since the earliest days of human existence and, more importantly, fails to capture the critical integrative element that distinguishes the new approach. Adding to the confusion, however, is the fact that though the term 'intermodalism' captures the essence of the process, it does not take into account all elements involved (i.e. security, sustainability). This is evident if we consider some of the ways in which the term has been defined.

For example, consider the following popular definition: 'the coordinated passage of goods and people by way of two or more of the primary modes of transport (sea, air, rail, road) from origin to destination as defined by the passenger or the shipper and consignee, with a single travel directive bill of lading or ticket and a single price covering the entire trip' (Alt et al., 1997, p. 36ff). This definition captures the integration dimension well but it fails to include other critical elements – choice and inclusiveness – that many consider to be integral dimensions. Thus, intermodalism has also been defined more broadly as: 'a system that is both safe and efficient and productive and flexible in responding to the needs for good movements and . . . offer(s) people choices and flexibility in their personal movements. This system must also be "international, intelligent and inclusive"' (Jeff, 1998, p. 13). Yet many would argue that even this definition is inadequate because it does not recognize explicitly the externalities of a transportation system. It is obviously possible to develop an integrated system that is safe, efficient, flexible, intelligent, international and inclusive but which continues to pollute the environment and waste energy. Nor does it consider the critical elements of safety and security, elements that are essential in today's world.

Accordingly, it is necessary to expand the definition to include such factors as safety, security, efficiency, cost-effectiveness and long-term sustainability. Thus, we suggest the following definition: An intermodal system is one in which the individual modes are linked, governed and managed in a manner that creates a seamless and sustainable transportation system. Such a system should be economically efficient, environmentally sound, safe and secure, and ethically based.

Implicit in such a perspective is the idea that each mode should be utilized for the purpose for which it is best suited in terms of these considerations. Thus, as many containers as possible should move by rail and not by road and the aviation mode should be used only for high-value long-distance and trans-oceanic trips. Furthermore, every effort should be made to minimize the negative impacts that are inherent in each mode. Such a system maximizes efficiency, offers more choices for personal and freight mobility and minimizes environmental impacts and the use of energy – a critical point given transportation's heavy reliance on petroleum and its contribution to global warming.

Powerful forces created the need for this new approach to transportation. Most obviously, the process of globalization has impacted transportation in many ways. New economic units such as the EU and NAFTA were established and competition between countries and regions intensified, creating increased demand for transport – the role of which became more and more critical at the same time that the existing patterns were demonstrating major weaknesses. These structural changes in the global economy were accompanied and intensified by the emergence of new consumption patterns which created new pressures to distribute goods to global markets. As a result, new patterns of international trade emerged, creating opportunities for innovation and change. Production patterns were also affected as firms everywhere sought to minimize costs and eliminate inefficiencies in various ways. Such concerns led to the introduction of 'just in time' production, an approach that reduced costs by eliminating much of the need for warehousing and storage. As a result of these changes, national development now requires not only sound domestic economic policies but the ability to export and import products rapidly and efficiently to numerous foreign markets. This can only be achieved through integrated global supply chains.

1.   INTERMODAL SECURITY

However defined, the new complex transportation infrastructure which has emerged creates difficult new security challenges that are a major concern for governments everywhere. No mode – land, sea, water and air – has been immune as subway systems, airports, buses, ships, railroad stations and airplanes in many countries have been targeted, often with devastating consequences in terms of human lives and in economic terms. Attempting to ensure that people can continue to avail themselves of various mobility options and that trade can continue to flow smoothly and economically has become an international priority because intermodal transportation networks are a major sector in any economy and a significant contributor to national growth.

Thus, new security measures have been implemented everywhere and these have enhanced the security of various modes to varying degrees. However, transportation security requires going beyond safeguarding the individual modes to ensuring the security of the intermodal terminals, the nodes that link and integrate passenger and freight flows. Their importance has continued to grow as globalization and technological developments have accelerated in recent years, particularly in the fields of transportation and communications. These trends have made the world a smaller place. As technological progress has continued to shrink distance and time, an ever-expanding flow of people and goods across national frontiers further accelerates the process of economic and financial integration. Today companies produce in many countries, ship components from one subsidiary to another, distribute finished goods to markets in many countries and use the transportation system as a warehousing system. To accommodate the growing demands these developments place on the transportation system, new intermodal facilities have been built everywhere. Airports have proliferated throughout Asia, new road and rail links have been established through the Channel and the Trans-European Network, and many countries are modernizing and expanding their port facilities. Such projects facilitate and enhance interdependence and interconnectedness, but at the same time present new and attractive targets for terrorists who have become increasingly sophisticated in recent decades, understand the inner workings of transportation systems and are developing new weapons and capabilities.

Intermodal terminals are very attractive targets because of their economic and social significance and the difficulties that are involved in safeguarding them. Traditional security challenges are multiplied by numerous new problems of coordination and integration, such as clearly defining the roles of the many different types of personnel working in these terminals, and ensuring that they understand their proper roles in the security program and can manage them effectively. For example, the new emphasis on direct rail connections to airports means that security practices for the railways and those for aviation modes need to be harmonized. Of course, ensuring that all rail passengers are subject to rigorous aviation screening standards is no simple matter. Thus, intermodalism greatly complicates security procedures, particularly when there is a continuing tendency to think of security purely in intramodal terms within one mode at a time.

Modal thinking is reinforced by the tendency of virtually all governmental agencies (even those which have overarching responsibilities across modes of transportation) to function in a reactive manner by responding to particular threats, rather than taking a more holistic view of the situation. For example, the airline hijackings and the problem of bombs aboard airplanes that emerged in the late 1950s and 1960s resulted in government-mandated, stepped-up security measures by the airlines and at airports. By contrast, little focus was given at the time to security measures in road, rail or sea-going modes.

The global freight system which is vulnerable at many points is of particular concern because of the devastating economic consequences, nationally and internationally, that would follow from a successful attack. As Robert Bonner, the Commissioner of the US Customs Service has noted: 'If terrorists used a sea container to conceal a weapon of mass destruction and detonated it on arrival at a port, the impact on global trade and the global economy could be immediate and devastating – all nations would be affected. No container ships would be allowed to unload at U.S. ports after such an event.'[1] Consequently, the economies of all countries would receive a major shock as international trade would not return to its normal state for months. In the meantime, economic growth throughout the globe would slow, imposing a heavy burden on all states, especially upon those least able to bear it.

Another factor of concern lies in the awareness that terrorists have adopted new tactics and now seek to inflict as many casualties as possible. Intermodal nodes such as train stations, airports and metros which are often crowded with people are therefore attractive targets. The March 2004 attacks on the Madrid train stations in which over 170 people were killed and many more injured, and the July 2005 attacks on London's underground system which killed 56 people, including the four suicide bombers, and injured about 700 other people, provide vivid and tragic proof of the appeal of these targets. These attacks only involved a tragic human toll but a series of such attacks could produce significant changes in mobility patterns and hence on the quality of life as well as on economic activity.

Transportation facilities are often national and international icons and the demolition of a famous bridge or tunnel would possess great symbolic significance. Transportation security is thus an essential counter-terrorism tool. Terrorists have to travel to their targets with their weapons or to a place where they can obtain them. A secure intermodal system can obviously limit the mobility of terrorists, an issue of growing concern to law enforcement agencies everywhere. It can also increase the security of vehicles which can be, and often have been, used as weapons. The tragedy of 9/11 was the result of airplanes that were transformed into missiles. Most common are truck bombs which have been launched against intermodal terminals, bridges and tunnels, vessels in ports, trains and buses. Terrorists are also exploring the potential of other weapons including nuclear materials. The acquisition of 50 kg of Highly Enriched Uranium (HEU), would permit terrorists to assemble a nuclear weapon, albeit an inefficient one. However, building a bomb is a difficult task, even with the necessary materials and the technical know-how. More likely is a radiological attack using a 'dirty bomb' or other radiological dispersal device (RDD) that explodes and disseminates radioactive materials in transportation facilities or disperses such materials in powdered form, perhaps from a plane.

Even more likely are chemical and biological attacks. Terrorists may be able to acquire numerous agents that cause such diseases as plague, botulism and smallpox. The deployment of a few grams of these microbes in a passenger intermodal hub would suffice to cause death and create panic. Many other virulent toxins can be identified, some of which such as sarin gas and anthrax have actually been used. Each of these substances poses unique challenges that require particular countermeasures and responses that also depend on the nature of contexts and resources.

Cyber-attacks, which are commonplace, also pose an ever-growing threat. These can take many forms. A specific database of a transportation owner/operator can be attacked in order to gain information, or an attacker can seek out a weakly defended pathway for access to a network in order to shut down service or to introduce harmful instructions. Attacks can be launched against train control centers and air traffic control systems, ports, power and telecommunications systems, and railroad signals. A successful attack would have devastating consequences.

Since attacks against transportation systems can take many forms and involve a variety of weapons, safeguarding transportation systems is a challenging but essential task. Safeguarding this system is no easy matter for several reasons. First, its sheer size creates difficulties. Shipping freight in containers has proven to be a reliable and inexpensive way of sending goods from one corner of the world to another and container freight has grown exponentially in the few decades since its introduction. Today, about 90 percent of the world's cargo movements involve containers. Almost 50 million full containers are shipped between the world's major ports each year, six million of these arrive in the US each year (Szyliowicz, 2009). Another ten million arrive by road or rail.

Second, the economic and technological integration that has been achieved has not been matched by an equal degree of political coordination and cooperation. There is a growing discrepancy between traditional political borders and economic boundaries that continue to expand outward as a result of various international trade agreements. As a result, new questions have emerged to complicate the already complex and difficult issue of border security. There is an obvious trade-off between efficient trade flows and enhanced security risks.

Thus, the problem of safeguarding intermodal transportation systems is further complicated because it is an international as well as a national issue. But world politics continues to be largely characterized by the interactions of independent international states with varying degrees of power and influence. Thus, national and international security concerns require a strong measure of cooperation, reaching agreements, often a difficult and challenging task when attempting to create a new regime.

Since the system is characterized by a lack of agreement on responsibility and overlapping claims to jurisdictional authority, policy makers in national governments confront substantial challenges in such areas as port and aviation security since numerous national agencies and actors are involved as well as private sector firms and other non-governmental organizations and international organizations such as the International Civil Aviation Organization (ICAO) and the International Maritime Organization (IMO). Coordinating all these international, transnational and domestic actors and stakeholders is extremely difficult. Globalization, thus, poses difficult challenges for transportation security. It has created a system whose disruption can have catastrophic consequences for the entire world economy.

Still, international, and transnational, actors have attempted to enhance transportation security. Asia Pacific Economic Cooperation (APEC), for example, has adopted various measures to enhance transportation security among its member states. These include the establishment of the Secure Trade in the APEC Region (STAR) initiative by which member economies are to take action to screen people and cargo better, as well as to protect ships, planes, airports and seaports better more generally. To achieve these goals, a Counter Terrorism Task Force has been established along with a Transportation Security Experts Group with task groups for such areas as cyber, maritime and aviation security. Although helpful, the full impact of these activities remains to be seen. Nor should one overlook the policies that have been adopted by the two key international organizations whose areas of responsibility include shipping – the IMO – and aviation – the ICAO.

Though their activities involve the security of intermodal nodes, the traditional concern with enhancing the security of individual modes, especially aviation, continues to be the principal area of concern. Prior to 9/11, the other modes received what might be considered, at best, limited consideration. Today, governments recognize that attention must be paid to the intermodal dimension but transportation systems everywhere are still largely organized by modes and the key private and public actors continue to think and act along modal lines, often nationally. Such an orientation does not facilitate the development and implementation of appropriate policies to safeguard intermodal transportation systems. It is now essential to view transportation security from an intermodal or systems perspective and to be sensitive to the global reach of a transportation system. But, like globalization, its very characteristics – such as the increased number of stakeholders, the functioning of terminals, and the increasing reliance of information technology – further complicate the task of dealing with terrorism. Of particular significance are the great problems of coordination since different modes have different security practices and involve large numbers of private and public stakeholders.

Essentially, intermodal transportation can be divided into two obvious categories: passenger systems and freight systems. Though they are interrelated, they must be considered separately for each has distinct and separate features that present particular security problems.

2. INTERMODAL PASSENGER SYSTEMS

By their very nature, intermodal passenger systems are especially vulnerable. They are complex, large in terms of both the areas they cover and the number of people who utilize them, and they are designed to be easily accessible. As a result, it is difficult, if not impossible, to screen passengers and their luggage as is done at airports everywhere. Moreover, any attempt to enhance security is likely to conflict with the ease of access that all intermodal terminals are designed to provide to large numbers of users. Thus, there is always a tension between security and convenience. A report by Horowitz and Thompson (1994) ranked the maximization of security as the second most desirable goal (in a list of 70) for the evaluation of the quality of an intermodal passenger transport facility.

All new passenger transport hubs should then be built with a very clear security focus both in terms of design and construction and in terms of operations and response. With respect to the former, all available technologies should be used in order to maximize the screening capability of the infrastructure. Operations and response should, on the other hand, be aimed at minimizing the probability of occurrence of (a lack of) security related episodes and, given the virtual impossibility to reduce this probability to zero, the minimization of casualties, damages and disruption involved in such episodes. The training of intermodal hubs personnel is a very important factor if this objective is to be achieved. For very large intermodal hubs (i.e. airports and ports) devoted to international transport, the coordination among country systems and strategies plays a pivotal role in increasing the effectiveness of security systems. In this respect, the best practices adopted in one country and for a specific transportation mode should be extended and, where necessary, adapted to the other countries and transport modes. The main components of a security plan for intermodal passenger systems should include a clear identification of goals, assets and choke points, where security should be maximized and conceived as the primary goal of the system. This goal can be reached by a flexible and efficient security scheme that takes into account the evolution of transport systems and works to enhance security standards continuously. The dissemination of information and the involvement of private stakeholders is very important in this respect along with public awareness campaigns that target the overall society (Tarr et al., 2005).

3.   INTERMODAL FREIGHT SYSTEMS

The intermodal freight systems which, as noted above, are a critical infra-structure that undergirds national economies, present perhaps even more daunting security challenges. Ensuring the security of ports is particularly difficult. Ports are a critical element in the modern supply chain, handling thousands if not millions of containers a year. Like all other elements of the transportation system they also possess inherent characteristics that make them vulnerable and attractive targets. They are accessible by both land and water, have large numbers of workers and visitors, are in crowded metropolitan centers, cover large land areas that often contain (petro) chemical and other hazardous facilities, and are intermodal nodes that link shipping to rail and road nodes and thus provide ready access to other locations. The flow of trade enhances all these vulnerabilities.

Ports are not the only highly vulnerable nodes. Air freight is an enormous business that is handled not only in specialized airports but in regular airports as well. In fact, there is a significant volume of freight carried in the belly of passenger aircraft. This so-called belly freight poses serious potential risk to air passengers and any explosion at altitude would result in maximum fatalities. And, once cargo has arrived at a port, the container continues its journey by road or rail creating additional opportunities for a terrorist attack. Given the volume involved, checking each container or even a statistically significant percentage at a large port is an impossible task, since it would bring commerce to a standstill. Consequently, it is important to devise contingency plans aimed at minimizing the effects of security related attacks. These should take into account all measures that are both efficient and effective, such as the decision of which transport corridors to shut, how to divert traffic to other similar infrastructures, the downstream effects to the attack on an intermodal transport hub, and so on. As in the case of passenger transport, the coordination among all economic stakeholders involved is vital in order for a security system and/or a contingency plan to function smoothly. In this respect, a proper regime of incentives (i.e. conditional facilitation of procedures) and sanctions (i.e. slow lanes of custom clearance procedures for non-complying firms) should be promoted. Moreover, security protocols should not be based on the response to single episodes but they should rather rely on a strategic vision that integrates security as one of the most important elements in the supply chain. Finally, the efficient exchange of information among stakeholders should be fostered and facilitated.

4. STRUCTURE OF THE VOLUME

Clearly the emergence of multimodalism/intermodalism has created dangerous new security challenges. This volume is designed to provide an overview of these issues and the ways in which different countries have defined and dealt with them. Given that there are some homogeneities but also significant differences between the freight and passenger sectors, we consider each separately. The theoretical parts of the book (Part I devoted to freight transport and Part III to passenger transport) discuss the relevant issues in each sector. The empirical and country policy related parts of the book (Part II for freight transport and Part IV for passenger transport) comprise various case studies that cover Africa, Asia, Europe, North America and South America. By presenting the context, policies and strategies from a diverse range of cases we seek to develop, both at the theoretical level and with respect to specific countries, information about commonalities and peculiarities in approaches, procedures and strategies that can provide a basis for the development of sound, effective and efficient intermodal transport security policies.

Part I of the book begins with Chapter 2 where Gerrit Nieuwenhuis provides a general overview of the challenges confronting multimodal freight transport. Following a discussion of the various definitions for multimodal and intermodal transport, he emphasizes standardization as a necessary condition for the efficient and seamless transportation of goods at both the continental and intercontinental scale. He then discusses the large number of economic and transport firms and agents that are involved in multimodal transport on the demand side and on the supply side of the market, one of the main factors complicating efforts at securing any supply chain. The chapter also discusses how the container, the most important innovation that has allowed a large diffusion of intercontinental maritime transport and the consequent globalization of trade, creates its own problems. Although several loading units can alternatively be used (i.e. trailers, swap bodies) for continental multimodal transport, these too pose security challenges. The chapter then considers all possible categories of security related events that can pose a risk to the supply chain and considers cargo thefts, acts of terrorism and piracy as the most relevant ones. Finally, the chapter presents the EU regulations that seek to increase the degree of security with the least possible cost in terms of seamless transport flows and concludes by discussing the trends and innovations in the sector.

In Chapter 3, 'Economic issues in multimodal freight transport security', Luca Zamparini proposes an economic analysis of several topics related to multimodal freight transport security. The chapter first provides an economic analysis of the various container security measures that have been implemented in the last decades, especially after 9/11. This is followed by a detailed discussion of the important economic issues related to the main national and international initiatives that have been implemented since 2002 in an effort to increase the degree of multimodal transport security. Moreover, the economic impact of some private multimodal transport security programs is considered and is critically analyzed.

Chapter 4, 'Assessing vulnerability in multimodal supply chains' by Jyri Vilko, Lauri Lättilä and Jukka Hallikas, begins by proposing a clearly defined distinction between risk and vulnerability in the context of the supply chain and then discusses the main differences between these two concepts. It then clarifies that risk analysis and vulnerability are conceptually different and highlights the various steps that are necessary in a vulnerability analysis study (definition of scope, description of context, selection of methodology, scenario/model development, analysis and prioritization, interpretation of results and limitations, and selection of proper actions). The chapter then provides a taxonomy of possible risks in the various phases of a supply chain and posits the need to consider the quality and the amount of available data if a proper method of vulnerability analysis is to be selected. The second part of the chapter illustrates how this should be done by presenting and discussing a hypothetical case of vulnerability analysis in intercontinental multimodal transport. It discusses all possible causes of risk along the supply chain, their probability, and the implied costs in terms of delay to the shipment. Finally, the chapter concludes by considering the necessity of optimizing the supply chain management in order to minimize the connected risks and vulnerabilities.

Part I concludes with Chapter 5 on insurance issues. Eric Depré, Genserik L. L. Reniers and Luca Zamparini begin by defining insurance and partitioning it into two categories – indemnity insurance and fixed sum insurance. They then provide a taxonomy of all the possible types that can be related to a supply chain and all the related physical infrastructures. Moreover, the chapter considers the most relevant topics that are connected to single mode transport modes by discussing the peculiarities of each mode. The chapter concludes with a consideration of the themes and issues related to the insurance of the multimodal transport option, emphasizing that each single mode involved in a multimodal chain has its peculiar risks and that these have to be carefully considered. Finally, it highlights the most important elements that have to be taken into account when insuring a multimodal shipment.

Part II of the book is devoted to national policies that deal with multimodal/intermodal freight security. Chapter 6 by Brent Shapiro considers how the US seeks to ensure that imported freight does not pose a security threat, especially during its inland stages. For many years that responsibility has lain with the Customs and Border Patrol (formerly the US Customs Service). The chapter describes the various security initiatives that have been implemented by the US administration since 9/11. These include the Customs-Trade Partnership Against Terrorism, the Container Security Initiative and the 24 Hour Advance Manifest Rule, and the Importer Security Filing and Additional Carrier Requirements (commonly known as the 10+2 Rule). Moreover, the chapter analyzes the procedures and protocols that are related to security once a cargo enters the US. These measures relate to both hubs (such as ports) and to the other legs of the transportation shipment, including the electronic data interchange for the clearance of shipments bound at ports. The importance of tracking goods during their final stages is explained in detail.

Chapter 7 provides an analysis and discussion of Italy's policy. Luca Talarico and Luca Zamparini first describe the evolution of the multi-modal freight transportation system in Italy by highlighting the modal split and the difference between domestic and international multimodal freight transport. They then consider the existing logistic infrastructure network which can be integrated under the multimodal perspective, describing both the main multimodal hubs and the road network with its high traffic and medium traffic routes as well as the main multimodal firms. The criticalities for a consistent development of multimodal transport in Italy are then discussed. The second part of the chapter is devoted to the analysis of the security aspects in the multimodal freight transportation. The critical principles, legislations and rules which impact the Italian logistic system are then presented. Moreover the multimodal freight transportation security related events that occurred in 2013 are also reviewed and analyzed. Lastly, the chapter suggests that a discussion be held about the many best practices and innovative technical solutions which have been proposed in Italy, since doing so would help guarantee both the efficiency of the multimodal logistic nodes and the security of the overall logistic supply chain.

In Chapter 8 Olli-Pekka Hilmola describes the security improvement potential of Rail Baltica investment. The chapter begins with an analysis of the transportation sector's development including the evolution of fatalities and its downward trend in the last two decades in the Baltic States and Poland. After discussing the dependency of these countries on energy (mainly oil imports) and the consequent importance of fostering multimodal transport, the chapter discusses the existing security and safety controls in the rail sector. This mode has failed to adequately implement a common signaling and traffic control system (the European Rail Traffic Management System [ERTMS]), though doing so would ease interoperability and facilitate rail transport. The factors for this delay are then accounted for. The chapter then analyzes and discusses the most important threat to the mode, the growth in crime. It concludes with a consideration of the potential future growth of road transport due to increasing private car and truck traffic as well as the readiness of the railway sector to take care of south-north general cargo transports.

Chapter 9 by Evaristus Irandu deals with the situation in Kenya. The chapter begins by analyzing the development of its transport network over time and the problems faced by multimodal transport in sub-Saharan Africa. It then highlights the importance of multimodal freight transport within Kenya, and along the relevant regional transport corridors, as a means of reducing the high transport costs in the country and improving its economic competitiveness. The various challenges for the improvement of multimodal transport (an inadequate legal framework, institutional capacity and investments, lack of capacity at the port of Mombasa and in the railway network itself) are then discussed. The chapter then considers the security of the freight transport system, the factors that are threatening it and the policies and strategies that have been implemented in order to increase security along with the legal framework that has been issued over time for each transport mode. Finally, the chapter considers the role of ICT in multimodal freight transport security in Kenya.

Chapter 10 by Chunyan Yu and Yihong Ru discusses the Chinese situation. It begins by describing the current status of the transport sector in China with respect to both transport flows and the degree of infrastructural development for all transport modes, including the rail links with neighboring countries. The second part of the chapter discusses the main security issues for all transport modes, including a series of examples and a detailed description of the relevant security regulations and agencies. The last part of the chapter describes the security measures (prevention activities and optimal response strategies) that have been put in place in the main multimodal hubs and assesses their strengths and weaknesses. The chapter concludes by assessing the main similarities and heterogeneities of the various security measures across modes.

Part II closes with Chapter 11 by Michael J. Williams on the Brazilian case. Following some general data about Brazil the author turns to the development of its transport network in the last decades, including road, water, rail, pipeline and aviation. It then considers the government's initiatives to improve the conditions of transport infrastructures and the efficiency of freight movements. The challenges conditioning such policies and their degree of success and effectiveness are discussed. The second part of the chapter looks closely at the factors affecting freight security and emphasizes cargo thefts as the most relevant and recurrent issue. The last part of the chapter is devoted to a discussion of the initiatives and measures that have been implemented in order to increase the system's security.

Part III of the book begins with Chapter 12 on the 'Challenges for multimodal passenger transport' by Monika Bak and Jan Burnewicz. They start by clarifying the different concepts of multimodal and intermodal passenger transport and conclude that multimodality is more developed for freight while it is evolving in the context of passenger transport. They then consider all the important themes involved in meeting the infrastructure and technology needs for the efficient development of multimodal passenger transport. The relevance of transferability of good practices is also considered. In the second part of the chapter, the links between multimodality and sustainability of transport are explored, with particular emphasis on the need to reduce the environmental impacts. The increase in regional accessibility due to efficient multimodal transport solutions is also considered. The last part of the chapter discusses the policies and legal frameworks that facilitate intermodal cooperation including a comparative viewpoint on the actions and strategies adopted by the EU, the US, Japan, China and Russia.

Chapter 13 by Luca Zamparini concludes Part III and considers the economic and policy issues related to multimodal passenger transport security. It first stresses the homogeneities and, above all, the differences with respect to freight transport security and notes that relatively fewer analyses have been devoted to passenger transport security. It then discusses the economic issues in multimodal passenger transport security, two specific initiatives that have been developed by the International Road Transport Union and by the Transit Cooperative Research Program of the Transportation Research Board, and the multimodal passenger security policies of the EU and of Australia. The aim of this chapter is to highlight some relevant issues that will be thoroughly discussed in the country-specific chapters that constitute the next part of the book.

Part IV of the book – which is devoted to multimodal passenger transport security policies – begins with Chapter 14 by Joseph S. Szyliowicz which discusses the US case. The chapter begins with a description of how its transport network developed along unimodal lines and the attempts to adopt a holistic and multimodal perspective over the last 25 years. It then discusses the current state of multimodality, noting that it is more developed for rail transport than for air transport. The chapter then discusses the most vulnerable parts of the multimodal transport networks – the intermodal hubs – a vulnerability exacerbated by the wide array of weapons that terrorists can employ to attack such facilities. Another criticality is represented by the fact that security protocols need to mediate among different organizational cultures, structures and operating procedures. The second part of the chapter discusses the policies that have been adopted by the agencies created by the US administration, over time, to secure the multimodal hubs. Both airports and surface transport terminals are considered in a historical perspective.

Chapter 15 by Coen van Gulijk, Megan Anderson and Genserik L. L. Reniers considers the Dutch situation. It first describes the structure of the transport network in the Netherlands with a particular emphasis on the two main hubs – the port of Rotterdam and Schiphol Amsterdam Airport – and the general transport networks that serve them. In the second part, the management of transport security is described and analyzed, including the major role played by the 'national coordinator for anti-terrorism and safety' agency of the Ministry of Security and Justice. Moreover, the prioritization of strategies according to the national risk assessment multi-criteria strategy is considered in detail. After a description of the main security related episodes in the Netherlands, the security arrangements in the Port of Rotterdam and in Schiphol Amsterdam Airport are described and the mixed results of the national risk assessment strategy are thoroughly discussed.

Chapter 16 by Yair Wiseman and Yahel Giat considers the situation in Israel. The chapter begins with a description of the Israeli transport networks, the critical infrastructures pertaining to each mode and the agencies and authorities responsible for transport security. It discusses how policies evolved more as a consequence of security episodes than as a planned strategy. The most relevant cases of security related episodes in the various transport modes (air transport, rail and bus transport) and the policies adopted to decrease their probability and to reduce their impact are then discussed in detail. Various security challenges including road blockages, shooting from cars, and the use of ambulances as terrorists' tools are considered. The chapter then describes security in multimodal hubs and considers the occurrence of terror attacks and of missile strikes from a historical perspective.

The Indian case is analyzed in Chapter 17 by Jay B. Kshirsagar and Pawan Kumar. They note that passenger security in multimodal transport is a very relevant issue in India given that it has 53 cities with more than one million inhabitants. They specify that the software and hardware of the entire transport system are key elements in security. Particularly important, in this respect, is the planning strategy for the different infrastructures. The chapter then describes the current practices for the enhancement of security in public transport (where particular care is reserved for women travelers) and in its multimodal options. In the second part of the chapter, the main issues related to passenger security are discussed. These involve all phases of the transport chain and all possible means of transport. Lastly, the role of public campaigns to increase public awareness and to influence travel behavior is discussed.

Part IV closes with Chapter 18 on the Brazilian case by Dawna L. Rhoades. Following an overview of the country's general economic and geographical data she provides a precise description of the transport sector, particularly its air, inland waterways, road, rail and public transport. The regulatory and policy framework is then considered. The second part of the chapter starts with a discussion of the main bodies and agencies responsible for security in Brazil, at the national, state and local levels, and then considers the security challenges Brazil faces in terms of both border and interior security and crime and infrastructure.

The concluding chapter of the book provides a comparative analysis of the freight and passenger transport sections and highlights homogeneities and heterogeneities among the many countries that have been discussed. Moreover, it integrates the various case studies by comparing their regulations, policies and strategies and presents the best practices. It ends with proposals for possible future directions of research that will further our understanding of the factors that shape multimodal/intermodal freight and passenger security and the kinds of measures and policies that can further enhance their security.

NOTE

1. Remarks by Commissioner Robert Bonner, Council on Foreign Relations, January 11, 2005.

REFERENCES

Alt, R., P. Forster and J. King (1997), 'The great reversal: information and transportation infrastructure in the intermodal vision', in National Conference on Intermodal Transportation Research Framework, Washington, DC: Transportation Research Board.

Horowitz, A. J. and N. A. Thompson (1994), *Evaluation of Intermodal Passenger Transfer Facilities*, Washington, DC: US Department of Transportation.

Jeff, G. (1998), 'Welcoming remarks', in *Intermodal Education and Training*, Washington, DC: National Academy Press.

Szyliowicz, J. (2009), 'Terrorism, mobility and transportation security', in *Transportation Security against Terrorism. Proceedings of the NATO Advanced Research Workshop on Transportation Security Measures to Counter Terrorism*, Amsterdam: IOS Press.

Tarr, R. W., V. McGurk and C. Jones (2005), 'Intermodal transportation safety and security issues: training against terrorism', *Journal of Public Transportation*, **8** (4), 87–102.

PART I

Multimodal freight transportation security: themes and frameworks

2. Challenges for multimodal freight transport

Gerrit Nieuwenhuis

INTRODUCTION

Multimodal transport and especially intermodal transport is continuously developing nowadays. The containerization, globalization and increase of capacities of transport units are trends which not only have an impact on the modes of transport, but also on the security in transport systems. In this chapter the focus will be on the intermodal part of multimodal freight operations. Both the effects of the trends in intermodal transport on the system itself and on the security aspects will be described.

Definitions

Multimodal freight transport is the concept of using more than one mode of transport for moving goods from origin to destination. On longer distance and especially on intercontinental transport multimodal transport is almost inevitable. In intercontinental transport the deployment of sea transport or air transport will be necessary and this mode of transport has to be combined with a mode of transport to bring goods from or to the (air)port. Iron ore from southern America to the steel works in Germany will have to be transported by more than one mode.

In the case of multimodal transport an exchange of goods has to be part of the total chain of transport. The transhipment of goods takes place in terminals. The transhipment is possible by transferring the goods from one mode to the other mode of transportation or by leaving the goods in the loading unit and transfer of the loading unit. The last concept is called intermodal transport.

In this chapter the focus will be on intermodal transport. Gerhardt Muller (1995) defines intermodal transportation as 'the concept of transporting passengers and freight in such a way that all the parts of the transportation process, including information exchange, are efficiently connected and coordinated, offering flexibility'.

More specified for freight transport the United Nations Economic Commission for Europe (UN ECE) defines intermodal transport as 'the movement of goods in one and the same loading unit or road vehicle, which uses successively two or more modes'.

Following those definitions of intermodal transport some characteristics should be mentioned. First of all, intermodal transport is not just a mode of transport, like railways, barges or trucks are, but is a concept for organizing the logistics chain. As bundling is an important element of creating efficient and effective transport chains, the character of intermodal transport enables this feature.

The most important elements of intermodal transport are:

- Two or more transport modes are used in a transport chain.
- The goods are transported in one loading unit that is standardized in order to be used on several modes of transport.
- The exchange of the loading units between modes of transport makes transhipment in terminals necessary.

The most important feature of the definition of intermodal transport is the use of a standardized loading unit. Important for transport management is the possibility of bundling cargo to obtain an efficient way of transporting goods. Bundling takes place on two levels. The first level is the bundling of loading units on a high capacity mode of transport (ship, barge, train). The second level of bundling takes place by combining different shipments in one loading unit. Intermodal transport enables transport managers to combine different shipments on the majority part of the transport chain. Efficiency is further improved by using the standardized loading units.

Shipments of goods may be sent intercontinental or continental. The requirements for organizing intermodal transport will depend on the character of the route. For an intercontinental flow of goods mostly sea ships or airplanes are used. Both modes of transportation need a port for loading and unloading. In sea transport standardized ISO-containers are often used. This container meets all standards for intermodal transport: apart from a sea ship more modes of transport will be used for pre-haulage and post-haulage, and the container will be standardized and therefore to be used on all modes of transport. Containers for air freight are not standardized and cannot be used for other modes of transport. Transport of goods in air freight containers can be considered as multimodal transport. In this chapter, intercontinental intermodal transport is always considered as the transport of goods in maritime containers by sea.

Continental intermodal transport occurs within a continent or between two continents without using ocean shipping. All transport with an origin and destination in Europe is considered to be continental. Further, short-sea shipping between Europe and the coast of northern Africa is a form of continental transport. Continental intermodal transport is operated in different forms using the following loading units:

- Containers.
- Swap bodies.
- Semi-trailers.
- Trucks including tractors.

Continental intermodal transport of containers, swap bodies and semi-trailers is often called Huckepack or piggyback transport. The transport of trucks is called Rollende Landstrasse, or Rolling Road in the case of rail transport, or Roll on-Roll off in the case of short-sea shipping.

In the intermodal market many parties are involved both at the demand and at the supply side. At the demand side the most important actor is the shipper, who wishes to have freight transported. The shipper may organize the whole transport chain himself, but normally the organization of the transport chain is outsourced to a forwarding company. The forwarding company will book capacity on services offered by the companies at the supply side of the market. Capacity booking is done on behalf of the shipper in a way that the forwarding company has no risk of utilizing the capacity of a transport unit. By bundling the shipments of different shippers the forwarding company might find an opportunity to negotiate better prices from the transport companies involved. Some forwarding companies have developed into logistics service providers, which have the opportunity to offer services in road transport, warehousing and value-added logistics.

At the supply side of the market the transport operators are offering transport services for deepsea shipping, short-sea shipping, rail and barge. The transport operators develop intermodal networks in which regular capacity is offered to the demand side of the market. For these services, the operators provide transport units and staff.

In intermodal rail services it is usual to have an intermodal operator between the supply and demand sides of the market. The intermodal operator procures both transport as transhipment services and offers the capacity to their customers (shippers, forwarding companies or logistics service providers). The intermodal operator orders a regular train service between terminals and takes the risk of utilizing full capacity.

Last but not least the terminal operator is an important actor in the market. The terminal operator is responsible for transferring the loading units from one mode of transportation to another. The terminal operator provides the transhipment equipment and often offers additional capacity for storage of the loading units.

The structure of the multimodal market with several transport modes and several actors in one transport chain causes high security risks. Following the attacks of 9/11 in New York and Washington more attention was paid to measures to reduce security risks in transport chains. Since 2005 some ships have been attacked by pirates in the Gulf of Aden, which could be considered to be a new form of security risk. Since then several security initiatives have been taken, which also have influence on multimodal transport chains. On 1 July 2004 the so-called International Ship and Port Facility Security (ISPS) Code came into force, which applies to all member states of the International Maritime Organization. The ISPS Code is applicable for both sea vessels and port facilities, and also influences the maritime container transport operations.

For container transport to the USA the US Container Security Initiative (CSI) was launched in 2002. Based on the CSI, important container ports are involved in sending an advance message for containers that will be sent to the USA.

These two initiatives will be described in more detail in this chapter.

Maritime Intermodal Transport

The most important transport revolution of the 20th century is without doubt the introduction of containers in maritime transport. The displacement of general cargo in intercontinental maritime transport has always been very labour intensive, especially in ports. By bundling the cargo in boxes and by standardizing those boxes for all modes of transport the efficiency of freight logistics was raised. In the 1950s one port worker was able to load or unload 0.627 tons of freight per hour. Due to the introduction of the container, productivity increased to 4.234 tons per hour in the 1970s. The rotation of ships also improved. In the 1950s a ship spent three weeks in the port; in the 1970s, only 18 hours. Ultra-large container vessels with a capacity of more than 10000 twenty-foot equivalent units (TEU) nowadays spend around 36 hours in a port.

Containers are boxes, mostly constructed of steel, for the transport of goods. Containers have to meet requirements of legislation and standard dimensions as established by the International Organization for Standardization (ISO). Maritime containers are quite often called ISO-containers. Containers can be lifted by cranes or mobile transhipment equipment like straddle-carriers or reach stackers. The container is equipped in all corners with so-called corner fittings to enable the lifting of the containers. The standardization of containers enables the use of corner fittings for lifting the container and for securing containers on all modes of transport (sea vessel, truck, train and barge).

The most common container lengths are the 20-, 30-, 40- and 45-feet containers, of which the 20- and 40-feet containers are normally used for ocean transport. The 30-feet containers are mostly designed as tank containers for the transport of liquid freight. The 45-feet container is used in continental transport in combination with short-sea shipping. Containers are 8-feet wide and 8- to 9-feet high.

Capacities and statistics of container transport are referred to as TEUs. Ultra-large container vessels may have a capacity of around 14 000 TEU. The largest generation of vessels has a capacity of over 18 000 TEU.

Since the 1990s, the globalization of economies has had an important impact on worldwide transport in general and container transport in particular. The development of new economies like China and India has resulted in an increase of transport connections from those countries to high-consuming continents like North America and Europe. The production of goods can be done efficiently in Asian countries and the final products or elements are transported in containers to the assembly plants and consumer markets. As it was necessary to combine low production costs with low distribution costs a distribution and transport strategy was necessary to produce lower cost structures. Containerization and an increase of the scale of means of transport were the instruments to increase efficiency in the global transport of goods.

Thanks to the container, the handling of freight in the ports could be done in a more efficient way, resulting in lower costs and faster handling times in the ports. The efficient way of handling container vessels in the ports made it possible to reduce the turnaround times of ships, resulting in more round trips and a better use of available capacities. Innovation in maritime terminals resulted in high-quality handling of freight in the ports. Employee numbers could be reduced and systems were automated as far as possible.

In the same period, shipping companies found ways to reduce the costs of sea transport by increasing the capacities of ships. The first container ships of the 1970s had capacities of around 1000 TEU. In 2013, the first ships with a capacity of more than 18 000 TEU were introduced.

Logistics chains for the transport of goods between different continents need many actors involved in the management of the chain. For example, the following actors may be observed in the chain between the Far East and Europe:

● The shipper, who in many cases is the owner or producer of the goods and wishes to have the goods transported in a container from the Far East to Europe.

- The forwarding company in the Far East, who is commissioned by the shipper to organize the transport from the Far East to Europe.
- The transport company in the Far East, which is responsible for the transport from the shipping address to the port of departure. This transport can be done by truck, rail or barge.
- The shipping line, which is responsible for maritime transport between the port of departure in the Far East and the port of arrival in Europe. Shipping lines are represented in the port by agents or shipbrokers.
- Customs authorities, both in the port of departure and the port of arrival.
- Container terminal operators (stevedores) in both ports, who are commissioned by the shipping lines to transfer the containers between the ocean vessel and the mode of inland transport.
- Forwarding companies, which organize the hinterland transport from port to the receiving address in the hinterland of the port. Worldwide operating forwarding companies will be able to offer services on both continents. Examples of such companies include DHL Global Forwarding, DB Schenker, Kuehne + Nagel.
- Transport companies, which are responsible for the hinterland transportation between the port of arrival and the final destination of the goods. Transport might be by truck, train or barge.
- Inland terminal operators. Especially in the case of hinterland transport from the port by train or barge there will be another terminal to transfer containers between the modes of transport: from train to truck, or from barge to truck.

In the ports containers are handled in container terminals. As shipping lines are the customers of container terminals the first priority for a terminal will be the unloading and loading of the ocean vessels. Those vessels should be able to leave the port again as quickly as possible. Container handling is divided at the terminal process, at the sea-side of the terminal to load and unload the vessels, and at the terminal process to load and unload the units of hinterland transport (truck, train and barge). In between the two processes containers are stacked in the terminal. Throughout this whole process customs control has to be organized. Customs will control papers and select containers for further inspection by opening the container or by using container scans.

From the container terminal in the port the boxes have to be transported to the final destinations. This can be done by short-sea connections, and containers will leave the port again by sea. In most cases the containers leave by truck, train or barge into the hinterland. In the case of transport by road, the container can be sent directly to the final destination. However, the shipments are restricted to two or three TEU per truck. This makes truck transport rather expensive. For longer distances, or for large quantities of containers bound for one destination, it would be more efficient to transport containers by train or by barge for a significant share of the total distance. Both modes of transport offer networks of connections from the port in the hinterland.

In the hinterland transport of containers, the distance between the seaport and the hinterland regions might be quite substantial. The seaports in the so-called Hamburg and Le Havre range have the complete territory of Europe as a hinterland. Those seaports are competing in the quality and efficiency of the organization of hinterland connections. The ports of Hamburg, Bremen, Rotterdam and Antwerp offer extensive networks with rail connections. Rotterdam and Antwerp also offer high-quality barge connections with regular services.

As railways and inland shipping lines miss the opportunity to deliver containers to the final destination directly, the transfer of containers in inland terminals will be necessary. In those terminals, containers are transferred between trains and trucks or between barges and trucks. Terminals with connections to barge, train and truck are called trimodal terminals. In many cases those terminals develop as important logistic centres with terminals and warehouses, with which logistics service providers offer value-added services to their customers.

According to David Lowe (2005) the most important requirements for an efficient inland terminal are:

- Strategic location to serve key industrial and commercial catchment areas.
- Adequate road access for heavy freight traffic.
- Direct links into the international rail freight network (and if possible into waterway networks).
- Secure space for container storage, and vehicle manoeuvring.
- Suitable equipment for effecting quick and efficient transfer between road and rail, and between road and waterway vessel.

Examples of well-developed regions with terminals and logistics functions are Venlo in the Netherlands, Genk in Belgium, Duisburg, Cologne, Mannheim/Ludwigshafen in Germany, and Basle in Switzerland. Those regions are not only connected to the European main ports, but also are situated alongside or close to important rivers. In Austria, the port of Vienna developed as an important logistics region alongside the river Danube.

Continental Intermodal Transport

Maritime intermodal transport (container transport) has followed the process of globalization in trade. The development of international trade and supply chain management has resulted in a steady growth of container transport over the last few decades.

However, the concept of intermodal transport had already been introduced before the container entered the transport markets. In the 1930s continental intermodal transport was developed in the USA in order to gain greater efficiency in flows of transport over long distances. Sending 20 truck drivers with 20 trucks from the east to the west coast is not considered to be efficient. Possibilities such as bundling the 20 trucks or trailers in one shipment loaded on a train was the founding idea of intermodal transport.

Continental intermodal transport can be defined as the transport of goods originating and terminating in one continent. For this transport a standard loading unit is used for more than one mode of transport. A swap body or trailer might be used as the loading unit, but containers are also to be found in continental traffic. Even complete truck-trailer combinations can be transported by train or ship (barge or short-sea vessel).

The transport of trailers, swap bodies or containers is possible by train, barge or short-sea vessel. This form of intermodal transport by train is often called piggyback or Huckepack. The transport of (unaccompanied) trailers by barge or short-sea vessel is called Roll on-Roll off (RoRo). The accompanied transport of trucks and trailers is known as a Rolling Highway or Rollende Landstrasse in the case of rail transport or ferry service in short-sea transport.

The transhipment of loading units takes place in terminals. Inland terminals normally have a lesser capacity compared with maritime container transport in the main ports. However, the operation is comparable. The handling of loading units is carried out by portal cranes or movable equipment, like reachstackers or fork trucks.

In continental intermodal transport most of the players on the maritime market are also responsible for the operation of continental transport flows.

- The shipper is still the owner of the goods transported and may decide to use intermodal transport or to outsource transport decisions to a freight forwarder. The Incoterms will define the responsibility of the sending or receiving company.
- The freight forwarding company may decide to bundle different shipments and loading units in intermodal transport in order to gain efficiencies in the total transport.

- Further, the trucking companies may decide to bundle loading units in intermodal transport for efficiency reasons.
- Railways, inland waterway shipping lines or short-sea shipping lines operate the transport routes and offer the equipment to the market.
- In the European railway market the intermodal operator plays an important role as it mediates between the railway companies and market demand.
- The terminal operator is the owner of terminal facilities and offers the handlings of loading units to the market.

As already mentioned different loading units might be used in continental intermodal transport. Swap bodies are mostly used in road and rail transport. This equipment is owned by the trucking companies and forms the superstructure of a truck, which can be transferred on a railway wagon. The units are secured both on road vehicles and on rail wagons by means of twistlocks. In the base frame of the loading unit, corner castings are built in that fit on the twistlock cones mounted on the vehicle or wagon. Unlike ISO-containers, swap bodies cannot be stacked in terminals. Instead, they are fitted with folding legs in order to load and unload this equipment at loading bay height. Swap bodies can be operated in three length categories: 12.2 to 13.6 metres length, 9.125 to 10.216 metres length, or 7.15 to 7.82 metres length.

Trailers used in intermodal transport normally have a length of 13.6 metres. Trailers have to comply with European standards in order to be able to be lifted by a crane. The special trailers have a higher tare weight and, for that reason, lower payloads.

In addition to the maritime ISO-container other types of containers are operated in continental intermodal transport, for example tank containers (many containers with a length of 30 feet), reefers, open top, half-height etc. In short-sea transport the 45-feet container is in common use. This type of container has the advantage of a load capacity of 33 Euro-pallets.

As in North America the continental intermodal transport developed in Europe in its bigger countries, where trucks had to move cargo across long distances. Companies like Kombiverkehr in Germany and Novatrans in France developed inland networks in the 1970s. In Alpine countries such as Austria and Switzerland intermodal transport was an instrument for a modal shift of transit flows. For political reasons trucks in transit through those countries were forced to pass by train, and in those countries the Rollende Landstrasse was strongly promoted. However, in the Alpine countries this transport could not be operated profitably and governments had to subsidize the railways and operators for their losses. In smaller countries like Belgium and the Netherlands the continental intermodal transport was only operated in international flows and often in combination with maritime container transport.

Security in Intermodal Transport

As described, intermodal transport is characterized by a transport system that integrates many modes of transport. In logistics the door-to-door concept is part of the total supply chain of industries. Within this concept, transport is derived from production and distribution processes. In most chains of transport, different modes of transport are operated by different parties. An important goal of intermodal transport is the integration of different modes, and the technical harmonization and interoperability between infrastructure and operations.

In a seamless chain of intermodal or multimodal transport the development of an integrated level of security is important. This means that all parties in the chain have taken adequate measures for security. Security in the transport chain is under pressure because of events like terrorist attacks and the theft of cargo and/or means of transport. The events mentioned result in costs of damages, loss of revenues and the disruption of product flows. The result will affect all partners in a transport or supply chain. To reduce the costs that result from security events it is necessary for all partners in a chain to analyse the security risk, which can be defined as the probability of an incident attempt, times the vulnerability of the target, times the damage costs of a successful breach of security (Polzin, 2002).

Three types of security acts in transport can be recognized:

1. Cargo theft.
2. Terrorist acts.
3. Piracy.

Cargo theft is a security problem for all modes of transport. Terrorist acts also affect all modes of transport. Terrorism has to be considered as an act against human life and is not specifically focused on transport chains. However, transport infrastructure and transport facilities are often targets for terrorists. Piracy mostly affects maritime transport and is an act against commodities transported.

In Europe it was the European Commission (EC) which initiated a security policy. The objectives of the EC were:

- To increase the level of security along the supply chain without impeding the free flow of trade.

- To establish a common framework for a systematic European approach without jeopardizing the common transport market and existing security measures.
- To avoid unnecessary administrative procedures and burdens at European and national levels.

According to the principles of the Commission's policy, transport operators are responsible for their own security performance, to allow 'secure operators' to benefit from facilitations where security controls are carried out. A secure operator is an operator who has proven their compliance with minimum security requirements.

The EC published a 'Communication on enhancing supply chain security' on 27 February 2006 for the first time (Commission of the European Communities, 2006, 79). The Commission referred to security measures already introduced by the USA, an important trading partner for EU member states.

For intercontinental transport, measures have also been introduced, especially for maritime transport. This chapter has already made reference to the ISPS Code (see p. 24 above) – ISPS stands for International Ship and Port Facility Security Code and forms a set of measures concerning the security of both ships and port facilities. The Code follows the approach that ensuring the security of ships and port facilities is a risk-management activity. This means that in each case an assessment of risks has to be made. The Code provides a standardized and consistent framework for evaluating risk. It also prescribes responsibilities to governments, shipping companies, shipboard personnel and port and facility personnel to detect security threats and to take preventive measures against security incidents affecting ships or port facilities used in international trade.

In the European Union (EU) the Code has been taken in EC Regulation 725/2004 on enhancing ship and port facility security. The Regulation was complemented by Directive 2005/65. In the ports, all facilities involved in the handling of containers (and other forms of loading units) are obliged to present risk analysis studies and a security plan, based on the risk analysis. Most ships that arrive in ports have to send information before entering the port. This information concerns the International Shipping Security Certificate, the actual security level of the ship and the security measures taken to guarantee the security level.

Regulation 725/2004 and Directive 2005/65 are part of a framework, and member states carry out their own risk assessments and are free to determine appropriate responses. The EC will monitor whether member states are giving consideration to security measures for their ports and the ships that use them. This might result in a situation whereby two similar ports in two different member states have different measures in place.

For continental transport another approach has taken place with the creation of a Land Transport Expert Group, consisting of delegates from member states and industry stakeholders. This expert group had its first meeting in January 2013.

Intercontinental and continental transport have some fundamental differences. In intercontinental transport (both maritime and air transport) there are a limited number of transport operators whereas in continental transport there are more than half a million operators in the EU. However, within continental transport different modes have different operational characteristics, which will result in different risk profiles.

The security risks of continental intermodal transport are limited to the theft of goods during the transport process. This can be done by breaking open the loading units during parking or by stealing a complete loading unit with or without the complete vehicle. Stealing of a loading unit is possible in parking places or terminals that are not secured and guarded. In many countries guarded parking places along important highways are opened to prevent the theft of vehicles or cargo. In rail and water transport the risk of having a loading unit stolen is less high, but the possibility of a loading unit being broken into does exist when the train or ship is not moving or is waiting on a railway yard or in an inland port.

Security risks still take place during transport both on sea and in the hinterland of the ports. Incidents with ships and piracy still happen, although not regularly. The theft of containers or even trucks with containers takes place in road transport. Unauthorized opening of containers may happen on inland terminals or railway yards. For Europe different standards have been introduced, to be applied for all modes of transport:

- The Customs Security Programme (CSP), which introduces proper security controls. The CSP tries to find an equilibrium between security standards on the one hand and the protection of the internal European market on the other.
- The Authorised Economic Operator (AEO), which can be granted to companies, entered into force on 1 January 2008. In 2009, the EU and the USA agreed the reciprocal recognition of each other's AEO programmes.
- Regulation 1875/2006, which was accepted to establish a framework of harmonized risk security assessment in order to achieve an equivalent level of security for customs inspections.

Information Exchange

The flow of goods through a chain of transport is accompanied by a flow of information. Due to the fact that many actors in the market are involved in intermodal transport, the system to exchange information is an important part of the intermodal service. The exchange of information is also important for reasons of security. Customs authorities want to be informed about the content of intermodal loading units as early as possible. Shippers, who are often the owner of the goods, want to be kept informed about the location of the goods at a given moment. For that reason, tracking and tracing systems have been introduced. Tracking and tracing may also help to optimize processes in cases of disturbance to services. Information exchange also helps in planning all the different processes, such as terminal planning and the planning of loading trains or barges.

Information exchange makes it necessary to invest in the standardization and harmonization of information, and in new techniques to read information on loading units and identify freight and loading units during handling processes. In main ports containers nowadays are scanned by customs authorities, which enables the process of handling containers on major maritime container terminals to be carried out more quickly.

Trends and Innovation

Intermodal transport is considered to be an instrument to solve environmental and congestion problems with transport in Europe. For that reason, one may expect a further growth of intermodal transport, both in the maritime and in the continental market. In the maritime market growth will result from a further trend towards containerization and globalization. With the increase in the scale of ocean vessels more containers have to be handled in a restricted time in port terminals. To prevent congestion in terminals, containers have to be transported into the hinterland quickly. Thus, customs control and further security controls have to be moved from port terminals towards inland terminals.

In order to expedite the transfer of containers into the hinterland it is likely that an increase in the scale of the means of transport will be required. In Europe there is already discussion concerning the Longer and Heavier Vehicles (LHV) with a capacity of 3 TEU per vehicle. In addition, railways are also discussing longer trains (1000 metres plus, rather than 650 metres) on European networks. Barges on some European waterways will also show an increase in scale.

For continental intermodal transport there will be a trend to accept more trailers on railway wagons. Instead of a transhipment with cranes, terminals are looking for possibilities to introduce forms of horizontal loading and unloading of trailers. Trailers can be accepted in intermodal transport without special facilities.

Currently, the transhipment of containers and swap bodies without cranes is the subject of research projects. In some countries this development has resulted in the introduction of new equipment like ACTS-containers or mobiler.

Both increases in scale and the simplification of handling systems should result in a lower cost structure for intermodal transport, and a quickening of logistical processes in the flow of goods.

REFERENCES

Commission of the European Communities (2006). Communication to the Council, The European Parliament, The European Economic and Social Committee and the Committee of the Regions on enhancing supply chain security (Com(2006), 79), Brussels.
Lowe, David (2005). *Intermodal Freight Transport*. Oxford: Elsevier Ltd.
Muller, Gerhardt (1995). *Intermodal Freight Transportation*. Landsdowne, VA: Intermodal Association of North America and Eno Transportation Foundation.
Polzin, Steven (2002). *Security Considerations in Transportation Planning: A White Paper*. Southeastern Transportation Center.

3. Economic issues in multimodal freight transport security

Luca Zamparini

1. INTRODUCTION

The last 50 years have been characterized by a relevant increase in world trade that makes use of a variety of transport means to ship intermediate and manufactured goods from one country/continent to others. One significant driver for the development of such massive amounts of international trade has been due to the invention and use of containers. These enable the reduction of terminal costs at the various multimodal hubs. It is thus possible to move a large number of containers from one mode to another (ship, truck, railway and so on) reducing variability in transhipment time and costs. This has led to a massive increase in multimodal transport, especially for medium- and long-distance haulages, as it appears that for distances of less than 500 miles, multimodal transport is not normally an economically efficient alternative.

The relevance of multimodal transport is matched by an enormous number of economic agents that interact at various stages in this market (ECMT, 2005). It is possible to divide them into several categories: a) primary customers (sellers and buyers of intermediate or of merchandised goods); b) transaction facilitation agents (buying agents, freight forwarders, customs brokers); c) transport firms (empty container depot operators, warehouse/warehouse container freight station operators, inland terminal operators, road carriers, rail carriers, barge operators, ocean carriers, port terminal operators, airport operators, among others); d) authorizing or regulatory agencies (transport authorities, customs authorities, import/export licensing authorities, sanitary agencies, import/export statistical agencies, among others); and e) financing agents (banks and insurance providers).

The multimodal transport chains have to be interpreted as complex networks that are physically centered on the main international hubs but whose development depends on the interactions among all of the above-mentioned economic agents. In this respect it is important to consider that shipments can either be intra-firm movements of (normally intermediate) goods or the result of transactions among different firms. The former normally pose fewer threats on the security of the supply chain given that the firm tries to exert full control of the shipment, while the latter present a greater number of potential threats given that a larger number of economic agents is involved, with different degrees of knowledge with respect to all stages of the supply chain. Moreover, it should be noted that, in general, the central legs of a multimodal shipment are carried out by international/large firms which have the economic/financial resources to invest in security protocols and improvements. On the other hand, the first and last legs of a shipment are normally performed by small and medium sized enterprises which cannot have the same level of expertise and financial resources to devote to security (for the discussion of a particular case, see Zamparini and Reniers, 2013). Another important element is related to the above-mentioned number of players in the supply chain; each of them normally characterized by a particular vision of security and, more importantly, each aiming to optimize its profit function. These issues give rise to a series of important problems in the case of uncoordinated security practices. Consequently, regulatory frameworks should take into full consideration the possible incentive schemes that can lead to the cooperation of the economic actors in the supply chain.

This chapter aims to assess the economic relevance of a series of issues that arise when multimodal freight transport is considered. It is structured as follows. The next section will provide an analysis of the various container security measures that have been implemented over the last few decades. It will be followed by section 3 which presents a discussion of the main public initiatives to improve multimodal transport security. This will be followed by section 4 in which the two most important private initiatives for multimodal freight security will be analyzed. Section 5 concludes the chapter.

2.   THE ECONOMIC RELEVANCE OF CONTAINER SECURITY MEASURES

According to a review proposed in the above-mentioned ECMT (2005) publication, the measures targeted at increasing the security of container shipments can fall into one of five possible categories: 1) scanning and inspection; 2) the physical integrity of the container; 3) the container environment; 4) tracking and tracing; and 5) trade documents, data and intelligence. The first set of measures – scanning and inspection – is considered to be the most effective given that the content of the container is directly checked, either via an intrusive or a non-intrusive inspection. This was one part of the measures proposed in the aftermath of 9/11, by means of the Container Security Initiative. Although very effective, this measure has been proved to be almost impossible to implement consistently; the problem being related to the high costs, from both an economic and a time perspective, for firms. Moreover, the efficacy of screening depends heavily on the skills of the personnel employed; however, training can be very costly. The EU Commission (2010) has estimated that at the EU level, full compliance to the container security initiative would have implied a relevant financial burden of approximately €430 million. A possible alternative, which can be more economically viable, is represented by a combination of screening and scanning activities; where screening consists of a prior selection of the containers that may have a high degree of risk according to a series of parameters (ports of call, shipper, and so on). Although it is very unlikely that a 100 percent degree of effective screening is accomplished, its use would reduce the time and cost components of the shipments by at the same time increasing the security level of the supply chain.

The second set of measures is aimed at guaranteeing the physical integrity of the container in order to avoid an intrusion into the content of the container. This set of measures originated in the early 1970s, aiming to minimize the risk of theft of the container's content. However, the same measures can be used effectively to prevent terrrorist acts. The integrity of containers is mainly obtained through the use of seals and through the related checking protocols. The first generation of seals was mechanical in nature and, over time, firms have resorted to stronger materials in order to reduce the possibility of damage to them. The second generation of seals was electronic and encompasses a physical sealing device and an electronic data interchange device that can signal whether the seal has been attacked or broken by thieves/terrorists. From an economic viewpoint, electronic seals are definitely the best option given that their extra cost can be justified not just by the reduction in the probability of container tampering but also because, in a wider supply chain perspective, their use can allow the optimization of other cost components of the supply chains (i.e. custom clearance).

A further possible measure to increase the security of containers' shipments deals with securing the container environment. This is the most costly strategy given that it implies securing all the possible sites in which the container is stored, transported and handled. First, it is necessary to bear in mind that the security of the container environment depends on the private investments of the firms that are involved in the supply chain, but the role of the public administrations is also very important. It is

related for example to the provision of efficient and secure border crossing facilities, where it is important to invest in the training of personnel
and on the infrastructures. Moreover, all public intermodal hubs (airports,
ports, and so on) need to be designed or, in most cases, updated to take
into account the deployment of security protocols and procedures. In this
respect, an important element would lie in the cooperation between the
public sector and the private firms. It would be beneficial to devise a set
of economic incentives that might motivate firms to participate in plans
like the Customs-Trade Partnership Against Terrorism (C-TPAT) that
was conceived as a joint government–business initiative. Moreover, the
most vulnerable sites along the supply chain should be identified by means
of multicriteria or risk analyses to maximize the security of containers
flowing along the supply chain.

The fourth set of measures is related to tracking and tracing containers.
This goal can be obtained by the use of two different strategies. The first
requires the identification of a series of checkpoints that should record
the passage of containers. The second strategy makes use of transponders
or of others' Radio-frequency Identification (RFID) devices to follow the
containers all along the supply chain. This second option means not only
that containers can be followed during their normal shipments but also
that containers that may have been stolen or lost during the shipment can
be retrieved. The first option was the one commonly used in past decades.
However, the widespread diffusion of satellite GPS has substantially
lowered the costs of using RFID which has proliferated in the freight
transport sector. All tracking systems need to mediate between the need
for public agencies to monitor the movement of containers for security
reasons and the privacy issues of firms that may be reluctant to share such
data.

The final set of measures is aimed at managing and checking trade documents and information. One initiative that falls into this category in the
aftermath of 9/11 is that related to the role of the Authorised Economic
Operator (AEO) that was envisaged by the World Customs Organization
and applied by several countries or areas (the EU, New Zealand, Singapore,
Taiwan and the United States, among others). The status of AEO is
granted to firms that can demonstrate that they meet precise information and security requirements. At the firm's level this implies some costs
in order to obtain such certification. However, in a cost–benefit analysis,
the costs incurred are normally more than justified by the gains in terms
of the facilitation or simplification of customs controls, priority in cargo
checks and reduced transit times (see, for a description, Papa, 2013). At
the market level, this strategy has been questioned over the possibility
that small and medium sized enterprises may not have sufficient financial

resources to adapt to the requirements of the AEO initiative and thus would be excluded from the market.

This section has considered the specific container-related strategies that can be adopted to increase supply chain security. The next section will discuss the economic issues related to the most important initiatives that have been adopted by the United States, by the EU and by some Asian countries to improve multimodal freight transport security.

3.   THE ECONOMIC ISSUES OF THE MAIN PUBLIC INITIATIVES TO IMPROVE MULTIMODAL FREIGHT TRANSPORT SECURITY

This section will provide a detailed discussion of the main economic issues related to the main national and international initiatives that have been implemented since 2002 to increase the degree of multimodal transport security in various regions of the world. It will first consider the United States. Then it will take into account the EU, and finally it will discuss the STAR (Secure Trade in the APEC Region) conferences that have involved the countries belonging to the Asia-Pacific Economic Cooperation (APEC) forum.

3.1   The Main US Multimodal Security Initiatives

The United States is definitely the country that has proposed the largest number of multimodal security initiatives since the tragic events of 9/11. The main initiatives are: a) the Container Security Initiative (CSI) which began in 2001; b) the Customs-Trade Partnership Against Terrorism (C-TPAT) which began in 2002; c) the Food and Drug Administration Bioterrorism Act that also began in 2002; d) the Megaports Initiative that entered into force in 2003; e) the 24-hour advance vessel manifest rule that also started in 2003; f); Importer Security Filing (ISF) or '10+2' which began in 2009; and g) the 100 percent scanning initiative that was issued by the US legislation in 2007 and that should have come to existence in 2012. Alongside these specific initiatives, it is also worth mentioning the Operation Safe Commerce program. This program was funded by the US Congress and aimed at fostering public-private partnerships to identify supply chain vulnerabilities and to propose new technologies and processes to enhance the security of the supply chain. Table 3.1 proposes a brief description of these initiatives by focusing on the types of program that are described in section 3.2 and on their main goals.

Table 3.1 shows that the various initiatives that have been proposed

Table 3.1   The main US initiatives for multimodal freight security

Initiative	Type of program	Main aim of the initiative
CSI (Container Security Initiative)	Tracking and tracing cargo	Increasing security related to ocean-going sea containers through the targeting and screening of high-risk containers bound for the US before they are loaded
C-TPAT (Customs-Trade Partnership Against Terrorism)	Managing and checking documents and information	Transferring some of the customs control responsibilities to importers and exporters in order to reinforce overall security levels
FDA Bioterrorism Act	Managing and checking documents and information	Firms must register their supply chain partners and describe the content of the containers they ship at least eight hours before importing the goods
Megaports Initiative	Tracking and tracing cargo	Reducing the illicit trafficking of special nuclear and other radiological materials of proliferation concern
24-hour advance vessel manifest rule	Managing and checking documents and information	Implementing the cargo-related information at least 24 hours before a container is loaded aboard the vessel at the foreign port
ISF (Importer Security Filing) '10+2'	Managing and checking documents and information Screening	Integrates the previous initiative by requiring supplemantary information to be provided to the Customs and Border Protection office in order to screen for suspicious cargo
100% scanning initiative	Physical integrity of the container	Inspection of 100 percent of all inbound containers in order to prevent the entrance of any illegal or dangerous goods
Operation Safe Commerce	All measures considered in section 3.2	Conduct vulnerability assessments of sample supply chains and serve as a benchmark for new business processes and security technologies to increase the security of container shipments

Sources: Papa, 2013 and author's elaboration.

and implemented by the United States have dealt with all possible series of measures that were described in section 2. Most of the initiatives have related to the management and checking of documents and information. Moreover, the tracking and tracing of containers has been an option that has been considered by three out of seven initiatives. The main issue that characterizes all the above-mentioned initiatives is the existing trade-off between the security and efficiency of the supply chain (see, among others, Brooks, 2008). It is recognized that, in the aftermath of the 9/11 episodes, US regulations have put an emphasis on security as their main objective, considering cost and trade issues as a lower objective. However, the combined reading of Limao and Venables (2001) and of Leonard (2001) allows us to consider the relationship between security-related measures and the increase in the costs of trading, and the elasticity between the latter and world trade flows (of an approximate value of 3). In a global perspective, the economic costs of many of these initiatives have constituted a specific entry barrier for a large number of small and medium sized shipping firms that have lacked the necessary financial and human capital endowments to comply with the higher security standards required by these initiatives. Moreover, this has implied that many developing economies need to resort to shippers from developed countries to deliver their goods to the final markets, delaying the promotion of a system of local supply chain firms.

3.2 The Main EU Multimodal Security Initiatives

The main EU initiatives aimed at increasing the security of the supply chain have also been implemented since 2001 and have emerged, as in all other sectors of EU legislation, out of the necessity to balance general EU objectives and country interests. From an economic viewpoint, it must be emphasized that the EU regulations have tried to follow an approach that would enhance security but would also consider the trade effects (and, particularly, the need to avoid the discrimination of some of the ports, and to avoid competition among all ports belonging to member states). Moreover, all EU initiatives have tried to tackle operational efficiency by aiming to contain time losses and relevant cost increases.

The main initiatives that have been related to the enhancement of multimodal transportation security are: a) the AEO initiative; b) the Advance Notification System; and c) the Secure Operator Proposal. These initiatives were outlined in the EU's Customs Security Programme that was proposed by the EU Commission to the EU Parliament at the end of 2003. The main characteristics of the above mentioned initiatives are summarized in Table 3.2.

An initiative which was proposed in 2006 but which was withdrawn

Table 3.2   The main EU initiatives for multimodal freight security

Initiative	Type of program	Main aim of the initiative
Authorised Economic Operator (AEO)	Container environment; trade documents	Grant the status of AEO to firms which can prove their economic stability, their security control systems and their capability to abide by existing customs rules. The AEO will gain the right to a lower frequency of inspections and to simpler formats for entry and exit declarations
Advance Notification System	Trade documents	Allow the EU customs authorities to gain extensive advance information on the goods that are bound to one of the EU countries, or that will be exported from one EU country

due to the criticisms it received from several business associations was the 'Secure Operator' proposal. This had the aim of making every single supply chain operator responsible for the security of its shipments, the objective being to enhance the security level of the overall supply chain with a low cost to the public administration. The economic benefit would be similar to that related to the AEO in lowering the economic and time costs of the security controls.

The economic effects of the AEO and of the Advance Notification System initiatives are connected to the fact that they can hamper seamless trades for small and medium sized firms that may face huge difficulty in complying with the extensive information that is required by this initiative (Altemoller, 2011). The long-term effect may be one of market discrimination for the firms that are not able to efficiently manage the requirements of this system.

3.3   The Asian STAR (Secure Trade in the APEC Region) Conferences

The countries belonging to the APEC have tackled the security issues related to (international) multimodal transport mainly by means of a series of conferences that have been taking place since 2003.[1] The main aim of this series of conferences has been the identification of an integrated and comprehensive approach to enhance the security of trade in the region by also taking into account the need to guarantee the efficiency and resilience of regional commerce. These conferences have also aimed to gather governments' representatives of all the APEC region countries, of private firms and of multilateral institutions. On the basis of the STAR conferences, several dedicated working groups have been established to tackle specific problems related to freight transport security. Table 3.3 provides essential information related to the first nine STAR conferences.

As can be seen, all the STAR conferences placed a considerable emphasis on the need to integrate enhanced security with the containment of economic costs related to all initiatives. On the other hand, the need to involve private institutions in the development of security initiatives appears to have been the most important element of success. The next section will discuss the economic impact of the main security initiatives that have been based on private cooperation.

4. THE ECONOMIC IMPACT OF PRIVATE MULTIMODAL TRANSPORT SECURITY PROGRAMS

The previous section has discussed the main multimodal freight transport security initiatives that have emerged in several regions of the world on the basis of public initiative. This section is aimed at discussing two of the most relevant security related initiatives that have emerged from private cooperation.

4.1   The Transported Asset Protection Association (TAPA) Initiative

The Transported Asset Protection Association (TAPA) initiative was initially conceived in the United States but was then diffused through the EU and Asia (National Board of Trade, 2008). It is focused on the supply chain of high-value goods. It then addresses companies producing and/ or transporting particular brands (initially only high-tech brands but later including other high-value goods merchandise categories) that may incur very high economic costs in the case of the theft of their shipments. Within the TAPA framework, three main programs were developed: 1) the incident information service; 2) the freight suppliers' minimum security requirements; and 3) the freight suppliers' minimum trucking security requirements. The first program – the incident information service – aims to rapidly diffuse information regarding thefts and, consequently, to lower the average costs of the recovery of stolen goods. Moreover, the database related to all thefts enables the implementation of a statistically sound risk analysis in order to identify the main problem areas and to channel the

Table 3.3   STAR conferences

Venue and date	Main proposals, issues and criticalities
Bangkok (Thailand), 23–25 February 2003	Need for a strong partnership between governments and private firms. The various countries have different levels of resources and skills to implement the initiatives
Viña del Mar (Chile), 4–6 March 2004	Advance compliance with the International Maritime Organization initiatives; development of a regional movement alert list system; machine readable documents
Incheon (Korea), 25–26 February 2005	Enhancement of the private involvement on security initiatives. Strong focus on aviation and maritime security
Ha Noi (Vietnam), 23–24 February 2006	Reducing the adverse impacts of security initiatives on trade and investments in the APEC region. Private involvement in security initiatives
Sydney (Australia), 27–28 June 2007	The main theme of this fifth conference was the consideration of costs of security initiatives and the need to achieve a mitigation of risks jointly with the containment of costs
Lima (Peru), 20–21 August 2008	Enhancement of security with a low impact on trade. Consideration of the vulnerability of the region. Benchmarking on successful experiences in other regions
Singapore, 30–31 July 2009	Security threats to the global economy. Security, resilience and effective trade recovery. Integrated approach to secure trade. Building trust and transparency
San Francisco (USA), 15–16 September 2011	Need to develop a risk based approach with multiple layers of security. Sharing of advance information. Collaboration with multilateral institutions (i.e. IMO, WCO)
Beijing (China), 6–7 August 2014	Discussion of APEC countries' initiatives to control threats in marine transportation. Sharing of experiences and best practices in container transportation security

Source: APEC website (http://www.apec.org/Groups/SOM-Steering-Committee-on-Economic-and-Technical-Cooperation/Working-Groups/Counter-Terrorism/Secure-Trade-in-the-APEC-Region.aspx).

resources related to investments efficiently so as to improve the security of the supply chain.

The freight supplier minimum security requirements initiative fosters the implementation of technologies that avail sound security routines. Such measures are related to both internal and external security. The economic benefit emerging from such measures was evaluated by a study by Purtell (2007) which estimated that the average company would reduce its losses from thefts by 40 percent.

The freight supplier minimum trucking security requirements initiative was introduced in 2006 due to large increases in the number of truck hijackings in the previous years. One difference between this latter initiative and the previous one is the emphasis placed on the training of personnel. All sets of possible measures of security from loading to unloading of trucks were taken into account. Moreover, the economic benefit of the efficient flow of information (in terms of, for example, advance notification, reports and scheduled routes) was given a high priority.

4.2   The Business Alliance for Secure Commerce Initiative

The Business Alliance for Secure Commerce (BASC) program emerged from the initiative of a private company that imported goods from Latin American countries. The aim was to establish a set of protocols and procedures that would impede the use of legitimate cargo for the smuggling of illicit or dangerous goods. During its existence, this program has developed more than 100 security measures that are related to personnel, to physical security, to electronic security systems, to document and data security, and to seals and stamps. The incentive for firms to join the BASC program is that it has established itself as a signalling mechanism that is required by the most important suppliers and customers.

A study conducted by Gutierrez et al. (2007) has estimated the costs for private companies to join the BASC program. It has emerged that such costs amount to more than 50 percent of the yearly turnover for small firms (whose yearly turnover is below US$50 000). They amount to between 3 percent and 34 percent for firms with a turnover between US$50 000 and US$500 000, between 1 percent and 3 percent for firms with a yearly turnover between US$500 000 and US$1 million, between 1 percent and 6 percent for firms with a turnover between US$1 million and US$5 million, and below 1 percent for the largest firms (whose yearly turnover is above US$5 million). It is evident that they represent a huge burden for small firms while, for the largest firms, the relatively low investment costs are justified by the threat of losing important market segments. The main benefit pursued by most companies was, in fact, the improvement of the company image and credibility. Other important stated goals of participation to the BASC initiative were the reduction of smuggling, theft and supply chain vulnerability. Of lesser importance seemed to be the indirect cost savings and the reduction of insurance premiums. One issue that characterized all firms surveyed in the Gutierrez et al. (2007) sample was the difficulty in quantitatively estimating the benefits related to participation in the BASC initiative. Only 40 percent of the firms were able to provide a quantitative estimation and most of them were unable to certify where and how they originated. However, no clear relationship was demonstrated between the cost of the security measures and their effectiveness; while a mild positive relationship between the number of implemented applicable measures and the obtained/expected benefits appeared to be present.

5.   CONCLUSIONS

This chapter has discussed the main economic issues related to the multimodal freight transport security. Section 2 has discussed the main contexts in which container/supply chain security can be applied by highlighting the different costs and impacts on trade and on firms' costs. The analysis in section 3 has shown that there has been a heterogeneity of approaches in the various regions of the world to tackling the security problem. A higher emphasis on security has been demonstrated by the United States, while the strategies adopted by the EU and by the Asian/Pacific countries have placed a higher emphasis on the costs of implementing security measures and on the importance of proactively involving private firms. These latter economic actors have in some cases promoted initiatives to enhance security. Throughout the chapter, it has emerged that in most cases these initiatives work as signaling institutions for international trade and, therefore, firms are eager to abide by these initiatives in order not to lose important market segments. The analysis of this chapter will be complemented by the discussions that will be carried out in the chapters that constitute Part II of this book. They will try to describe in detail the particular approaches to security that were followed in several countries located in various regions of the world.

NOTE

1.   This subsection will discuss the conferences that took place before this chapter was written (end of 2014).

REFERENCES

Altemoller, F. (2011), 'Towards an international regime of supply chain security: an international relations perspective', *World Customs Journal*, **5** (2), 21–34.

Brooks, M. R. (2008), *North American Freight Transportation: The Road to Security and Prosperity*, Cheltenham, UK and Northampton, MA, USA: Edward Elgar Publishing.

ECMT (European Conference of Ministers of Transport) (2005), *Container Transport Security Across Modes*, Paris: OECD.

EU Commission (2010), *Secure Trade and 100% Scanning of Containers*, European Commission Staff Working Paper.

Gutierrez, X., J. Hintsa, P. Wieser and A. P. Hameri (2007), 'Voluntary supply chain security program impacts: an empirical study with BASC member companies', *World Customs Journal*, **1** (2), 31–48.

Leonard, J. (2001), 'Impact of the September 11, 2001 terrorist attacks on North American trade flows', Manufacturers Alliance/MAPI e-Alerts, Arlington, Virginia.

Limao, N. and A. Venables (2001), 'Infrastructure, geographical disadvantage, transport costs and trade', *World Bank Economic Review*, **15** (3), 451–479.

National Board of Trade (2008), *Supply Chain Security Initiatives: A Trade Facilitation Perspective*, Stockholm: Kommerskollegium.

Papa, P. (2013), 'US and EU strategies for maritime transport security: a comparative perspective', *Transport Policy*, **28**, 75–85.

Purtell, D. (2007), Best Security Practices in Outsourcing the Global Supply Chain, 2007 Performance Conference, 30 October 2007.

Zamparini, L. and G. Reniers (2013), 'A comparative study of hazardous material transportation security issues in Flanders and in Apulia', *Security Journal*, **26**, 142–156.

4. Assessing vulnerability in multimodal supply chains

Jyri Vilko, Lauri Lättilä and Jukka Hallikas

INTRODUCTION

Global supply chains are comprised of a multitude of companies acting as part of a long and complex, multimodal logistics system that is increasingly vulnerable to various disturbances (Wagner and Neshat, 2010; Vilko, 2012). The length and complexity of supply chains are derived from the many parallel physical and informational flows that are in place to ensure that products are delivered in the right quantities, to the right place, in a cost-effective manner (Jüttner, 2005). The increased length and complexity of multimodal transportation chains is attributable to multiple sources and this complexity, in turn, drives supply chain vulnerability (Mason-Jones, 1998; Harland et al., 2003; Brindley, 2004; Hult, 2004; Craighead et al., 2007; Waters, 2007; Narasimhan and Talluri, 2009; Thun and Hoenig, 2011).

Transport logistics have become increasingly significant in an era of international trade (Beresford et al., 2011). Although logistics were previously seen as purely operational, they are now regarded as a strategic issue for many organizations (Gattorna, 1998; Frankel et al., 2008). In order to be competitive, companies are leaning towards complex logistics networks that act more as an extension of their core competitive advantage. As such, supply chains are becoming more agile, with the purpose of getting products to customers more quickly and at a minimum total cost (Gunasekaran et al., 2008). Thus, the level of logistics service provision can determine how competitive an organization is and whether it will retain its customers or attract new ones (Oflac et al., 2012).

Multimodal transportation systems have increased inter-organizational dependency, and inter-organizational relationships have become increasingly important (Soosay et al., 2008). Integrated and seamless logistics can play a crucial role in facilitating global transportation processes (Banomyong, 2005). Yet, in practice, greater integration increases dependency between companies, which can have the undesirable effect of increasing vulnerability. It is essential that actors collaborate and share information within their network to avoid interruptions in logistics flows (Edwards et al., 2001; Svensson, 2001).

Many recent events have highlighted the vulnerability of long and complex chains. A risk realization affecting operations anywhere in the supply chain can have a direct effect on the progress of operations, thus endangering the security of supply to the market and to customers. A prime example of the effects of disruptions was the ten-day shutdown of 29 ports in the US in 2002 that wound up costing the US economy USD1 billion per day (Jüttner, 2005; Park et al., 2008). Furthermore, investor reactions can be significant, in that companies admitting to major supply chain difficulties have seen their shareholder value drop by 10 percent on average (Handfield and McCormack, 2008; Hendricks et al., 2009).

It is clear from the above that logistics has been undergoing continuous, considerable and rapid change and that the primary focus has been on supply chain vulnerability (Frankel et al., 2008). In the past decade, scientific discussion has focused on supply chain risk management. However, while some scholars (e.g. Peck, 2005; Sheffi, 2005) have contributed to the issue of vulnerability, the concept has received only limited attention in the context of supply chains. Therefore, we aim to shed light on vulnerability assessment in multimodal supply chains by first presenting different methods of analysis and, second, by illustrating a picture of supply chain vulnerability.

THEORY

This section presents the main concepts – namely supply chain, vulnerability and risk, and supply chain risk management and analysis – in terms of multimodal transport logistics.

Supply Chain, Vulnerability and Risk

A supply chain is defined as a system of suppliers, manufacturers, distributors, retailers and customers in which material, financial and information flows connect participants in both directions (Fiala, 2005). According to Waters (2007) a supply chain consists of a series of activities and organizations through which material moves on its journey from initial suppliers to final customers.

To define supply chain vulnerability, it is essential to first examine the characteristics of risk. The literature defines risk in a multitude of ways. Waters (2007) defines it as a threat that something might happen to disrupt normal activities and prevent things from happening as planned. Typically, risk is defined as to have negative impact, leading to undesired results or consequences (Harland et al., 2003; Manuj and Mentzer, 2008). A standard formula for the quantitative definition of supply chain risk is:

$$Risk = P \times I \tag{4.1}$$

where P is the probability of a risk event, and I is the impact of the risk event (Mitchell, 1995).

Supply chain risk can be seen as originating from any unwanted event that concerns the material, information or cash flow from the initial supplier to the end customer. Risk can arise from organizations, supply chain partners or from the external environment (Waters, 2007). How sensitive a supply chain is to these disturbances is measured by its vulnerability.

According to Wagner and Bode (2008, p. 304), 'supply chain vulnerability is a function of certain supply chain characteristics, and the loss a firm incurs is a result of its supply chain vulnerability to a given supply chain disruption'. Asbjørnslett (2008) defines vulnerability as 'the properties of a supply chain system; its premises, facilities and equipment, including human resources, human organization and all its software, hardware, netware that may weaken or limit its ability to endure threats and survive accidental events that originate both within and outside system boundaries'. Previous definitions have differed somewhat from this. For example, Peck (2005) describes vulnerability as 'exposure to serious disturbance, arising from risks within the supply chain as well as risks external to the supply chain'. Furthermore, according to Waters (2007), 'supply chain vulnerability reflects the susceptibility of a supply chain to disruption and is a consequence of the risks to the chain'. Jüttner (2005) describes supply chain vulnerability as the propensity of risk sources and risk drivers to outweigh risk-mitigating strategies, thus causing adverse supply chain consequences and jeopardizing the supply chain's ability to effectively serve the end customer market. Synthesizing from the above definitions, we define supply chain vulnerability as *the supply chain system's exposure to unwanted and unexpected risk events that originate both within and outside the supply chain system.*

According to Asbjørnslett (2008), the difference between vulnerability analysis and risk analysis is the focus of the analysis. While vulnerability analysis focuses on the holistic supply chain perspective in terms of system mission and the security of supply, risk analysis focuses more on the impact of individual events. When examined from a quantitative perspective, the difference between risk and vulnerability is expressed in terms of the exposure-element; here we define the supply chain vulnerability formula as follows:

$$Vulnerability = \Sigma(P \times I \times E) \tag{4.2}$$

where P is the probability of a risk event, I is the impact of the risk event, and E is the exposure to the risk.

In reality, when considering supply chain vulnerability, actors can better affect the probability of a risk event when they have control over the operations (risk emanating within the supply chain) or affecting the exposure of the supply chain to the risk events (risk coming from outside the supply chain). Thus, when analyzing appropriate responses to supply chain vulnerability, the origin of the risk event needs to be taken into account.

Vulnerability Analysis in Multimodal Supply Chains

Vulnerability analysis is an integral part of supply chain risk management processes. Supply chain risk analysis is a component of supply chain management and refers to a proactive relationship and integration among various tiers in the chain (Trkman et al., 2007). A comprehensive view of a supply chain is necessary for management to construct a holistic understanding of the sources of risk. Jüttner et al. (2003) define supply chain risk management as 'the identification and management of risks of the supply chain, through a coordinated approach amongst supply chain members, to reduce supply chain vulnerability as a whole'. Thus, supply chain risk management aims to identify and assess potential sources of risk and implement appropriate action to avoid or contain supply chain vulnerability. The vulnerabilities affecting the supply chain should take the source of the risk into account so that contingencies can be devised to mitigate their effects or prevent their occurrence. All supply chains carry some risk, but the extent depends on a multiplicity of factors, including the density, criticality and node density of the network as well as the transportation modes used (Vilko, 2012).

Multimodal supply chains are international combinations of various modes of transport, such as ship, rail and road. In essence, there are two main characteristics of multimodal logistics: first, there is typically more than one means of transport from one place to another; and, second, the chain includes loading/unloading facilities in order to transfer from one means to another and to/from transport tools of different types (Hu, 2011).

Figure 4.1 illustrates the various steps of a vulnerability analysis of multimodal supply chains. In the first step, the scope of analysis is

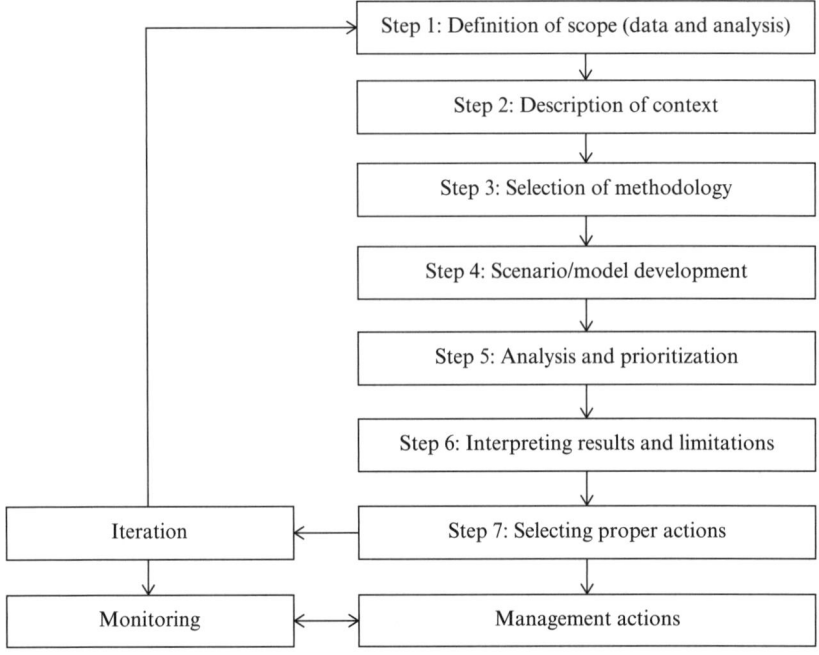

Source: Modified from Asbjørnslett, 2008.

Figure 4.1 Steps of vulnerability assessment in multimodal supply chains

defined on the basis of the available data and its quality. In the second step, the context of the multimodal supply chain is described. The third step is the selection of an appropriate methodology based on the two earlier steps. Based on the methodology and data, the scenario and/or model is created in the fourth step, followed by analysis and prioritization in the fifth step. The sixth step includes interpreting the results of the analysis and discussing its inherent limitations, after which appropriate actions are selected in the seventh step. The vulnerability analysis continues with the selected management actions, followed by iterative rounds and results monitoring.

In multimodal supply chain vulnerability analysis, it is essential to select an appropriate method based on the available data and its quality. Among other things, the results depend directly on the data input. The next section will present on the selection process of an appropriate method for vulnerability analyses.

Security of Supply in Multimodal Supply Chains

There are several ways to ensure the security of supply, which typically differ according to country. The concept of security of supply was developed by the Finnish National Emergency Supply Agency (Finnish Council of State, 2008), and 'The objective is to ensure the continuity of production and infrastructure vital to society under all circumstances in such a way that the living conditions of the population and the critical functions of society are secured also in the event of disruptions and emergencies, such as state of defence' (author's translation). Similarly, in the case of managing supply chain vulnerability, the concept of security of supply can be seen as the continuation of operations whereby organizations can identify and analyze the vulnerabilities and contingencies in normal situations and manage them in case of disruptions.

To ensure the proper management of security risk, it is essential to identify the risk factors that may have significant impact on the operational or financial performance of the multimodal logistics system. In the modern multimodal transport chain, the sources of security risk are vast. Transport chains are exposed to criminal actions, terrorism, climate conditions, work safety and personnel-related security risks. The leaner the global supply chains in terms of material and capacity buffers, the more vulnerable companies become to the security risks.

There are specific techniques that provide a structured framework for risk identification and the analysis of vulnerabilities in the transportation chain. For example, the FMEA (Failure Mode and Effect Analysis) framework can be used for investigating potential security-related failure modes and their causes and effects in a supply security case and for identifying actions that can reduce or eliminate the likelihood of potential failure (Chuang, 2007).

SELECTING AN APPROPRIATE METHOD FOR VULNERABILITY ANALYSIS

A complete understanding of the consequences of a risk is impossible to analyze because of data-related limitations and uncertainty that offer only a limited view of the vulnerabilities facing a supply chain. In many cases, supply chain information sharing is limited, which can hinder exposure to the vulnerabilities and processes in the supply chain. In these cases, the method of analysis has to be carefully selected in order to obtain relevant results. Selecting an appropriate analytical method can improve the accuracy of the assessment. Conversely, selecting an inappropriate method can hinder the results of the supply chain.

Table 4.1   Example of vulnerability analysis method selection based on the amount of data and its certainty levels in operational security events

	High amount of data	Moderate amount of data	Limited amount of data
Data with probabilistic certainty	Mathematical models with focus on optimization	Mathematical models with focus on robust solutions	Mathematical models with focus on scenario testing
Data with parametric uncertainty	Statistical analysis with focus on intervals	Statistical analysis with focus on parametric causalities	Simulation with focus on parametric estimation
Data with structural uncertainty	Supervised data mining techniques with focus on improving the holistic understanding of operational events and causalities behind them	Cause-and-effect diagrams with focus on improving the understanding of local causalities formed by operational events	Flow chart with focus on improving general structural understanding
Data with procedural uncertainty	Unsupervised data mining techniques with focus on finding correlations	Affinity diagrams with focus on finding relations	Intuition

Several factors contribute to the success of a vulnerability analysis, such as the personal skills of the logistics managers and the availability of software. More essentially, however, the accuracy of the analysis is based on the data, namely the amount (and availability) of it as well as its quality – in other words, the uncertainty it holds. Table 4.1 illustrates an example of selections based on these two factors.

The amount of data in the analysis is divided into three categories: a high amount, a moderate amount and a limited amount of data. The uncertainty of the data is divided into four categories (Vilko and Ritala, 2012). The first category is the certainty of probabilities whereby the available data is very accurate, and the structure and objective mathematical probabilities of future events are known. The second category is parametric uncertainty whereby the structure of the future is known, but the probability parameters are not certain. The third category is structural uncertainty whereby there is only imperfect knowledge of the structures, and the future and analysis rely mostly on subjective beliefs. The fourth and final category is data containing procedural uncertainty whereby there is severe limitation in understanding the structures of the supply chain processes and the causalities of events.

VULNERABILITY ASSESSMENT ILLUSTRATION IN MULTIMODAL SUPPLY CHAINS

In this section, we utilize simulation to understand, in a holistic way, vulnerability deriving from operational security events in multimodal transportation. If one simply analyzes individual nodes or trans-shipment, or simply combines separate analyses, it would not be possible to understand the risks to the supply chain as a whole. In this section, a conceptual simulation model is presented, which can be used to understand the manner in which exposure impacts on the functionality of the supply chain. Robinson (2004, p. 4) defines simulation as 'experimentation with a simplified imitation (on a computer) of an operations system as it progresses through time, for the purpose of better understanding and/or improving that system'. In this section, we present a model that has been developed using Discrete Event Simulation (DES) as it is suitable for the problem domain.

Simulation Model Structure

The simulation model consists of a supply chain in which a container is transported from Asia to a European facility. The supply chain starts with a truck transport from the manufacturer to a local Asian feeder port. The container is then transported from the smaller feeder port to a major Asian port. From there, the container is transported on a large container ship to a major European port. From the major port, a smaller feeder ship transports the container to a local port, and, finally, a truck delivers the container to its final destination.

The supply chain is converted in the simulation model as individual nodes which represent warehouses and seaports and the forms of transport connecting these together. One node and the associated forms of transport are presented in Figure 4.2. In the simulation model, the transport modes are modeled as delays (transportation). The transportation time might include a degree of stochasticity, which would represent daily differences in the transportation process. When the transport reaches its destination, the model will check whether there is additional delay due to risk realization (excessDelay). This additional delay would represent the risk factor

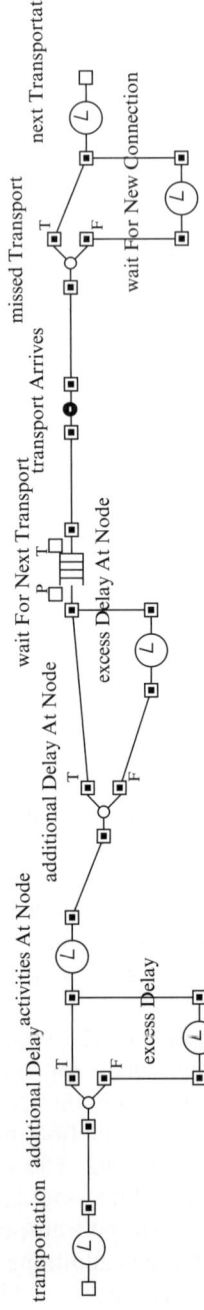

Figure 4.2   A node in the simulation model

of the specific transport (for example, the probability and impact of the risks). The vulnerability of the supply chain is considered by multiplying the stochastic delay with the exposure level of the organization. This is presented in (4.3):

$$excessDelay = D_t \times E_t \qquad (4.3)$$

where, D_t is the stochastic delay for transport t, and E_t is the exposure level of the organization for transport t.

When the transport finally reaches its destination, there might be some additional activities at the node (activitiesAtNode). These include stevedoring, customs etc. These locations might have excess delays due to various reasons (excessDelayAtNode). The container will then wait at the node for the next available transport (waitForNextTranport). When the scheduled transport leaves (transportArrives), the container is also allowed to leave the node. If the container does not reach the node on time, it will miss the transport (missedTransport). This would create an additional delay in the transportation process (waitForNewConnection) and will also include stochasticity. After these steps, the container returns to the transportation part of the supply chain (nextTransportation).

Simulation Model Parameters

The simulation model consists of three different types of random distributions: delivery delays, delays due to waiting for a substitute transport and exceptional delays due to realized risks. In the simulation model, we utilize a triangular distribution for most of these (the only exception are container ships from Asia to Europe). Triangular distribution has a minimum value, a maximum value and a mode value. All of these values are presented in Table 4.2.

In addition to the delays, the probability of risks occurring has a high impact on the results. Different parts of the supply chain will have different risks. The probabilities for the exceptional delays are presented in Table 4.3.

The supply chain might also be buffered at the main nodes (Asian feeder port, Asian major port, European major port). This can be done by planning the entire journey to include potential storage at these nodes. In the simulation model, we use 24-hour buffers at all of the three main nodes to incorporate minor delays in the supply chain.

In order to analyze vulnerability, we use different exposure levels to test the sensitivity of the multimodal supply chain to risks. We use exposure levels from 10 percent to 100 percent with an interval of 10 percent on two

Table 4.2   Transportation delays (in hours)

Part of supply chain	Normal operations delays			Additional delays due to risk realizations		
	Min	Mode	Max	Min	Mode	Max
Truck to Asian feeder port	3.5	4	6	0	2	24
Operations at Asian feeder port	1	1.5	2	0	24	168
Asian feeder ship	72	74	76	0.5	24	48
Operations at major Asian port	0.5	1	1.5	0	24	48
Container liner from Asia to Europe	744	744	744	0	72	240
Operations at major European port	1	2	3	0	48	96
European feeder ship	96	98	100	0	5	10
Operations at European feeder port	2	3	5	0	48	96
Short-term depot waiting for truck	0.5	3	12	–	–	–
Final truck delivery to destination	2.5	3	4	2	12	48
Wait for Asian feeder ship				12	24	168
Wait for container liner from Asia to Europe				12	24	168
Wait for European feeder ship				0	24	48

Table 4.3   Probability of one or more risks occurring

Part of supply chain	Probability (%)
Truck to Asian feeder port	2
Asian feeder port	5
Asian feeder ship	5
Major Asian port	0.05
Container ship from Asia to Europe	0.10
Major European port	1
European feeder ship	5
European feeder port	1
Final truck delivery to destination	0.30

different nodes of the supply chain. Each exposure level will be used in 10 000 simulation runs since even with high exposure levels, the number of cases in which the transport is delayed is relatively small. In this case, we assume that the transport is delayed if it arrives later than the calculated maximum time, assuming no exceptional delays occur.

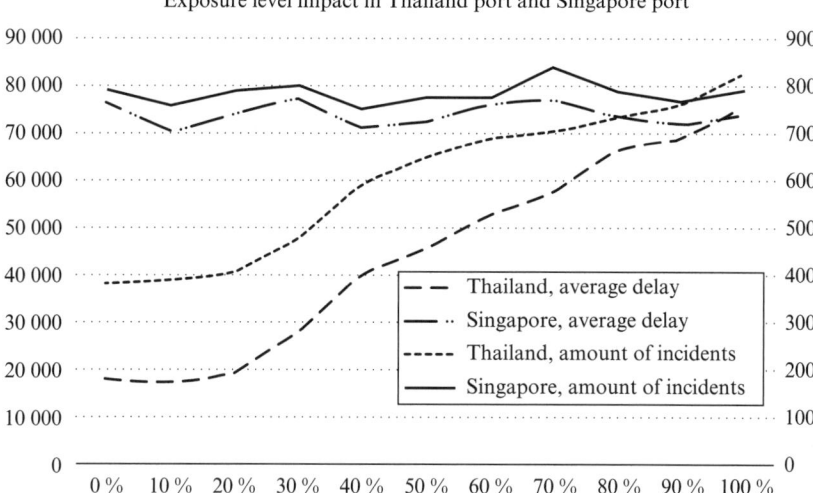

Figure 4.3 *Impact of exposure (level on the average delay and amount of incidents)*

Results of the Model

By varying the exposure level on operational security issues, it is possible to have a better understanding of the performance of the supply chain with different kinds of investments in risk management. Figure 4.3 shows the average delay of the transport. According to the figure, operational security issues in Thailand are much more sensitive to the various exposure levels than in Singapore. When the exposure level is between zero and 20 percent in Thailand, there is basically no impact in relation to the average transport delay. However, security issues in Singapore seem to have no impact in relation to the average delay. This highlights the importance of understanding operational security issues in determining control actions for the vulnerability of the whole supply chain system.

SUMMARY

Multimodal supply chains have become increasingly important to the global economy. Numerous trends have affected the development of complex logistics systems in the last decade, many of which have exposed supply chains to various risks and have made them more vulnerable than ever before (Wagner and Neshat, 2010). In many ways, coping with this vulnerability is still in its infancy.

It is clear from earlier studies on supply chain security and risk that the field would benefit from greater attention from practitioners and researchers (Acciaro and Serra, 2013). This chapter aims to increase understanding of the current level of knowledge of vulnerability analysis by means of a twofold contribution. First, we improve the clarity of the current academic discussion on vulnerability in supply chain risk management by taking into account both the risk and exposure elements and by illustrating their impact in a simulation. Second, we put forward a managerial framework for choosing appropriate vulnerability analysis methods using available data.

An understanding of the causalities at the theoretical and practical levels is essential in order to analyze vulnerability. As part of supply chain risk management, the conceptual maturity of supply chain vulnerability is still very much developing. Our scientific contribution is drawn from synthesizing previous literature (e.g. Peck, 2005; Waters, 2007; Asbjørnslett, 2008; Wagner and Bode, 2008) and putting forward our own definition of supply chain vulnerability. Furthermore, we improve the clarity of the scientific discussion by differentiating the concepts using an exposure element in supply chain vulnerability.

In order to properly analyze supply chain vulnerability, supply chain operations and risks need to be identified by the actors involved. The importance of a comprehensive perspective is vital, especially in the case of multimodal supply chains where there are several different modes of transportation in different environments, reflecting the variation in vulnerability, with different exposure to some risks and different probabilities of other events occurring. In order to attain a comprehensive view of an international, multimodal supply chain, extensive knowledge about the different phases of operation is required. This issue becomes more complex when multiple actors are involved. As different amounts of information are available from different parts of the supply chain, vulnerability assessments require different kinds of tools. Finally, individual vulnerability assessments of operational events need to be combined in a holistic manner in order to gain a complete view about the risks involved in the supply chain.

By limiting exposure to disruptions in the supply chain, it is possible to minimize the total vulnerability of the supply chain. Depending on the nature of the operations, the security of supply can cope with different levels of vulnerability. For instance, if the supply chain is part of some sort of critical infrastructure like energy production, vulnerability needs to be carefully managed. However, even in critical infrastructure environments, different supply chains handle exposure differently. The vulnerability of a multimodal supply chain can thus be directly connected to the security of supply, and this should be reflected in the decision-making process.

In supply chains, the management of vulnerability is a delicate act. The limited availability of resources requires efficient and effective supply chain risk management processes. If an organization has a firm understanding of the vulnerability of its supply chains, it is possible to concentrate scarce resources in the most appropriate areas. In an optimal situation, risk management efforts are balanced with the size of the risks involved in the supply chain of the organization.

In reality, it is virtually impossible to list every conceivable risk. Typically, risk identification gives a list of the most significant risks that can have an impact on the supply chain. Inter-organizational employees typically have the most intimate knowledge of the organization and its conditions but not necessarily the capability to identify risks (Waters, 2007). This illus-trates the benefits of having a holistic perspective on individual security events, which is also essential for supply chain vulnerability analysis. By understanding the importance of using the appropriate methodology to analyze different kinds of data, organizations are able to more efficiently cope with vulnerabilities in their supply chain, and resources can be liber-ated for other uses.

REFERENCES

Acciaro, M. and P. Serra (2013), 'Maritime supply chain security: a critical review'. International Forum on Shipping, Ports and Airports (IFSPA) 2013: Trade, Supply Chain Activities and Transport: Contemporary Logistics and Maritime Issues.

Asbjørnslett, B.E. (2008), 'Assessing the vulnerability of supply chains', in G.A. Zsidisin and B. Ritchie (eds.), *Supply Chain Risk: A Handbook of Assessment, Management and Performance*, NY: Springer, pp. 15–34.

Banomyong, R. (2005), 'The impact of port and trade security initiatives on maritime supply chain management', *Maritime Policy and Management*, **32** (1), 3–13.

Beresford, A., S. Pettit and Y. Liu (2011), 'Multimodal supply chains: iron ore from Australia to China', *Supply Chain Management: An International Journal*, **16** (1), 32–42.

Brindley, C. (2004), *Supply Chain Risk*, Aldershot, UK: Ashgate Publishing.

Chuang, P. (2007), 'Combining Service Blueprint and FMEA for service design', *The Service Industries Journal*, **27** (2), 91–104.

Craighead, C.W., J. Blackhurst, M.J. Rungtusanatham and R.B. Handfield (2007), 'The severity of supply chain disruptions: design characteristics and mitigation capabilities', *Decision Sciences*, **38** (1), 131–156.

Edwards, P., M. Peters and G. Sharman (2001), 'The effectiveness of information systems in supporting the extended supply chain', *Journal of Business Logistics*, **22** (1), 1–28.

Fiala, P. (2005), 'Information sharing in supply chains', *The International Journal of Management Science*, **33** (3), 419–423.

Finnish Council of State (2008), Finnish Council of States Decision about the Goals of Security of Supply (Valtioneuvoston päätös huoltovarmuuden tavoitteista), 21.8.2008/539.

Frankel, R., A.B. Yemisi, A.E. Reham, A. Paulraj and G.T. Gundlach (2008), 'The domain and scope of SCMs foundational disciplines – insights and issues to advance research', *Journal of Business Logistics*, **29** (1), 1–30.

Gattorna, J. (1998), *Strategic Supply Chain Alignment: Best Practice in Supply Chain Management*, Hampshire, UK: Gower Publishing Limited.

Gunasekaran, A., K. Lai, and T.C.E. Cheng (2008), 'Responsive supply chain: a competitive strategy in a networked economy', *International Journal of Management Science*, **36** (4), 549–564.

Handfield, R.B. and K. McCormack (2008), *Supply Chain Risk Management: Minimizing Disruptions in Global Sourcing*, New York: Auerbach Publications, Taylor and Francis Group.

Harland, C., R. Brenchley and H. Walker (2003), 'Risk in supply networks', *Journal in Purchasing and Supply Management*, **9** (2), 51–62.

Hendricks, K., V. Singhal and R. Zhang (2009), 'The effect of operational slack diversification, and vertical relatedness on the stock market reaction to supply chain disruptions', *Journal of Operations Management*, **27** (3), 233–246.

Hu, Z.H. (2011), 'A container multimodal transportation scheduling approach based on immune affinity model for emergency relief', *Expert Systems with Applications*, **38** (3), 2339–2632.

Hult, G.T.M. (2004), 'Global supply chain management: an integration of scholarly thoughts', *Industrial Marketing Management*, **33** (1), 3–5.

Jüttner, U. (2005), 'Supply chain risk management: understanding the business requirements from the practitioner's perspective', *International Journal of Logistics Management*, **16** (1), 120–141.

Jüttner, U., H. Peck and M. Christopher (2003), 'Supply chain risk management: outlining an agenda for future research', *International Journal of Logistics: Research and Applications*, **6** (4), 197–210.

Manuj, I. and J.T. Mentzer (2008), 'Global supply chain risk management', *Journal of Business Logistics*, **29** (1), 133–155.

Mason-Jones, R. and D.R. Towill (1998), 'Shrinking the supply chain uncertainty cycle', *The Institute of Operations Management*, **24** (7), 17–22.

Mitchell, V.W. (1995), 'Organisational risk perception and reduction: a literature review', *British Journal of Management*, **6** (2), 115–133.

Narasimhan, R. and S. Talluri (2009), 'Perspectives on risk management in supply chains', *Journal of Operations Management*, **27** (2), 114–118.

Oflac, B.S., U.Y. Sullivan and T. Baltacioglu (2012), 'An attribution approach to consumer evaluations in logistics customer service failure situations', *Journal of Supply Chain Management*, **48** (4), 51–71.

Park, J., P. Gordon, J.E. Moore II and H.W. Richardson (2008), 'The state-by-state economic impacts of the 2002 shutdown of the Los Angeles–Long Beach Ports', *Growth and Change*, **39** (4), 548–572.

Peck, H. (2005), 'Drivers of supply chain vulnerability: an integrated framework',

International Journal of Physical Distribution and Logistics Management, **35** (4), 210–232.

Robinson, S. (2004), *Simulation: The Practice of Model Development and Use*, West Sussex, UK: John Wiley & Sons.

Sheffi, Y. (2005), *The Resilient Enterprise: Overcoming Vulnerability for Competitive Advantage*, Cambridge, MA: MIT Press Books.

Soosay, C., P. Hyland and M. Ferrer (2008), 'Supply chain collaboration: capabilities for continuous learning', *Supply Chain Management: An International Journal*, **13** (2), 160–169.

Svensson, G. (2001), 'A conceptual framework for the analysis of vulnerability in supply chains', *International Journal of Physical Distribution and Logistics Management*, **30** (9), 731–750.

Thun, J.-H. and D. Hoenig (2011), 'An empirical analysis of supply chain risk management in the German automotive industry', *International Journal of Production Economics*, **131**, 242–249.

Trkman, P., M. Indihar Štemberger, J. Jaklič and A. Groznik (2007), 'Process approach to supply chain integration', *Supply Chain Management – An International Journal*, **12** (2), 116–128.

Vilko, J. (2012), *Supply Chain Risk Management: Identification, Analysis and Control*. Acta Universitalis Lappeenrantaelis, Lappeenranta, Finland.

Vilko, J. and P. Ritala (2012), 'Uncertainty in supply chain risk management', International Symposium on Logistics, Cape Town, South Africa.

Wagner, S. and C. Bode (2008), 'An empirical examination of supply chain performance along several dimensions of risk', *Journal of Business Logistics*, **29** (1), 307–325.

Wagner, S.M. and N. Neshat (2010), 'Assessing the vulnerability of supply chains using graph theory', *International Journal of Production Economics*, **126** (1), 121–129.

Waters, D. (2007), *Supply Chain Risk Management: Vulnerability and Resilience in Logistics*, London: Kogan Page Limited.

5.   Multimodal transport insurances

Eric Depré, Genserik L. L. Reniers and Luca Zamparini

1.   INTRODUCTION

An insurance approach assumes that a loss can be suffered by the insured party or by another party (in case of a loss for which the insured is liable). In such liability insurances a distinction is made between the parties who have a contractual relationship and those who have not (extra-contractual liability).

A definition of insurance is: 'The pooling of fortuitous losses by transfer of such risks to insurers, who agree to indemnify insured for such losses, to provide other pecuniary benefits on their occurrence or to render services connected with risk in exchange for a premium. Pooling is the sharing of total losses among a group and is thus the spreading of losses incurred by a few over an entire group' (Rejda and McNamara, 2014).

Hence, insurance is the transfer of risk; the sharing of a loss; a contract between two parties (the insured and the insurance company). It should be noted that the insurance broker is an important player but not a contracting party. An insurance is thus a written contract between two parties providing a promise of reimbursement in the case of loss due to a covered trigger; and purchased by people or companies so concerned about hazards that they have made pre-payments, or premiums, to an insurance company for such protection.

There are actually two distinguishable groups of insurances with their own characteristics:

● Indemnity insurances: such as property, liability, transport:
 This type of insurance indemnifies the damage and there cannot be any profiting out of a damage allowed for the insured (= no better situation than before the loss).
 The occurrence of the risk has to be accidental, unintentional and sudden.
 The performance of the insurance is restoring the same financial situation as before and it is based on the pooling principle.

- Fixed sum insurances: such as pension funds, life insurance:
  This type of insurance pays a stated sum when a predefined trigger (pensioning, death) occurs or happens. People can have different insurances for the same trigger and they all pay the contractually agreed sums.

In fact, insurance aims at restoring, indemnifying, or compensating the insured, should the insured risk (described, where there has been a premium payment for it) occur. Legally, insurance cannot bring the insured to a better position than before the loss (Rejda and McNamara, 2014). In such a case, it would be called fraud. Insurance is based on probabilities – the risks may or may not occur. If the occurrence is certain, there is no risk and the issue is not insurable in indemnity insurances. Insurances are not the total solution nor a protection against reputation and market losses or image destruction. There is also no guarantee that a risk would not materialize or that all costs of a damage will be paid.

An often-encountered problem with insurances is that within a policy there is only an exchange of a minimum amount of information instead of a maximum amount of information due to the misconception that exchanging a maximum amount of information will lead to an increase in the premium. This is because there is a significant misunderstanding about the real value of insurances. Other problems that occur when claims are made include for example that insured sums are too low, that the wrong guarantees or extensions have been subscribed, or that there was no use made, or a bad use made, of specific conditions.

The logic of the different insurance lines can be demonstrated by looking at the matters they cover, which are given hereafter as:

- Transport (Marine): to cover the risk arising out of the transport of the construction parts or the raw materials.
- CAR – Construction all risk/Contractors all risk: to cover the risk arising out of the construction period, as well to the construction itself, as the liability towards damage to third parties due to the construction.
- EAR – Erection all risk: to cover the risk of loss arising out of the erection and installation of machinery, plant and steel structures, including physical damage to the contract works, equipment and machinery, and liability for third-party bodily injury (BI) or property damage (PD) arising out of these operations.
- Property (or Fire): to cover the risk arising out of fire or related risks to the property.
- Machinery breakdown: to cover the risk arising out of a breakdown of the machinery.

- All risks electronic equipment: to cover the risk of damage to electronic equipment caused by operation; electrical energy (short circuit, excess voltage or induction), human element (faulty operation, lack of skill, negligence), the manufacturer (faulty design, defects in material, faults at workshop, faults in erection).
- Liability (or Casualty): to cover the risk arising out of the exploitation, or product or performance to third parties.
- Transport (Marine): to cover the risk arising out of the transport of finished goods.
- Business interruption (sometimes called Advanced Loss of Profit [ALOP] or Delay in Start-up [DSU]): to cover the risk arising out of financial losses due to the incapacity to make turnover because of an insured incident.
- Other insurances: D&O (Directors and Officers), E&O (Errors and Omissions), workman's compensation, fleet, etc.

2.   TRANSPORT OR MARINE INSURANCE

In this chapter the insurances for the transport of goods by different modes and means will be treated. To understand this well, a description of the different important elements of insurances on single transport modes and means is needed, before explaining multimodal transport insurance.

2.1   Transport Insurance Context

In transport insurance there are fundamental differences between three types of insurance: (1) insurance of the means of transport, (2) insurance of the goods themselves, and (3) the liabilities of the participants towards the owner(s) of the goods and third parties. Damage to the means of transport, to the goods, to the cost of transport (freight), the liabilities involved and the consequential losses incurred, all have to be dealt with.

Due to the value of the means of transport, insurance is needed for its liability for damage to third parties as well as in Casco (damage to the ship; compare this to car insurance). The insurance of the goods is the choice of the owner of the goods. He/she has to pay particular attention to covered and uncovered risks and to the exclusions in the insurance policy/policies. The indemnity is calculated on the insured value of the merchandise and depends directly on covered risks.

The liabilities of the participants towards the owner(s) of the goods are further described. These liabilities and compensations are ruled and determined by the different conventions and the regulations ascertained for each form of transport. In the case of deep sea (ocean) marine transport, one of the seminal references is the Marine Insurance Policy of Antwerp which came into force on 1 July 1859. Its Article 2 mentions contraband; illicit and clandestine commerce are causes of limited liability. Another reference is represented by the Hague-Visby rules as amended by the Brussels Protocol in 1968. In clause 4 this states what are the limits to the liability of the carrier or the ship in case of the loss or damage of the transported goods; three instances mention security related causes, namely: act of war, act of public enemies, and riots and civil commotions. Another important reference in marine transport are the Institute Cargo Clauses[1] that directly mention several security related episodes as causes of limited liability. At clause 4.7, it is stated that the insurance will not cover the loss, damage or expense arising from the use of any weapon of war employing atomic or nuclear fission and/or fusion or other like reaction or radioactive force or matter. At clause 6.1 war, civil war, revolution, rebellion and civil strife are mentioned. Clause 6.3 takes into account derelict mines, torpedoes, bombs or other derelict weapons of war. Finally, clause 7.3 cites the loss or damage caused by any terrorist or any person acting from a political motive. In the case of inland waterway transport, the main reference is represented by the Budapest Convention on the Contract for the Carriage of Goods by Inland Waterway that was issued on 22 June 2001. In its Article 18 (special exonerations from liability), there is one clause that is related to the safety/security issue. Namely, a limitation of liability exists in case the loss, damage or delay originates from rescue or salvage operations or attempted rescue or salvage operations on inland waterways. In the case of road transport, the main reference is represented by the Convention on the Contract for the International Carriage of Goods by Road that was issued by the United Nations in Geneva on 19 May 1956. For railroad transport, the Convention Concerning the International Carriage by Rail (COTIF) and the uniform rules concerning the Contract of International Carriage of Goods by Rail (CIM) are the most important international references. Finally, in the case of air transport, the Warsaw Convention (12 October 1929) and the Montreal Convention (28 May 1999) for the unification of certain rules for international carriage by air represent the benchmarks.

In general, and for all transport modes, the indemnity is limited in these conventions by the weight of the goods, and a maximum value is determined. If the value of the goods exceeds the mentioned values, the owner of the goods has to insure them separately in a specific policy to be insured for the whole value of the transported goods. Indemnity is also ruled and only given if the transporter was unable to evade responsibility, and depends on the value of the goods.

2.2 Participants on the Transport Activity and Consequences for the Insurances

In order to understand the different insurance products one needs to consider the different participants and aspects of the transport of goods.

We can distinguish the following participants:

- The owner of the goods, at different stages being the producer or the buyer.
- The shipper.
- The freight forwarder.
- The owner of the means of transport/the carrier.
- Third parties: people, other companies, terminal operators, owners of infrastructure (e.g. station, port).

We can also distinguish the following damages/liabilities as aspects of the transport of goods:

- Loss to the means of transport, as owner.
- Loss to the goods, as owner.
- The following liabilities:
  - To third parties due to the means of transport.
  - To the goods and owner as shipper.
  - To the goods and owner as carrier.
  - To the storage facilities.
  - To third parties due to the goods.
- The consequential loss or business interruption of all participants.
- The cost of the transport (freight).

The following sections will provide a more extended description of the single transport mode and of the multimodal transport insurances.

3.   SINGLE TRANSPORT MODE INSURANCES

Freight transport today can be carried out by different modes of transportation, such as road, rail, air, ocean, sea, river. The insurances are further treated and described on that basis.

3.1 Transport by Water: Ocean, Sea, River

3.1.1 Ocean

Insurance for sea and ocean transportation is indicated with the term 'ocean marine insurance'. Ocean marine insurance has the following types of coverage, related to the main interests to be insured on an ocean voyage. Compensation is determined by the regulations ascertained for each form of transport, and indemnity is limited by the weight of the goods. Indemnity is only given if the transporter was unable to evade responsibility and depends on the value of the goods. The responsibility of the carrier (or/and shipowner) is limited contractually according to different Acts for Carriage of Goods by Sea.

The shipping company is not responsible for losses of, or damage to, the goods if he/she proves that they arise from:

- The merchandise's own defect(s) and loss in weight during transport.
- A nautical mistake by the crew.
- A fire.
- Acts of war.
- Quarantine.
- The ship not being seaworthy.
- An Act of God.
- Strikes or a lock-out.
- A mistake by the loader.
- Hidden defects on board the ship, which went unnoticed during rigorous inspection.
- An attempt to save lives or goods at sea.

The four main interests to be insured in an ocean transport are:

- The vessel or the hull, called Casco.
- The cargo.
- The freight.
- Legal liability or protection and indemnity.

3.1.1.1 The vessel or the hull These policies cover the vessel itself and not the transported goods.

'Hull' means in fact the outer body of a ship, but this name is a historical fact. For today's ships the insurance has been widened to 'hull and machinery', which follows the original intention of granting cover for the skin and the propulsion equipment in the ship. Hull and machinery insurance is to protect the shipowner's investment. This policy is also called Casco, and can be compared with the Casco of a car (own damage). This insurance can be subscribed in different ways.

The policy may cover the ship during only one transport or during a given period of time, usually not exceeding one year. These policies are commonly subject to geographical limits and/or war zone lists, which are regularly adapted. To qualify as a valid exclusion zone, the war zone must be in the list before the start of the journey. Also, if the ship is anchored in a port for an extended period of time the policy may be subscribed at a reduced premium under the condition that the ship remains in the port (reduced risk).

Furthermore, the insurance covers some liabilities – normally a collision liability with other ships (known as RDC – 'Running Down Clause'), and sometimes also a liability for colliding with objects other than another ship (known as FFO – 'Fixed and Floating Objects') (see also protection and indemnity cover below). The third part of the insurance represents the cover for salvage and general average contributions.

Typical hull and machinery claims include:

- The total loss of the ship.
- Damage to the ship, engines and equipment.
- Explosions and fires.
- Groundings – damage to the ship, salvage of the ship.
- General average contributions.
- Collisions – damage sustained to the ship.
- Liability towards the other ship (RDC).
- Striking other objects: damage inflicted to own ship.
- Liability towards the owners of the other object (FFO).

The policy can cover a builder's risk (damage to the vessel and liability) while the vessel is under construction or conversion.

3.1.1.2 The cargo   The cargo insurance is a policy that covers the transported goods against the perils mentioned in the policy. This means that the physical integrity or the loss of the goods is insured. Note that the policy concerns solely goods and not human beings. There is a further differentiation by how easy or difficult it is to steal the goods. Any cargo with a value/weight ratio exceeding that of silver (450.00 €/kg) is called 'valuables' and must be insured specifically.

The cargo insurance may cover the goods during a specific voyage (as in case of the hull) or on an open basis, which is nowadays probably the most common type of policy. Under the open policy, there is no termination date, but either party may cancel upon given notice, usually 30 days. All shipments (this can be all kinds of means of transport), both incoming and outgoing, are automatically covered. The shipper reports to the insurer at regular intervals (normally mentioned in the specific condition of the policy) as to the values shipped or received in the previous period. The shipper declares the classes of goods and the ports (or destinations) between which the goods move. There is usually a limit of values that may be insured on a single vessel and a limit on the goods stowed on deck (higher risk). The insured must pay attention to the definition of the meaning of 'limit per transport'. If the insured discussed that with regard to truck or train loads, and then forgets that multiple trucks or trains can be put on one boat, there is a risk that the limit will be exceeded on the boat.

To summarize, 'it' must be carried by 'something' for the purpose of transportation to be a cargo within the definition of the transport insurer. If it moves on its own, it is not a cargo. To illustrate: when cars, trucks, planes, boats (even the space shuttle) are carried by other trucks, boats, planes, they are cargo. As soon as they are unloaded and move by themselves they are not cargo anymore.

3.1.1.3 The freight The cost or the money paid for the transportation of the goods (including preparation) is called the freight charge, and it is an insurable interest because in the event that freight charges are not paid, the carrier has lost income. Depending on the contractual arrangements it is possible that the freight costs are only paid on the delivery of the cargo. If the vessel sinks, the freight is lost and the owner loses the expenses incurred plus the expected profit. The carrier's right to earn freight may be defeated by the occurrence of losses due to perils ordinarily insured in an ocean marine policy. For example, the hull may be damaged so that it is uneconomical to complete the voyage, or the cargo may be destroyed in which case, of course, it cannot be delivered. Therefore the cargo owner has an interest in freight insurance arising from the obligation to pay transportation charges. Freight insurance is therefore often, indeed normally, included in the hull or cargo coverages instead of being subscribed as a separate policy.

3.1.1.4 Protection and indemnity Protection and indemnity insurance, or 'P&I' as it is usually called, is a shipowner's insurance cover for legal liabilities to third parties. 'Third parties' are any person, apart from the shipowner, who may have a legal or contractual claim against the ship. P&I insurance is usually arranged by entering the ship in a mutual insurance association, usually referred to as a 'P&I club'. The main coverages of a P&I policy are outlined in Table 5.1.

Table 5.1   Coverages of a P&I policy and their explanation

Cargo	Liability for cargo loss, shortage, damage, extra handling costs or delay occurring in relation to the carriage of cargo on the entered vessel
Crew, passengers and other persons	Loss of life, personal injury and life salvage claims in respect of members of the crew and third parties, e.g. passengers, crew, relatives, stevedores and other personnel on board required for the operation of the vessel. Hospital, medical, funeral and repatriation expenses (including owners' liability for wages as agreed) in respect of sick or injured crew members. Further, repatriation expenses, unemployment indemnities and loss of effects of shipwrecked crew
Pollution	Oil or any other polluting substance escaping from, or caused by, an entered ship resulting in pollution of sea, land or air
Collision and contact liability	Liability arising out of collision with another vessel, a fixed or floating object or property (e.g. docks, buoys, etc.) may be included when not covered under another policy. Further, liability with respect to damage to any other vessel or property thereon without actual contact is included in the cover. Full collision liability is available
Wreck removal and obstruction	Liability and costs of compulsorily removing, destroying or marking the wreck. Further, liability arising out of the entered vessel causing an obstruction
General average contribution	Cargo's proportion of general average and/or special charges not recoverable due to breach of the contract of carriage. Ship's proportion of general average and salvage charges not otherwise recoverable from excessive valuation of the ship in a foreign country
Fines	Fines imposed by authorities for short or over-delivery of cargo, cargo documents, pollution, smuggling, and breach of regulations, etc. Quarantine and disinfection requirements: extraordinary expenses incurred in cases of outbreak of infectious disease. Also quarantine and disinfection expenses
Liabilities	For stowaways, diversions, refugees, salvage and towage, container operations, mitigation costs including legal and associated costs

3.2 Rivers – Inland Waterways

This transportation mode uses the same insurances as the insurances mentioned in the previous section 3.1:

- The vessel or the hull.
- The cargo.
- The freight.
- Legal liability or P&I.

Hence, ocean and inland waterway transportation have similar policies. However, the latter are somewhat easier because some risks are lower (e.g. war) and/or better known (e.g. ports).

The responsibilities are ruled by the Budapest Convention on the Contract for the Carriage of Goods by Inland Waterway (CMNI), of 22 June 2001, which determines the responsibilities, the exclusions and the liabilities.

3.3 Road Transport

Insurance for transport by road is sometimes called 'Inland Marine' insurance. In the case of this transport mode, the following items need to be insured:

- The truck.
- The cargo.
- The freight.
- Legal liability or P&I.

For the insurance of this kind of transport, a distinction should be made between 'transport for own account' (with own transport means) and 'transport for third parties'. By the transport for own account (with own transport means), so-called 'Automobile liability' and 'Casco' insurance are needed for the means of own transport, and 'Cargo' insurance is needed for the own goods.

Transport for third parties needs 'Automobile liability' and 'Casco' insurance for the owner of the means of transport, and liability insurance for the third parties for whom the goods are transported. This liability is ruled by the CMR convention, Convention on the Contract for the International Carriage of Goods by Road (CMR) (Geneva, 19 May 1956). The CMR insurance is the transfer of the financial consequences of the liabilities foreseen in this convention towards an insurer. The CMR insurance policies have all exclusions of liabilities foreseen in the convention. For the coverage of possible damages exceeding the prescriptions of the convention, the owner of the goods needs to subscribe an own cargo insurance for his/her goods. An important element for insurance is that the liability for the goods is limited by the CMR convention to compensation limits based on 8.33 Special Drawing Rights (SDRs) per kilo of gross weight of the lost or damaged goods. The value of the SDR against major currencies is set out each day in the specialized media. The value of 8.33 SDRs is approximately 10.00 €. This means that for all goods exceeding a value of 10.00 € per kilo of gross weight, the owner of the goods must subscribe an additional cargo insurance, in order to be correctly insured. Some CMR insurance policies have coverage for two or three times the value of the goods as limited by the CMR convention but this needs to be checked by the owner of the goods.

3.4   Railroad Transport

For this transport mode, the following items require insurance:

- The train.
- The cargo.
- The freight.
- Legal liability or P&I.

This liability is ruled by the Uniform Rules Concerning the Contract of International Carriage of Goods by Rail (CIM) (CIT – Rail, 2010) and the Convention Concerning the International Carriage by Rail (COTIF) (CIT – Rail, 2010). Again, the liability insurance provides coverage for the liabilities foreseen in the rules.

3.5   Air Transport

Regarding this transport mode, the following items need to be insured:

- The plane.
- The cargo.
- The freight.
- Legal liability or P&I.

This liability is ruled by the Conventions of Warsaw (1929) and Montreal (1999) (Cheng, 2004). Again, the liability insurance provides coverage for the liabilities foreseen in the conventions.

3.6 Stock and Transit

It is possible that goods cannot be transferred directly from one transport mode to another and that the goods have to be stored temporarily. This can happen in a programmed way or due to an incident or delay in the voyage.

As with all other cases, this must be analyzed, foreseen and described in the insurance policies in cases of programmed and foreseen stock and transit, as well as for the unexpected ones. The insured has to think carefully about the length of the stock and transit cover, and about the possibilities and premium of extending the cover in a timely manner.

3.7 Charterers Liability

In the case that the means of transport would be chartered, specific charterers liabilities arise. A charterer is someone who charters something, for example the hire or lease of a ship. This marine policy is designed for vessel charterers and provides coverage for the charterer's legal or contractual obligation to a vessel owner as specified in a charter agreement. This coverage typically addresses liability exposures such as hull damage, safe berth, loading, unloading and stowage of cargo, damage to berthing facilities and other vessels and loss of life or bodily injury to third parties resulting from the acts of the charterer. Coverage can also be included for liability for cargo carried on the vessel for third parties.

According to the Charter Party, the charterer can, among other events, be held liable for the following exposures:

- Damage to the vessel.
- Bodily injury.
- Damage to the property of third parties.
- Damage caused by cargo.
- Damage to or loss of cargo owned by a third party.
- Stevedoring damage.
- Environmental pollution.
- General average. (Aon, 2014)

3.8 Project Cargo

Project cargo is a term used to describe broadly the national or international transportation of large, heavy, high-value or critical pieces of equipment. This includes shipments made of various components which may need to be disassembled for shipment and reassembled after delivery. The marine (or 'cargo') insurance industry generally considers a project to be a series of related shipments, some of which will be oversized or of high value, all forming part of a particular job. Regardless of whether it is a series of related or single shipments, these are risks which are often either too large or too perilous for the traditional market.

Project cargo insurance is coverage for the transport risks of equipment destined for infrastructure projects and industrial facilities. Policy coverage includes physical loss and damage and may include consequential loss, such as DSU and additional cost of working. It is used for large infrastructure construction projects such as: power generation facilities; liquid and gas pipeline projects; telecommunications installations (including those involving fibre optic networks, satellite ground stations, mobile phone cellular networks); highway, bridge and tunnel construction; seaport and airport development and improvement projects; liquefied natural gas (LNG) and petrochemical processing facilities.

4.   MULTIMODAL TRANSPORT INSURANCES

The definition proposed by the UN, at the Convention on International Multimodal Transport of Goods (Geneva, 24 May 1980), is used for international multimodal transport, that is, the carriage of goods by at least two different modes of transport on the basis of a multimodal transport contract from a place in one country at which the goods are taken in charge by the multimodal transport operator to a place designated for delivery situated in a different country.

A transport, and certainly a multimodal transport, has different involved parties or so-called stakeholders:

- The owners of the merchandise.
- The freight-forwarders.
- The carriers.
- The insurers (those who insure the cargo, 'cargo insurance', as well as those who insure the carrier, 'liability insurance').
- The 'sub-stakeholders', mainly the terminal operators, who have an important function in the connection of the different modes of transport.

Due to its very nature, multimodal transport is characterized by different modes and means of transport. The 'modes' are the methods that are used to transport people or cargo: transport by air, water, road and railroad. The 'means' of transport are the individual vehicles that are used: the airplane, the helicopter, the ship, the barge, the boat, the train, the truck, etc.

The transfer terminals also have to be considered, where the cargo passes from one mode of transport to another. In this case the stock and transit are considered to be the transfer activities. For the points of passage of responsibility between seller and buyer, the insurances should be fully compatible with the Contract of Carriage.

Moreover, multimodal transportation has a number of specific characteristics:

- In a circuit of international transport, the merchandise will be in the custody of different operators and subject to different laws and conventions that govern the 'Responsibilities of the Carriers' and of the 'Terminal Operators', with their eventual 'Monetary Limits of Liability'.
- Almost all of these have different bases of responsibility, limits of liability, different documents with different legal values, and different time-bars (periods of prescription of claims).
- Each mode of transport has its own laws with its basic principles. The following issues have to be taken into account: a) when case the carrier is considered to be responsible for damages or losses; b) when can he/she exculpate him-/herself; c) which are his/her maximum limits of compensation for damages; d) what value of evidence is given to the different documents that are used; e) who can make a claim and what are the different periods of prescription to present claims (time-bars).

The different interpretations of what is multimodal transport, the different stakeholders in the process, and the different liability regimes and conventions make the contracting (purchase/sales/transport/carriage/Incoterms used) and the insurances difficult and complex. Therefore a 'standard multimodal transport insurance' does not exist in the market. Hence, it will be a tailor-made policy considering all aspects of transport, liabilities, regulations, roles, etc. Furthermore, it is well known that transportation risks exist and losses may occur. Each mode of transport has its particularities and its own risks. There are also differences in the average values of the goods that are transported in each mode. The elements of single mode transport remain. The insurance contract has to be adapted to the particular purchase/sales/transport/carriage/Incoterms used contract terms. Stock and transit issues, and manufacturing issues, also should not be forgotten.

An important aspect of insurances is so-called business interruption damage. When damage occurs, there is a possibility that delivery may be prevented or there may be a delay in delivery, with a possible impact on the projects waiting for equipment or spare parts, or it may lead to goods that cannot be sold. This may lead to economic losses which are not covered in the insurances described above. These costs can be very substantial and sometimes more important than the material damage, because, due to the non-delivery or the delay in delivery, fixed costs remain and profit is not made. The existing insurance cover for this kind of loss is called Business Interruption, ALOP or DSU Insurance. This insurance provides indemnity for loss of earnings and/or profits (turnover) and brings the enterprise to the same financial situation in which it would have been had the insured damage not occurred.

The most important elements of this insurance are the insured sums, the indemnity period and the insured perils. An important element is the possibility of insuring the additional costs of working needed to reduce the delay time. This often-forgotten insurance is the life insurance of the enterprise.

5.   HOW TO PROCEED IN CORRECTLY INSURING MULTIMODAL TRANSPORTS

To be correctly insured, one must carefully analyze what the needs are, which covers are needed and wanted, and what the exclusions are, and all this before the loss occurs. This requires an in-depth risk analysis of all aspects. A distinction has to be made between the owner (in the broad sense of the term, who can also be the overall shipper or 'expediteur' commissioner) of the goods and the transport commissioner (the one who executes the transport, overall or partly). This distinction should be made because of the ownership on one hand and the liability on the other. If various operators execute different parts of the transport, attention has to be paid to verify whether the transfer activities of all transport means are correctly insured.

For the owner of the goods there are no major problems in multimodal transport: he/she may insure his/her goods in cargo in all risk policies for all possible goods for all transport means. However, care needs to be taken to ensure that the transport insurance contract includes detailed descriptions of the goods, of the destination, the transport means and the maximum value per transport mode.

For the transport commissioner it is more difficult to find coverage on the 'global' insurance market, due to the complexity of different responsibilities. Transport commissioners have to look for specific policies and coverages with specialized transport insurers such as TT Club, Post & Co., and Navigator, etc.

The broker and the insurance company also need to be chosen. The broker should be considered as a guide in a specific world. The insurance company has to provide reimbursement in case of a damage. Therefore, a relationship of trust with both parties needs to be established. Maximum communication is recommended before any loss occurs.

Transport insurances have to be adapted to transport contracts which exist in the organization. Transport contracts are ruled by purchase/sales/transport/carriage/Incoterms used contracts, and insurances need to be fine-tuned to all these contracts. The whole voyage from buyer to seller should be insured by at least one policy.

In the case of multimodal transport, care needs to be taken that all transfers from one transport mode and mean to another are also insured. Therefore, if possible, it is recommended that one insures the *whole* transport or makes one party insure the whole transport. This is the only way to be sure that all aspects have been considered and all exclusions are read, understood and known. If different parties are insuring their own part of the transport, one should be careful that the liability restrictions of the conventions are adapted to the value of the goods, and that the modes of transport are analyzed. Also, if several different policies cover the different transport modes and their exposures, and, moreover, if these policies are effected with different insurers, the risk exists that where one policy stops and another policy begins there is scope for either an overlap in coverage or a gap in coverage. This potential duplication or gap in insurance cover can cause a significant problem in the event of a loss, and this can be further aggravated if two different insurers are involved. The exclusions should also not be greater from one policy to another.

Furthermore, one needs to be careful with the insurance contract with regard to the maximum covered/insured value per transport (mode). For example, it is possible to put more than one truck on one boat or one train, and if the maximum value in the contract is the value of goods contained on one truck, there is insufficient insurance. One truck is one transport but a boat is also regarded as just one transport. Finally, if the broker and/or the insurer is changed or replaced, a thorough analysis needs to be carried out with regard to all the insurance covers.

6. CONCLUSIONS

Insurances need to be given the attention they deserve before a loss occurs. The right insurances need to be chosen, and care needs to be taken not to be insured twice for the same risks or perhaps not at all against other risks. Many insurance problems stem from the fact that the policies are not adapted to the seller/buyer and/or to the transport contract. The Incoterms used determine where liabilities change and the insurances have to cover all movements of the goods. All activities need an insurance. Insurance contracts have to provide protection taking into account all laws, conventions, contractual clauses, liabilities, and Incoterms. Insurance is one of the main drivers of world trade, and insurance is bought for asset and balance sheet protection, and for the requirements of the lender, the lease, contracts, legal rules and, last but not least, for peace of mind against security-related events.

NOTE

1. The Institute Cargo Clauses are a set of terms for cargo insurance policies voluntarily adopted as standard terms by many international marine insurance organizations, including the Institute of London Underwriters and the American Institute of Marine Underwriters.

REFERENCES

Cheng, B. (2004), 'A new era in the law of international carriage by air: from Warsaw (1929) to Montreal (1999)', *International and Comparative Law Quarterly*, **53** (4), 833–859.
Rejda, G. E. and M. McNamara (2014), *Principles of Risk Management and Insurance*, 12th edition, Upper Saddle River, NJ: Prentice Hall.

Electronic Sources

AON: http://www.aoncommoditytrade.com/products_and_services/commodity_traders/charterers_liability/.
CAP Marine: http://www.cap-marine.com/fr/produit-assurances-marchandises-2-EN.html.
CIT Rail: http://www.cit-rail.org/en/rail-transport-law/cotif/.
International Special Risks: http://www.isr-insurance.com/commercial-marine-insurance/isrcharterslegalliability.cfm.
TT Club (Through Transit Club): http://www.ttclub.com/.

PART II

Multimodal freight transportation security: policy applications

6. Multimodal freight transportation security in the United States

Brent Shapiro

Honest discussions regarding the secure movement of international freight into U.S. commerce must begin with the origin of the manufacturer and how those goods move through the various supply chains. When observed through a logistical security matrix, the presumed secure movement of goods/freight is at minimum degraded by time, distance, route, type of conveyance, carriers, number of carrier transactions and the combined vulnerabilities of each actor from freight origin to release of freight and delivery into U.S. commerce.

For many years Customs and Border Patrol (CBP), formerly known as the U.S. Customs Service, has employed agents, trade representatives, and investigators at numerous global ports. These representatives perform various tasks to include verification of treaty and trade agreements, commercial enforcement, the expedited movement of goods, and to help ensure cargo safety prior to entering U.S. ports.

Since the September 11, 2001 attacks on the United States, several security initiatives have been introduced to ensure, to the fullest possible extent, the safety of maritime freight destined for U.S. commerce. In November 2001, U.S. Customs developed and implemented Customs-Trade Partnership Against Terrorism (C-TPAT). Under this program, shippers make voluntary commitments to improve the security of their cargo by providing specific data regarding manufacturing and logistical operations. In return, their goods are less likely to be inspected at the port of debarkation or upon entering inland ports for freight release and distribution.

Beginning in 2002, the Container Security Initiative (CSI) was developed and mandated to pre-screen 100 percent of cargo for nuclear and radiological hazards at the ports of embarkation. Currently, CSI teams operate in at least 20 foreign ports alongside host government representatives. These teams share data pooled from multiple sources needed to help enforce security protocols and ensure cargo safety prior to embarkation.

Several programs have been implemented to improve maritime freight security and to help expedite the movement of goods. One of the first was the 2003 implementation of the 24-hour Advance Manifest Rule, also known as Advanced Cargo Manifest Filing. This program requires shipment data to be filed 24 hours prior to lading of cargo in order to assess possible risks or hazards and to keep specific cargo landed until customs and local law officials deem the freight fit for transport. This legislation helps in several ways by tightening freight reporting requirements to include but not to be limited to: (1) the elimination of dummy bills of lading, (2) freight must be specified per waybill and, (3) bills of lading must specify cargo consignee or their representative at port of destination. This ensures that cargo has two legally contracted parties responsible for cargo destined for U.S. markets. By closing these clerical loopholes, Customs lessens the possibilities of hazardous cargo being loaded for transit to the United States.

Effective January 2009, and in accordance with U.S. Code of Federal Regulations, Title 19, Chapter 149.1–6, Customs implemented a new regulation titled Importer Security Filing and Additional Carrier Requirements. Commonly referred to as the 10+2 Rule, it requires importers to transmit cargo data electronically through the Automated Commercial Environment (ACE), which replaced the Automated Commercial System (ACS) in September 2012. As a result, ACE is the only approved electronic data exchange by which sea and rail manifests can be transmitted to U.S. Customs. The 10+2 Rule requires that Importer Security Filings contain ten specific elements of cargo data that must be filed electronically with Customs more than 24 hours prior to lading of freight. The cargo data elements include:

1. Seller
2. Buyer
3. Importer of record
4. Ship-to name and address
5. Consignee IRS/EIN number
6. Manufacturer/supplier
7. Country of origin
8. Harmonized Tariff Number
9. Container stuffing location
10. Freight consolidator (stuffer).[1]

Once cargo is loaded and the vessel is on route to the U.S. port, manifests and stowage plans of the vessel cargo must be transmitted to the U.S. Coast Guard and the Port Director prior to entering port limits.

In 2009, approximately 14.571 million TEU's (twenty-foot equivalent containers) entered into U.S. commerce. Approximately 57 percent entered from the ports of Long Beach/Los Angeles and New York/New Jersey.[2] Combinations of data from human and electronic sources such as C-TPAT, Automated Manifest System (AMS), and ACE provide overlapping streams of data that gives Customs officials a fairly detailed and comprehensive overview of freight and its movement. Some of the methods specified above greatly enhance security and facilitate the smooth movement of freight through the global logistical chain. However, there are concerns of the quality and veracity of data provided by shippers at the port of embarkation and the inability to verify shipper cargo data in real time. At times, some shippers/exporters may fear closer attention and possible inspection of certain cargo or that from a particular manufacturer's point of origin. In these cases some may be tempted to fabricate or replace current manufacturer information with another identity in their export profile. Since it is not physically possible to verify source data on site, that data is submitted through ACE at the port of embarkation and is entered with additional information in different modules later in the inland transport and final entry process. In time, the freight profiles of shipper and importer and their combined supply chains become clearer. Then, discrepancies in exporter/importer profiles become more verifiable and proper actions can take place at either end of the freight movement process.

The secure movement of maritime freight does not end when it reaches U.S. seaports. The secure movement of goods continues from ports of debarkation to inland destinations for freight release. This secure movement of bonded freight to inland destinations is equally important – and more impressive – than the original import process.

The United States utilizes the most extensive and interconnected transportation and logistics network to connect major ports to the interior. This network is comprised of approximately 138 575 miles of cargo carrying rail,[3] 945 000 miles of paved roads which includes 46 036 miles of interstate highways,[4] and 25 483 miles of navigable waterways.[5]

To move the enormous amounts of bonded cargo through the inland transportation network, Customs issues licenses to many carriers and of different modalities to transfer cargo under Customs supervision (in-bond) to any one of the 361 Customs ports of entry for release and distribution. To that end, the most prevalent form of in-bond transportation is the trucking industry. As the primary mode of transportation this industry provides the means of delivery from the port of debarkation to final ports of destination. As a secondary mode, it provides movement of freight to and from port facilities to other modes of transport. In tertiary mode, it provides freight transportation to and from bonded facilities for final disposition at the port of entry and release to the ultimate consignee. In these varied modes, the trucking industry facilitates the coordination and smooth interaction of all types of freight regardless of modality.

For cargo entering port limits (usually a large geographic area of Customs operational responsibility), clearance data regarding merchandise may be submitted to Customs in person or through the Automated Broker Interface (ABI) module of ACE by the importer of record or its authorized agent. Based on data processing and analysis of importer/ exporter history a number of actions may occur. First, freight may attain electronic release, sometimes prior to entering port limits. Second, Customs may inspect all documents upon entering port limits and require hard signature release. Third, Customs may place an electronic ABI hold on cargo, thereby requiring the inspection of documents and cargo for safety, commercial compliance, or at the direction of the Port Director.

Measures available to Customs for freight in violation of security or commercial compliance are varied by means of fines, penalties, forfeiture of freight, or any combination. All actions taken by the Port Director, from electronic cargo release to seizure and destruction of property, are recorded electronically in real time into both shipper and importer profiles. By doing so, future shipper and importer cargo information is processed with current data and actions both favorable and unfavorable taken by Customs at all locations. By doing so, neither shipper nor importer will be able to skirt the ACE/ABI system to gain more relaxed treatment at another location since all data is collected, stored, and becomes part of the entry process nationally. This near instant processing of cargo gives Customs and other law enforcement elements the ability to track and/or prevent shippers or importers from having freight enter U.S. commerce simultaneously from multiple ports. In this regard, the ACE system and its attending modules greatly enhance Customs capabilities to combat threats of hazardous cargo and strengthen commercial enforcement capabilities by collecting, processing, and analyzing freight data from port to door.

Further conversations regarding international freight security within U.S. borders must involve the documentation and security protocols required by Customs for all freight carriers of all modalities (to include bonded warehouses) seeking licensure to traffic bonded freight destined for U.S. markets. In many instances, the documentation, operating, and security standards required for initial certification, which Customs considers minimal operational requirements for licensure, are considered to be the 'Gold Standard' *not operational standards* by many in the logistics industry.

Therefore, when speaking of operational and security requirements mandated by Customs, one must consider the regulatory environments in which the licensed/bonded carriers and warehouses operate. For all carriage types there are a myriad of state, local, and federal safety and operational standards. With the deluge of statutory requirements it is difficult if not impossible for carriers to be in full operational compliance at all levels for any length of time, if at all. Therefore, discussions of secure in-bond freight must include levels of compliance and non-compliance that Customs allows its licensed carriers and warehouses to operate. Security concerns in this area are further complicated when bonded carriers and warehouses have licenses to operate in more than one location and region of the country.

For example: Alpha Company operates three licensed and bonded transportation facilities in Seattle, WA, Chicago, IL, and Newark, NJ. If Alpha Company's hub in Chicago is cited for gross operational and security violations a number of questions arise. First, will Customs allow freight to be moved through this hub, and if so under what guidelines and restrictions? Second, if the carrier operates a separate bonded warehouse facility in conjunction with the transport operation will the warehouse facility be allowed to continue to operate as a separate entity? Finally, when the carrier is fined and censured by the proper regulatory authorities how much time will carriers be given to meet compliance standards, and under what circumstances will they be able to operate during the probationary period? At first glance these concerns seem manageable. However, added into this mix are the number of carrier exchanges, interchanges, and the very real possibility that bonded freight may be transported, warehoused, and co-mingled with general freight – a further cause for greater concern.

A frequently overlooked major security lapse that Customs has the regulatory ability to correct is the clerical processing of data into the ABI module of the ACE system by freight forwarders and customhouse brokers at ports of debarkation. When bond information is correctly submitted to Customs, cargo can be monitored by waypoints throughout the transportation process and released into U.S. commerce. If incorrect bond information is documented and submitted at the port of debarkation, freight moves within U.S. borders without Customs oversight or supervision. To be more precise, Customs does not know the freight exists. Many times these errors are corrected and electronic loopholes closed by customhouse brokers when they must reconcile all ABI elements to include bond information prior to Customs acceptance at the port of entry for either bonded warehouse entry or release of freight into U.S. commerce. The critical question that must be addressed is what happens to 'rogue freight', its mode of transport, and container during those unaccounted for periods of time? Many times the freight moves through the logistical supply chain on schedule and as planned. Usually at some point, ABI information is reconciled and freight is released by Customs for distribution.

Freight traveling multimodally further exasperates the security dilemma. Often the multimodal operator (MTO) contracts with more than one operator to move freight to ports of destination. In these cases the chances of interested parties losing freight during movement for any length of time dramatically increases with every carrier exchange. This could occur because not all interested parties may be tracking the freight in real time and/or the last handling party loses contact with the cargo and does not notify the MTO or Customs.

These scenarios highlight situations where Customs is not able to track freight electronically due to the most common of clerical errors made at ports of debarkation combined with the immediate carrier and MTO's inability to verify freight location or status. To further complicate matters, Customs' regulations continue to allow carriers between 15–60 days to deliver cargo to its final destination depending on mode of delivery.[6]

This issue of tracking, or lack of, in-bond freight across all modes of transport was illuminated by the General Accountability Office (GAO) Report 07-561 dated October 2007. In part, the GAO inspection concluded that the 'CBP does not adequately monitor and track In-Bond goods.'[7] They noted that at the ten major ports visited, the inspectors found many in-bond cargo shipments remained open with unreconciled and unknown dispositions.[8] The report continued and stated that,

> administrative (clerical) errors by shipping agents and CBP staff continue to inconsistently perform in-bond compliance exams with some stations not performing them at all and other ports only recently beginning to perform them. The results of those compliance exams when consistently performed can aid CBP management in identifying system weaknesses.[9]

The report also highlighted manpower restrictions with regards to priority of mission at some ports. Most of the ports dedicated more staffing resources to port security and immigration operations at the expense of commercial enforcement. This report among others found that though an enormous amount of data is collected through ACE and other systems, many times the volume overwhelms those working with the processed not to mention raw data.

The GAO concluded the report by recommending that

> the Commissioner of CBP take action in three general areas. (1) Collect and use improved information on in-bond shipments to enable better informed decisions. (2) Assess systemic problems associated with identifying open in-bonds and take measures to resolve these problems, and (3) ensure that compliance measurement system is performed to improve CBP's in-bond management.[10]

As a result of this testimony, Customs officials claim they are attempting to address this issue by cross-training their members in the different aspects of commercial operations and enforcement. As such, they are committed to cross-training personnel to provide enhanced mission capability and manpower flexibility while operating within its budget.

Over the past two decades, the improvement in the ability to track freight of all types in real time has been a boon for companies of all sizes and has become part of everyday life. In the past, companies had to rely on posted schedules and entities that dealt with international freight. They also had to contend with hard signature release by Customs before the electronic release of most freight became common practice. Presently, many MTOs offer one-stop-shop service from ports of origin to freight delivery. As part of this service, many MTOs offer the customer the ability to track the movement of their freight in real time. By using these tools, companies of all types, regardless of size, are able to streamline logistical and warehouse operations and use this tool as a mainstay of daily operations.

However, while convenient, the means of tracking cargo adds another unknown variable to the freight security equation. Presently, the ability to track freight in real time electronically combined with physical vulnerabilities of freight along its logistical route serves as a case in point. This ability to track freight combined with point surveillance techniques during freight movement provides an opportunity to use cargo, carrier, or conveyance to attack multiple targets of opportunity anywhere along the cargo's route to destination. The United States and other governments are aware of this vulnerability and may attempt to regulate who and at what levels among the general public retains access to real-time freight location. The real difficulty is whether the United States and other nations have the political will to restrict access to this information to which the public has grown accustomed. Additionally, will costs incurred by rolling back this access to cargo location make freight movement more secure or simply add to the public perception of increased freight security?

Currently, Customs effectively operate the most elaborate and sophisticated sets of security systems in the world, at times in conjunction with global trade partners. There are many features and aspects to these systems. The few systems listed in this chapter are responsible in part for the enormous amount of cargo entering into the United States and help identify hazardous cargo and freight in non-compliance on both ends of the logistical chain. As with any large organization operating complex sets of systems, there are functions that do not operate at peak efficiency. However, when observed procedurally from a holistic perspective these multi-layered operational and security protocols and systems do work. To that end, Customs continues to balance the security of freight entering

U.S. markets with cost-effectiveness. In this manner, Customs plays a dominant role in international freight security and by default is the major player in the global supply chain.

NOTES

1. 19 CFR 149.3.
2. U.S. Army Corps of Engineers, *U.S. Waterborne Container Traffic for U.S. Port/ Waterway in 2008*.
3. Association of American Railroads (2013), 'Overview of America's Freight Railroads', https://www.aar.org/keyissues/Documents/Background-Papers/Overview-US-Freight-RRs.pdf (accessed April 2013).
4. Department of Transportation, *Highway Statistics Series 2011*.
5. Department of Transportation (2013), *America's Marine Highway Program*.
6. 19 CFR 18.2 and 112.118.
7. United States Government General Accountability Office (2007), *Report to the Committee on Finance, U.S. Senate (Gao-07-561) International Trade: Persistent Weaknesses in the In-bond System Impede Customs and Border Protections Ability to Address Revenue, Trade and Security Concerns*, p. 3.
8. Ibid.
9. Ibid.
10. Ibid., p. 33.

7. Multimodal freight transportation security in Italy

Luca Talarico and Luca Zamparini

1. INTRODUCTION

According to recent studies carried out by the European Commission (2011a) it is expected that in Europe freight transport will increase by 80 percent by 2050 and the CO_2 emissions will decrease by 60 percent. The European Union (EU) is now making considerable efforts encouraging the integration of existing transport modes and the use of intermodal (and/or multimodal) systems to improve transportation flexibility, costs and effectiveness. This would stimulate competition among transporters rather than among transport modes.

However, this goal is still far from being completely achieved since a range of obstacles prevent an optimum use of the existing infrastructures. The research agendas developed by the European Commission in the last decades emphasize the need to adopt a new perspective integrating different logistic elements such as vehicles, trains, airplanes, vessels, transport networks and logistic infrastructures. A smarter approach of using the existing logistic components more efficiently has been developed at the European level and needs to be implemented at the national level. In Italy the competitiveness gap corresponds to €12 billion, due to inefficiencies in the transportation sector (Cassa Depositi e Prestiti, 2012). Therefore, the identification of strategic actions aimed at increasing the efficiency of freight transport is necessary to ensure the economic growth of the country.

While the competitiveness of Italy passes through a better reorganization of the current multimodal logistic network, the need to make transportation more secure through multimodal solutions is not an easy task. The country's air, land and marine networks are designed for accessibility and efficiency, two characteristics that make them highly vulnerable to intentional attacks. In fact, the usage of several modes of transportation for freight transport could increase the exposure of the goods to several risks such as toxic and/or radioactive releases, explosions of dangerous materials and cargo theft. It is worth noting that the majority of malicious acts which took place in Italy over the last few years were not related to terrorist attacks, but to intentional activities aimed at smuggling or illegally trading dangerous/not-dangerous goods.

This chapter analyzes multimodal freight transportation in Italy focusing on security aspects. After a short introduction on the evolution of multimodal freight transportation, the existing logistic infrastructure, which can be integrated under the multimodal perspective, is described. In the second part of the chapter, some security aspects are discussed, pointing out criticalities, principles, legislations and rules which interest the Italian logistic system. Further, multimodal freight transportation security-related events from 2013 are also reviewed and analyzed. The chapter concludes with a discussion about best practices and innovative technical solutions which have been proposed in Italy to guarantee both the efficiency of the multimodal logistic nodes and the security of the overall supply chain.

2. EVOLUTION OF MULTIMODAL FREIGHT TRANSPORTATION IN ITALY

According to a synthetic indicator used to measure the effectiveness of the national logistic system, Italy lies in 22nd place out of 155 countries, with a score of 3.64 on a 0–5 scale (World Bank, 2011). The top three countries are Germany (4.11), Singapore (4.09) and Sweden (4.08). A recent study by A.T. Kearney and Confetra (2011) estimates for Italy a total cost of logistics 11 percent higher than the European average resulting in significant inefficiencies and GDP losses.

In Italy, transportation cost is significantly influenced by a strong imbalance in the modal split. More specifically, 63 percent of the total cost of logistics is due to road transport (50 percent on average in Europe). Also the impact of ship transport is higher than the EU average (8.9 percent compared to 7 percent). Inversely, the incidence of rail transport is lower than the European average (0.8 percent versus 2 percent).

In the period 2009–2012, the transportation sector was significantly influenced by the decline of national and worldwide economies and in particular by the poor performance of the industrial sector (Centro Studi Confetra, 2013). After the financial crash in 2008, freight transportation services showed a substantial recovery which, however, was interrupted at the end of 2011 due to a new recession resulting in another significant reduction in freight flow. Nevertheless, in 2012 the positive trend in container traffic from/to Genoa harbor (+11.8 percent) continued, producing encouraging growth margins for the maritime sector. To date, the negative trend for the rail carriers remains, with relevant freight volumes being transferred from rail to road even for long distances and for the transportation of dangerous goods, in contradiction with the EU objectives for a sustainable mobility.

By analyzing the volume of goods transported in Italy over the last decades, it can be observed that road transport accounts for the lion's share of the total freight flows. In fact, 92.4 percent of the total shipments covering long distances (>50 km) is made by road, while the remaining 7.6 percent is divided between railroad (5.9 percent), air transport (1.3 percent) and waterways (0.4 percent). The share of ground transport is even higher for short distances within urban freight distribution (Ministero dell'ambiente e della tutela del territorio e del mare, 2014). Given the morphology of the country, in which only a few rivers are navigable for long distances (e.g. the Po River), inland waterway holds only a minor share of the total freight transportation.

Analyzing the flows, 73 percent of the total inbound freight movements are finished products (e.g. textile products, machines and vehicles), 22 percent are mineral raw materials and energy resources (e.g. natural gas and oil), 3 percent are agricultural goods, while the products resulting from waste treatment account for 2 percent. From the export perspective, finished industrial goods and agricultural products represent more than 96 percent of the exportations.

In 2012, more than 70 percent of the whole multimodal freight transportation was performed by using containers passing through logistic hubs located in Northern Italy. Multimodal freight transportation has had a growing trend over the last few decades which has increased the efficiency of the overall Italian logistic system. Freight transported at international level through the Alps represents about 150 million tons, of which 50 million are transported by train (17 million via traditional trains and 33 million via intermodal trains). In 2011, the total train flow from/to neighboring countries was divided as follows: 60 percent crossed Switzerland, 30 percent Austria and 7 percent France. In addition, 8 percent of the freight transported by train is represented by dangerous and hazardous materials.

Considering the current multimodal transportation network, additional security measures should be adopted to avoid potential terrorist attacks, with prior focus on radioactive materials, flammable products and pollutant substances. Despite the rarity of such events the risk remains for the population located in the neighborhood of logistic infrastructures being exposed to severe consequences. Other security threats commonly encountered in the Italian transportation system are related to crimes committed on the premises of transport operators (e.g. break-ins), to the illegal transport of forbidden substances (e.g. drugs) or dangerous goods such as weapons, toxic waste dumping, the theft of valuable cargos in transit, or armed piracy to national vessels in international seas.

3.   INFRASTRUCTURES FOR MULTIMODAL FREIGHT TRANSPORTATION IN ITALY

Recent experiences in many European countries, in the United States and in Japan have shown that an efficient multimodal freight transportation cannot be achieved only through the implementation of new (sometimes not really necessary) transportation infrastructures (European Commission, 2011b). It is necessary to act directly on the transportation demand, by distributing the traffic flow in a balanced manner between the various transport modes. In this way, it is possible to optimize the use of infrastructures allowing more secure, faster and cheaper shipments. An optimized transportation network which integrates several logistic nodes such as ports, railways and roads might allow Italy to benefit from its strategic geographical position in relation to worldwide freight flows. With exceptions made for pipelines (which can be hardly combined with other transport modes) and for air and inland waterways (which cover a small part of the total freight transportation), in Italy multimodality is mainly achieved through the integration of land modes (road and rail) and sea transport resulting in the following combinations: road-rail, road-sea, rail-sea, road-rail-sea (see Figure 7.1).

After the decline in traffic volumes in all transport modes due to the crises of 2009 and 2011, Italy is restructuring its logistic system with a significant rationalization of the companies operating in the logistics industry. As a result, the number of enterprises is constantly decreasing (4.8 percent a year over the last five years) and bigger companies are taking over smaller ones. In 2012, despite an increase in the tolls (+4.34 percent) and the high excise tax on fuel, the usage of highways increased by 3.51 percent. Road transport absorbs almost entirely freight transportation over a short distance (<50 km), completing and integrating almost all transport modes (e.g. maritime, rail and air). The predominance of road transport is due the following factors: population distribution; location and size of industrial plants; infrastructure limitations; and the pulverization of the retail system.

The primary road network is comprised of highways (6668 km), secondary roads (20773 km) and regional and provincial roads (151 583 km), with a total extension of over 179 000 km. In 2012, the total number of (heavy, light and special) vehicles registered in the Italian registry of auto-vehicles was 4.7 million (+1.15 percent compared to 2011). However,

Figure 7.1   Intermodal nodes in Italy

the registration of heavy vehicles is facing a considerable decrease (−29.4 percent compared to 2011). Analyzing the freight flow on the Italian road system, a prominent role is covered by four regions: Lombardy, Emilia Romagna, Veneto and Piedmont. Overall, these four regions generate 55 percent of extra-regional freight flows saturating the Italian primary road network. The most congested highway road segments are the following arterial roads: Milan–Padua, Milan–Bologna, Bologna–Ancona,

Trieste–Venice, each running more than 60 000 heavy vehicles per day (ANFIA, 2013; CENSIS and Unione interporti riuniti, 2010).

Crotti and Ramella (2012) estimated that about 190 million tons of freight currently transported by road (including the flows from/to harbours) could be moved by rail, thus reducing the number of accidents as well as the amount of congestion and pollution. The length of the Italian rail network in 2011 was 16 742 km, of which 7459 km were represented by double track electrified rail segments and 4472 km by single track electrified segments. Intermodality represents 45 percent of rail trips, at a total of 34.5 million tons. The reduced number of rides and the low cost of the road transport mode make the railway not competitive for in-country freight flows. For this reason, 65 percent of the total freight transported by train has an international destination. As a result, the Alps represent the cornerstone of the Italian railway network.

For a country like Italy, characterized by an industrial system having an international vocation and a significant reliance on foreign supplies of raw materials, the presence of an efficient port system is crucial for competitiveness and growth. The country presents a favorable geographical position in the center of the Mediterranean Sea, which is crossed by more than half of the worldwide cargo containers every year. Despite its strategic location, in recent years Italy has faced difficulties in intercepting international traffic flow due to increased competition from some ports located in North Africa (Egypt and Morocco) and in other countries such as Spain, Turkey and Israel. Despite these criticalities, Italian ports rank third at the European level, with a total volume of more than 470 million tons, contributing 2.6 percent to the Italian GDP.

The Italian port network consists of 24 big ports and many smaller commercial harbors. However, the biggest five ports handle more than 40 percent of the total freight traffic. A dual port system is adopted:

1. The southern ports, located along the Suez-Gibraltar axis, are specialized in transshipment. These ports devote more than 75 percent of their activities to handling containers and general cargo from ship to ship, relying on a favorable geographical position which allows them to intercept freight along the transoceanic routes. The transshipment traffic is mainly located in the ports of Gioia Tauro, Taranto and Cagliari (42 percent of the national container traffic in 2010). Gioia Tauro is the only Italian harbor built for the development of the transshipment mode, being the third Mediterranean port for transshipment after the ports of Valencia (Spain) and Port Said (Egypt).
2. The northern ports operate as gateways. Their strategic position enables access to the largest European markets and the main industrial

centers. The gateway port of Genoa (50 million tons in 2010) is the main Italian port and the fourth biggest hub in the Mediterranean Sea after Marseille (86 billion tons in 2010), Algeciras and Valencia (65.5 and 63.7 billion tons respectively in 2010).

Currently in Italy there are approximately 60 important multimodal terminals. Traditional terminals are increasingly becoming complex logistic hubs characterized by the proximity of arterial roads, rail stations and harbors. They are composed of a freight collecting center where incoming goods from different origins are transported via different modes and temporarily stored, consolidated and finally shipped to different destinations through different transport modes. The benefits of multimodality and intermodality are mostly exploited in the northern part of the country where approximately 70 percent of the Italian multimodal freight demand is handled. The boundaries of this macro-area are represented by the Livorno port on the western Tyrrhenian coast and the port of Ravenna along the eastern shore. In the northern part, this area includes the regions of Lombardy, Piedmont, Veneto, Emilia Romagna, Friuli-Venezia Giulia, Trentino-Alto Adige and the northern part of Tuscany.

In the central and southern part of Italy the conditions for the effective development of intermodality do not seem to be fully met yet. First, there is an excessive fragility in the economic and local production, which results in inadequate freight volumes. Second, even if the market size enables the adoption of intermodal solutions (e.g. in the case of important industrial cities such as Rome with a high number of inhabitants), there is a considerable fragmentation of freight traffic, a lack of facilities and appropriate strategies to replace the widespread road transport mode with alternative modes (e.g. rail and ship). In southern Italy the most interesting logistic areas with regard to multimodality are:

- the logistic centers gravitating around the port of Naples and the two freight logistic hubs of Nola and Marcianise;
- the logistic nodes connected to the port of Taranto and the freight logistic centers located in Bari.

4.   THE LEGAL FRAMEWORK FOR MULTIMODAL FREIGHT SECURITY IN ITALY

To a great extent, the deployment of intermodal freight transport concerns the international movements of goods among countries. This affects the role of the European countries as important trading partners of the globalized supply chains. Consequently, the harmonization of national laws is necessary to guarantee an adequate degree of security along the supply chain. The importance of security has been emphasized by the growing threat of terrorist attacks. In order to protect both citizens and firms, whose daily activities need to be secured, the minimization of vulnerabilities in the supply chain is required (Reniers and Zamparini, 2012).

Italy, as a member of the EU, is involved in the definition of policies and rules to increase the security of single transport modes and – in approaching the problem from a higher perspective – to consider the whole supply chain of multimodal interconnections.

In the following subsections we describe the EU framework that is implemented and translated into specific rules at the national level.

4.1 The European Legal Framework

At the EU level the general framework for multimodal transport security was set in 2006 by Communication No. 79 from the European Commission to the Council, the European Parliament, the European Economic and Social Committee and the European Committee of the Regions on enhancing supply chain security. This document acknowledged the main heterogeneities among air and maritime transports on one side and the road haulage segments of the multimodal supply chain on the other side, where the number of operators is limited in the former and much larger in the latter.

Aviation and airport security have been defined by a European Framework Regulation (EC) No. 2320/2002, while maritime and port security were targeted by Regulation (EC) No. 725/2004, and Directive (EC) No. 65/2005.

Due to their larger scale, air and maritime logistic operators normally have internally developed, formalized and advanced security strategies which the road operators lack. For this reason, the relevant document suggested that land transportation apply a framework of minimum security requirements that would gradually evolve in line with technological progress and risk developments to ensure satisfactory security levels. Those operators complying with the minimal security requirement set at the European level would be classified as a 'secure operator'. The security management system of a secure operator must be based on a risk assessment addressing the following aspects: physical security, access controls, procedural security, personnel security, documentation procedures, information security, education and training awareness.

The main advantages of the proposed secure schema are: a Europe-wide coordinated security drive, a better interconnectivity with secure maritime and air transport, a higher security performance, an enhanced business efficiency and resilience due for example to simplifications related to security control measures.

After stating the general needs to improve security, the document outlines the following objectives: (1) to increase the level of security along the supply chain without impeding the free flow of trade; (2) to establish a common framework for a systematic European approach without jeopardizing the common transport market and the existing security measures; (3) to avoid unnecessary administrative procedures and burdens at European and national levels.

The proposed measures to achieve such goals consist of:

- establishing a mandatory system for Member States to create a security ('secure operator') quality label that can be awarded to operators in the supply chain meeting the European minimum security levels, allowing a mutual recognition of the label on the internal market;
- introducing, within the mandatory provisions for the Member States, a voluntary scheme under which the operators in the supply chain increase their security performance in exchange for incentives;
- increasing the responsibility of supply chain operators for their own security performance in the European freight transport;
- granting benefits to 'secure operators' who positively distinguish themselves from other competitors in the area of security, giving them a commercial and competitive advantage;
- continuously updating and upgrading the security requirements, including recognized international standards.

The aim of these measures is to create a general and comprehensive framework for operators within the EU, instead of having particular measures that are adopted only for a limited number of key logistic areas (e.g. access facilities). The main objective in strengthening global supply chain security within multimodal and intermodal freight transportation is to guarantee that every operator of each link in the supply chain assumes responsibility for the security of its own activities. These individual security measures add up to the security of the complete chain.

An accompanying document annexed to the aforementioned Communication proposed a detailed cost-benefit analysis associated with the introduction of a mandatory security scheme, with an estimated investment for all the European logistic operators in security measures of €60 billion and an enforcement cost of €235 million per year to be paid by all EU Member States. An alternative security scheme was also estimated which would have required an implementation cost for industry of €2.42 billion per year, an auditing cost of €97 million per year, and an enforcement cost of €39 million per year.

4.2   The National Legal Framework

One of the first legal acts dealing with multimodal freight transportation in Italy refers to law No. 240 of 1990 in which a description of intermodal freight hubs is given. Moreover, such infrastructures are classified as first or second notch depending on their national relevance. Some considerations about safety issues such as environmental protection are contained. However, no security aspects are mentioned in the document. All the operational aspects and procedures including safety that apply to logistic operators are determined in the framework of the national long-term plans for transport and logistics which are issued every ten years.

The most recent plan was drafted in 2012, with a planning horizon to 2020. This document covers several strategic and operational aspects including combined transports, globalization, transport policies, intermodality and the environment. There is no specific section devoted to security. Nevertheless, security is a relevant factor that has to be considered by logistic operators and this concept is developed across the whole document.

At the national level, the Ministry of Internal Affairs and the Ministry of Environmental Protection are directly involved in defining and implementing security policies affecting multimodal freight procedures. Security also appears as a key driver in the development of the highways of the sea, especially in terms of port interconnections through physical and digital links.

At a wider level the continuous flow of information between economic actors involved in the supply chain is seen as an important prerequisite to guarantee multimodal freight transport security. At an operational level ICT technologies are useful in dealing with security during seal checks, container scans, access control, and track-&-traces. ICT plays a key role in securing not only the logistic nodes, but also the arcs along the whole supply chain, as stated within the context of the EU intelligent transport system endorsed by the EU Directive 2010/40.

Italy, as per the other members of the EU, transposed Communication 2006/79, mentioned above, into its legal framework by defining measures adopted at the national level to monitor national secure operators. A specific database, containing a risk index based on the characteristics of the secure operators and their infractions, was developed in the following years. The aim of this database is not only to create a blacklist of insecure operators, but also to harmonize classification and comparison among secure operators at the European level. The goals of this blacklist are to stimulate competitiveness among multimodal freight operators and to allow customers to compare different logistic operators on the same bases. Specific operative procedures to check the requirements and the application of the minimal security measures by national operators are also mentioned in the latest national long-term plan for transport and logistics.

This document also mentions territorial logistic platforms as an institution responsible for the trade-off between efficiency and security. These logistic platforms, alongside multimodal hubs, represent one of the pillars of the national framework law that is currently under approval by the Italian Parliament and that should replace the previous laws. Such a bill (No. 3257/2012) explicitly mentions security in the third article related to the requirements of the logistic infrastructures. In the fourth paragraph it is stated that the planning of the construction and the management of an intermodal hub must be in line with adequate security and control procedures. Article seven is devoted to waste and hazardous materials, emphasizing that their management should be aimed at enhancing freight transport security among territorial logistic platforms. A specific rule concerning hazardous materials within Europe was issued by the EU in 2008 (Directive 2008/68/CE) and transposed at national level by the legislative decree 35/2010.

5. A REVIEW OF MULTIMODAL FREIGHT TRANSPORTATION SECURITY IN ITALY

This section is devoted to the description of security-related episodes recorded in Italy in 2013. The database has been compiled through the official website of the Italian customs offices that register such occurrences on a monthly basis. In each report it was possible to elicit the location, the transport mode, the intermodal infrastructure involved and the security threat. Other information such as freight value and quantities were not always available and consequently they will not be part of the following analysis.

Figure 7.2 shows the number of episodes registered at each node/arc along the Italian multimodal transport network in 2013. It can be clearly observed that ports represent the most vulnerable places where security threats are concentrated. Road segments, intermodal hubs and airports are characterized by a lower number of events. In the case of road arcs this might be due to the difficulties of monitoring a dispersed and broad transportation network. In addition, the railway nodes/arcs were not involved in any freight security-related episode in 2013.[1]

Figure 7.2 also shows the breakdown of security-related episodes by

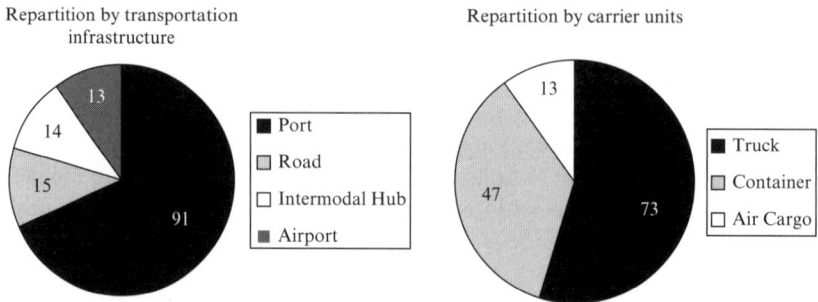

Figure 7.2   Security-related episodes per type in 2013

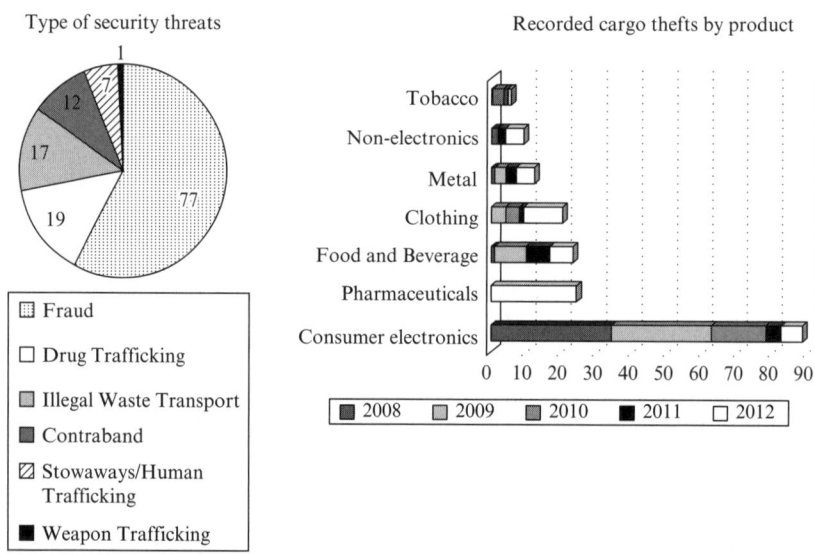

Figure 7.3   Major security threats in 2013

carrier unit. Coherently with the general statistics on modal split, the majority of events are related to trucks. It should be noted that in most of the cases these trucks opted for an intermodal Ro-Ro combination and their illegal activities were ascertained in a port facility. Moreover, all the airport-related cases concerned air cargo shipments.

Figure 7.3 reports the list of security threats on the basis of a taxonomy coherent with the framework described in Blümel et al. (2008). First, it can be seen that no terrorism-related event was reported in 2013.

However, in previous years, terrorism threats interrupted the Italian intermodal transport. Two notable episodes were registered in the Gioia Tauro terminal. The first one occurred in October 2001, when a supposed terrorist was found in a shipping container traveling from Egypt to Canada. The second episode happened in 2010 in the same intermodal node. The Italian police discovered seven tons of the powerful T4 explosive in a shipping container that was in transit from Iran to Syria, probably destined for a terrorist organization. This container arrived at Gioia Tauro inside a cargo ship named *Finland*, of the Swiss–Italian MSC shipping company, sailing under a Liberian flag. The explosive was hidden behind sacks of powdered milk and filled a good portion of the truck-sized container.

In 2013 the major security threats were related to fraud (mainly counterfeit merchandise and stolen goods), drug trafficking, illegal waste transport and contraband of cigarettes. The stowaways/human trafficking and weapon trafficking account for a limited number of episodes. Pilferage events are not included in the previously mentioned database, but other sources address this issue. According to a report published by the Transported Asset Protection Association (TAPA, 2013), the threat of cargo theft in Italy is severe. Criminals frequently target the major transportation hubs and follow specifically-selected loads before stealing the cargo – often standing in unsecured parking areas where unauthorized access to cargo shipments in transit does not appear to be a hard task. Consumer electronic goods – followed by pharmaceuticals, clothing, and food and beverage goods – represent the largest targeted categories between 2008 and 2012 (see Figure 7.3). The region of Lombardy recorded the highest number of episodes in that period (more than 27 percent) – theft from vehicles being the preferred modus operandi by criminals, followed by hijacking.

Considering the geographical dimension, it is possible to distribute the episodes into five main areas of Italy[2] as shown in Figure 7.4.

As expected, the North-West is the area with the majority of episodes with its share of freight transport and logistics activities. The other two relevant macro-regions are Central and Southern Italy. In both cases the largest share of security-related episodes was linked to security controls in port facilities. Finally, no clear pattern emerges from the monthly distribution of security-related events in 2013. However, the months of March, May, October and December registered the highest numbers of cases, with a dip in September.

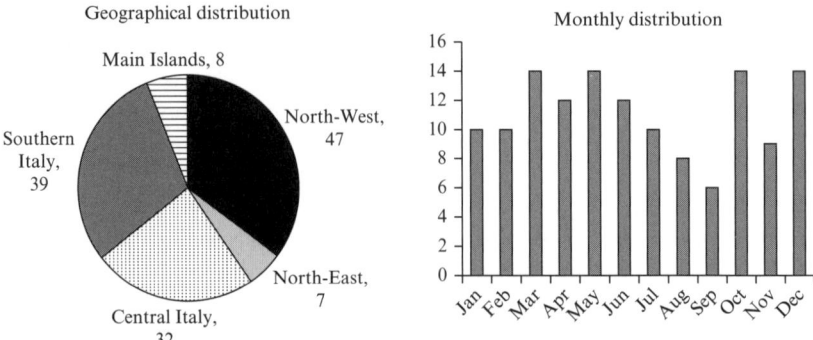

Figure 7.4   Spatial-temporal distribution of security-related episodes in 2013

6.   CONCLUSIONS

The main logistic nodes exposed to the highest security threats in Italy are represented by ports, and in the majority of the cases a truck is involved. Moreover, freight transported in containers through the Italian sea terminals is subsequently moved via other transport modes such as road (77 percent) and railway (23 percent) to reach its final destination. For these reasons, these multimodal patterns have been attracting the interest of both political institutions and scholars.

A section of the literature has investigated innovative solutions to increase security within intermodal transport chains with a particular emphasis on port terminal operations and truck monitoring and surveillance especially in parking areas. Blümel et al. (2008) have stressed a lack of efficient security systems interlinking maritime with land transports. For this reason, they proposed an integrated approach harmonizing security policy framework, physical security measures, intermodal transport security and ICT security. This approach aims at increasing the degree of security without a substantial reduction in the supply chain efficiency. ICT measures, as described by the National Association for Telematics for Transport and Safety (TTS, 2007), have the potential to increase the reliability and the synergies within a multimodal transport system. The Security Research Association in Italy (SERIT, 2011) proposed ICT technologies to sustain the following activities:

- detection of suspicious behaviors and early warnings;
- data exchange mechanism, satellite and GPS systems to track and trail shipments;

- analysis of anomalies by integrating different sources and heterogeneous multimodal transportation systems;
- improved detection rate of hazardous and illegal materials by adopting new generation scanning systems.

A recent comprehensive security strategy has been proposed by the SISTEMA project described in Coppolino et al. (2011). ICT is exploited to support operations management in container terminals. The main system's components are: land side security; sea side security; goods and vehicle security; and passenger security.

An important instrument for this strategy is represented by radiofrequency identification (RFID) systems which are also the basis of another interesting application proposed by Casola et al. (2013) for rail transport. Also in the latter security application, ICT can provide effective tools in which efficiencies of cost, easiness of installation, interoperability of information sources, and security requirements, are jointly pursued.

Another remarkable application aimed at increasing security along the national highways has been recently proposed by Carrese et al. (2011). They consider a whole array of different measures – from wired fences to the most innovative technologies such as RFID – to enhance the security of parking areas and to reduce episodes of theft in Central Italy.

NOTES

1. A relevant number of security-related episodes involving passengers happened in the same period. Nevertheless, passenger transport is out of the scope of this study.
2. North-West includes Aosta Valley, Piedmont, Lombardy and Liguria. North-East consists of Emilia Romagna, Friuli-Venezia Giulia, Trentino-Alto Adige/Südtirol and Veneto. Central Italy contains Tuscany, Umbria, Marche and Lazio. Southern Italy includes Campania, Apulia, Molise, Basilicata and Calabria. The two main islands are Sardinia and Sicily.

REFERENCES

ANFIA (2013), Transporto Merci su Strada. Associazione Nazionale Filiera Industria Automobilistica.
A.T. Kearney and Confetra (2011), La logistica italiana, Rome.
Blümel, E., Boevé, W., Recagno, V. and Schilk, G. (2008), 'Port and supply chain security concepts interlinking maritime with hinterland transport chains', *WMU Journal of Maritime Affairs*, **7** (1), 205–225.
Carrese, S., Mantovani, S. and Nigro, M. (2011), 'Safe, secure and comfortable

HGVs parking areas: an Italian experience', *Procedia-Social and Behavioral Sciences*, **20**, 732–740.

Casola, V., De Benedictis, A., Drago, A. and Mazzocca, N. (2013), 'SeNsiM-SEC: secure sensor networks integration to monitor rail freight transport', *International Journal of System of Systems Engineering*, **4** (3), 291–316.

Cassa Depositi e Prestiti (2012), Porti e logistica Studio di settore.

CENSIS and Unione interporti riuniti (2010), Il sistema interportuale nelle piattaforme logistiche territoriali, Rapporto Finale, Roma.

Centro Studi Confetra (2013), Nota Congiunturale sul Trasporto Merci. Anno XVI No.1 – February.

Coppolino, L., D'Antonio, S., Formicola, V., Oliviero, F. and Romano, L. (2011), On the security of the terminal operations for container shipping in multimodal transport: The SIS-TEMA project, *Proceedings of the 2011 6th International Conference on Risk and Security of Internet and Systems (CRiSIS)*, 1–6.

Crotti, A. and Ramella, F. (2012), Caratteristiche attuali del trasporto intermodale. Policy Sessions Il Trasporto Intermodale Merci, la Logistica e l'Economia Regionale. Università di Roma, Tor Vergata, Rome.

European Commission (2011a), *A Budget for Europe 2020*.

European Commission (2011b), Connettere l'europa le reti transeuropee di trasporto TEN-T, available at http://ec.europa.eu/italia/milano/documents/connet tere_europa__per_sito.pdf (accessed on 27 May 2014).

Ministero dell'ambiente e della tutela del territorio e del mare (2014), Il trasporto merci in Italia 2013.

Reniers, G.L.L. and Zamparini, L. (2012), *Security Aspects of Uni- and Multimodal Hazmat Transportation Systems*, Weinheim, Germany: Wiley-VCH.

SERIT (2011), Roadmap Strategica 2011, SERIT Perugia.

TAPA (2013), Cargo crime in Italy – lean or mean?, available at https://www.tispol.org/system/files/TAPA_EMEA_Vigilant_Newsletter_January_2013.pdf (accessed on 27 May 2014).

TTS (2007), I Sistemi ITS: proposte per una nuova mobilità del Paese. Associazione per la Telematica per i Trasporti e la Sicurezza.

World Bank (2011), *Trade Logistics in the Global Economy: The Logistic Performance Index and its Indicators*.

8. Security improvement potential of Rail Baltica investment

Olli-Pekka Hilmola

1. INTRODUCTION

Buchhofer (1995) predicted that the Baltic States' (Estonia, Latvia and Lithuania) railways would lose their traffic volume to road transport, particularly in the freight segment. The reason for the loss was that the countries' roads were in much better condition than the rail system after the Soviet era. Road traffic levels have in fact grown enormously since this prediction (Ojala et al., 2005; Kovacs and Spens, 2006; Hilmola, 2011). Buchhofer (1995) also argued that only one north–south corridor would exist. This is the Rail Baltica. Kovacs and Spens (2006) continued Buchhofer's research and concluded that road volumes had increased significantly during this time period, but questioned the sustainability of this trend since maintenance and investments to the road infrastructure had been minimal (compared to volume growth). Kovacs and Spens (2006) did not see much potential for rail-based solutions and were a little skeptical of the Rail Baltica project, as it lay in 27th place in the TEN-T priority list of the EU's railway/road projects.

Research into road transport has continued (Keshkamat et al., 2009; Komornicki and Miszczuk, 2010). Keshkamat et al. (2009) proposed that the Rail Baltica line be located near the Via Baltica road to enable intermodality in the region. Further, Keshkamat et al. (2009) noted that the Polish route for Rail Baltica was not a simple issue as major green areas exist in the north-east region (four national parks, 12 landscaped parks and 10 national reserve areas). A route through Bialystok was also problematic as it would eventually make the journey longer. From a spatial economics perspective, large-scale implementation of infrastructure investments in this area of Poland are seen as vital, since it is the poorest region in the country (Komornicki and Miszczuk, 2010) with low value-added per employee. In recent years, due to EU and Schengen area enlargement, traffic to Belarus and Ukraine has decreased considerably (trucks and passengers).On the other hand, Lithuanian (Baltic) traffic is experiencing a

significant and continuous increase. Komornicki and Miszczuk (2010) estimate this volume to have been approximately 4000 trucks per day between
Poland and Lithuania in 2007. It is no wonder that Laisi and Saranen
(2013) argued – based on city-/town-level interviews (upper management)
in the Baltic States (the theme being the possible effects and drivers of
Rail Baltica) – that expectations for freight were high in Lithuania, while
the importance of passenger transport had increased. Inside of Latvia
and Estonia, the expectation was that the passenger transport side would
experience increases in the north. In Finland and North-West Russia,
Rail Baltica was seen as an attractive alternative for the private sector and
freight, if realized (Henttu et al., 2012; Karamysheva et al., 2013).

Even if investments had been made in the road infrastructure (Schwab,
2011, 2013) it is in poor shape based on international rankings, for example
in Latvia and Poland. General cargo transported by road heads east, typically to Russia and its capital, Moscow. However, road conditions do not
get any better on this eastern end, although significant improvements have
been made on the road network. Road maintenance has also taken a huge
share of the budget in Poland (PKP PLK, 2011).

Over the years, numerous investment calculations and cost benefit
analyses (CBA) from Rail Baltica have been released (the main starting
point being European Commission, 2007). Jonaitis and Butkevicius (2005)
argued that the investments required on Lithuanian soil were simply
unprofitable, while Bröcker et al. (2010) argued that the overall investment was well justified, providing EU-wide and societal issues were taken
into account (investment having a clear wealth-increase effect). On the
downside, analysis of Rail Baltica shows very low 'spillover' effects for
large areas or for those at a greater distance. The TEN-T priority of Rail
Baltica (e.g. Kovacs and Spens, 2006) is questionable based on these fresh,
independent and neutral calculations. The EU and the Baltic States have
carried out several of their own studies into Rail Baltica's profitability. The
most recent AECOM (2011a, 2011b) studies argued that it is profitable
within different CBA calculations (the coefficient was 1.75). AECOM recommended a direct alignment through the Baltic States (see Figure 8.1) –
this serves the lead time performance, which is critical for both passengers
and freight, and is key to societal benefits. Direct alignment also supports
intermodality, as the main international road, the Via Baltica, is in close
proximity (Keshkamat et al., 2009).

In this chapter, the focus of the analysis is on the multimodal security
in the Rail Baltica alignment, which connects Tallinn, Estonia to Warsaw,
Poland. At present, multimodality is nonexistent since the Baltic States and
Poland do not have any official, operating international passenger train
connections. Domestic train service ends in the border areas, although

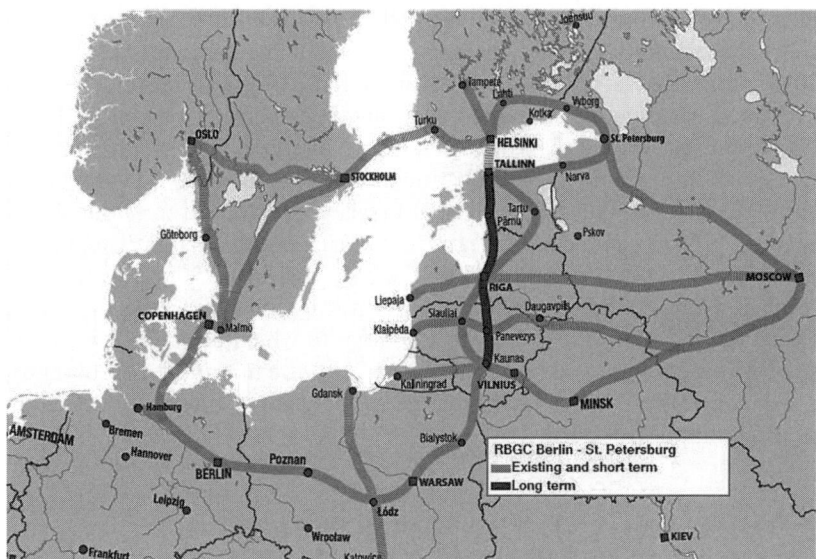

Source: Karttakeskus Oy/Aalto University, Cemat.

Figure 8.1 *Rail Baltica alignment plan for a totally new straight railway line (dark) and the current existing railway network (light) in the Baltic States and surrounding neighbouring countries*

there have been efforts to optimize them to serve international transport. However, travel times are long and average speeds occasionally only go above *biking* speed with this option (Hilmola, 2011; Lüttmerding and Gather, 2013). The frequency of passenger trains is one of the lowest in all of Europe. The situation is similar on the freight side. The railways carry domestic or international raw materials, with general cargo consigned to roadways. In the absence of an existing network on which to gather data, our analysis of the situation relies on observation from a number of different sources, using secondary statistics. However, hinterland transport is not an insignificant issue for Rail Baltica alignment countries as, recently, Nežerenko et al. (2015) showed with longitudinal statistical analysis that hinterland investments in roads and railways in this region have resulted in increasing imports and exports together with economic growth.

The Baltic States and Poland became members of the World Trade Organization (WTO) in 1999 and 1995 respectively. The Baltic States countries are also members of the EU (2004, as full members) and NATO (since 2004). Poland joined NATO in 1999. Even if the Baltic States and

Poland are members of the EU, membership of the Euro currency system splits these countries. The first country to join the Euro was Estonia in 2013, while Latvia became a member of the European currency system in 2014. Lithuania was accepted as a member of the Euro area in 2015. At the present time, Poland still retains its national currency. In general, transportation sector regulation and norms conform to EU directives across the region. Guidelines from Brussels are converted to national legislation. NATO membership means that border control is tightly regulated with non-EU countries and utilizes the best possible technical equipment (such as x-rays, as well as detectors of chemicals and radioactive material). Inside the EU area (the Schengen EU area, to which nearly all EU countries belong), freight and passenger movements are not under constant and direct control (only in cases of emergency or security threats are old style practices applied, if needed).

2.   HINTERLAND TRANSPORTATION CHARACTERISTICS AND CHANGE

Since the mid-1990s the freight market has grown in Poland and the Baltic States, but this has been fueled by increasing amounts of road transport. While the rate of road transport has slowed, the longer-term trend of this mode is still increasing. In Poland, the market share for road transport in 2012 was high at 76 percent. Latvia posted the lowest share in 2012 at 33 percent. Change has been significant over the years. In 1995, the Polish market share for road transport was below 40 percent, while Latvian market share was roughly 11 percent. Similar change is evident in passenger transport. Private cars currently dominate in all four countries. In this regard, the leader is Lithuania, where private cars accounted for over 90 percent of passenger transportation in 2012. The private car share of passenger transportation in the other three countries was around 80 percent market share. Again, change has been rapid. In 1995, the private car market share of Lithuania was 75.1 percent, while the market share in the other three countries was between 60–70 percent (European Union–Eurostat, 2014).

The Baltic States and Poland have been extreme examples of road freight transportation growth within the period of 1995–2008/2009 (European Union–Eurostat, 2014). Percentage growth ranges from 200–300 percent (e.g. see Komornicki and Miszczuk, 2010). In Poland, growth has risen steadily even though the crisis of 2009 severely affected almost all other aspects of transportation systems worldwide. Polish road freight has grown nearly 35 percent from 2008. The Baltic States have only grown by

3 percent from the high of 2008; however, over the longer term the Baltic States and Poland have shown similar growth rates in road freight. Freight volume in road transport was 4.3 times higher in Poland in 2012 than in 1995. For the Baltic States, growth was 4.8 times higher. Reasons for this growth could be related to international transports, as the manufacturing base in the Baltic States is limited.

The Polish international road freight share has increased from 36 percent in 2000 to 55–60 percent in the most recent data. Freight share growth continues in the Baltic States. Currently, Estonian road freight share is over 70 percent of international transports, with Latvia approaching 80 percent and Lithuania close to 90 percent. In general, international transport share is on a growth trajectory, with international transport growing at twice the rate of domestic transport. The only exception is Estonia, where growth was 'only' 30 percent in the period 2000–2012.

Passenger transport shows a pattern of growth similar to freight (European Union–Eurostat, 2014). In Poland, private car use has grown consistently even in the midst of the financial crisis of 2008–2009. In Poland and the Baltic States the use of private cars doubled between 1995–2012. Private car use in the Baltic States between 1995–2007 was actually higher than in Poland; however, the economic crisis was so severe in the Baltic States that it reduced private car use significantly (approximately −19 percent in the years 2007–2012) producing a decline that has only recently started to level off. On the other hand, growth in Poland accelerated from 2007. It should be noted that the Baltic States were not a homogenous group in terms of passenger car use after the crisis – in Estonia volumes did not experience a decline and even grew somewhat between 2007–2012 (up 8 percent). Lithuania and Latvia recorded severe declines of −22.3 percent and −27.7 percent respectively.

The collapse of railway sector demand due to a Soviet Bloc preference for this transportation mode and changes in the economic system (Blackshaw and Thompson, 1993; Tanczos, 1999; Lukasiak, 2001) is still present in the Polish railway freight markets as volumes for 2012 were still 28 percent lower than in the base year of 1995. In comparison, the Baltic States were able to utilize their valuable hinterland position in raw material transport from the east (Russia, Belarus and Ukraine). After the collapse in demand of the early 1990s, volumes increased rather rapidly and efficiently (Hilmola, 2007). They are actually double those of 1995 levels.

Unlike road transport, railway passenger transport has shown no evidence of growth as there is no upswing or tendency to greater volumes during the years 1995–2012 (European Union–Eurostat, 2014). Both the Baltic States and Poland are currently posting their lowest performance in at least two decades. The situation is most challenging in Lithuania, where only approximately one-third of railway passenger volumes remain as compared to 1995. In terms of railway use, Estonia is the strongest of the Baltic States countries (56 percent remaining from the volume levels of 1995), followed by Latvia (53.2 percent remaining from the 1995 volumes). Poland still has some advantage over these three countries as the decline from the base year of 1995 has been roughly only one-third. However, some positive signs have appeared in recent years. For example, Estonia renewed its rolling stock in domestic transport and improved its domestic rail network. This resulted in extremely favorable developments within passenger transport in 2014 (Statistics Estonia, 2015).

3.   ROAD TRANSPORTATION FATALITIES AND INJURIES

Earlier research and general press articles have highlighted the road safety challenges in Eastern Europe (Marquez and Bliss, 2013). This was verified with an analysis of the main Rail Baltica countries. Although the situation is still challenging, it has improved over the years. Fatalities have declined in the Baltic States and Poland with a reduction of approximately 75 percent in the period 1990–2012. In 2012, 565 people died in the Baltic States. In Poland, the number of deaths is now roughly half of the 1990 total, with 3571 deaths in 2012. Even if the improvements sound remarkable, the difference with neighboring countries in 2012 is apparent – Germany (3600 deaths), Sweden (285 deaths) and Finland (255 deaths) (European Union–Eurostat, 2014). Based on Eurostat data, the normalized death rate (deaths to population) is roughly three times higher than that of a comparison country such as Sweden. If comparison is made with Finland, four Rail Baltica countries are on average twice as dangerous as their northern neighbors. However, it should be remembered that all former Soviet Bloc countries still reflect a heritage from their past, with fatalities in Russia (scaled to population) still much higher than in Poland – in fact, they are nearly double based on official statistics (Russia in Figures, 2012).

In terms of fatalities, the global recession which started in 2008–2009 significantly improved road safety statistics. This is especially true in all of the Baltic States, which all recorded declines in the death rate of more than 55 percent as compared to 2012 and 2007. From earlier analysis, it is known that volumes in freight road transportation and private car use were modest or even declining after the crisis in these countries. In Poland, road volumes continued to increase and fatalities simultaneously declined by 35.9 percent. This development is not only due to declining transportation volumes (in the case of the Baltic States), but to increased fuel costs

Table 8.1   *Fatalities in the areas/districts within current Rail Baltica alignment of road transportation (Tallinn-Warsaw railway route, Rail Baltica)*

Country	Area / District	2005	2006	2007	2008	2009	2010	2011	2012
Estonia	Harju county	47	56	65	33	25	22	28	26
	Pärnu county	15	16	11	17	8	3	6	9
	Rapla county	9	12	13	1	3	4	6	4
Total	Estonia	71	84	89	51	36	29	40	39
Latvia	Zemgale region	67	57	78	51	37	42	35	32
	Pieriga region	132	121	128	92	76	54	47	39
	Riga region	66	70	70	46	39	32	28	31
Total	Latvia	265	248	276	189	152	128	110	102
Lithuania	Kaunas county					77	43	49	54
	Marijampole county					25	34	29	26
	Panevezys county					37	39	34	26
	Siauliai county					33	29	25	23
Total	Lithuania					172	145	137	129
Poland	Podlaskie						146	152	131
	Mazowieckie						655	712	587
Total	Poland						801	864	718
Total							1103	1151	988

Sources: Central Statistical Bureau of Latvia (2013); Statistics Estonia (2013); Statistics Lithuania (2013); Statistical Office in Szczecin (2013).

(resulting in more careful and planned driving), and general improvements in safety.

National statistics are one way to observe the safety and security aspects of new railway investment, but observation at the local and district level – where the railway connection of Rail Baltica is planned – gives a much better view. Table 8.1 presents recent statistics on fatalities and Table 8.2 presents the results for injuries. In general, 2010–2012 shows a slowly improving situation in road safety and security. It could be estimated that during 2012 the level of fatalities was slightly below 1000, while injuries were 12 times higher. Poland and the district (voivodship) around Warsaw, Mazowieckie, accounts for a significant portion of the fatalities and injuries. In the Baltic States, the highest absolute levels of fatalities and injuries were recorded in Lithuanian Kaunas and Latvian Pieriga. Other Lithuanian counties or regions also did not demonstrate good safety performance. In Panevezys, injuries have clearly increased during

Table 8.2　　*Injuries in the areas/districts within current Rail Baltica*
　　　　　　　　alignment of road transportation (Tallinn-Warsaw railway
　　　　　　　　route, Rail Baltica)

Country	Area / District	2005	2006	2007	2008	2009	2010	2011	2012
Estonia	Harju county	1136	1197	1081	828	670	607	723	729
	Pärnu county	210	262	266	189	143	162	141	89
	Rapla county	102	85	138	78	69	58	44	40
Total	Estonia	1448	1544	1485	1095	882	827	908	858
Latvia	Zemgale region	692	650	661	642	420	433	461	459
	Pieriga region	1095	980	1236	1193	766	772	862	879
	Riga region	2161	2123	2331	1932	1489	1632	1661	1659
Total	Latvia	3948	3753	4228	3767	2675	2837	2984	2997
Lithuania	Kaunas county					1213	1060	722	642
	Marijampole county					324	349	300	278
	Panevezys county					358	424	396	374
	Siauliai county					466	420	423	441
Total	Lithuania					2361	2253	1841	1735
Poland	Podlaskie						1125	1006	970
	Mazowieckie						6339	6148	5354
Total	Poland						7464	7154	6324
Total							13381	12887	11914

Sources:　Central Statistical Bureau of Latvia (2013); Statistics Estonia (2013); Statistics Lithuania (2013); Statistical Office in Szczecin (2013).

the observed four-year period, and in Marijampole county deaths have also increased slightly. Similar trends can be found in the Harju county of Estonia, where both fatalities and injuries have increased in the same observation period. The region of Riga has also experienced an alarming number of injuries.

4.　OIL DEPENDENCY AT NATIONAL ACCOUNTS

In addition to accidents and the associated fatalities and injuries, road transportation leads to higher oil use. This has unwanted consequences as oil prices have trended upward for the last ten years globally. In the early 1970s, one barrel of oil was priced below US$2. The days of cheap oil (US$10–20 per barrel) are over and oil has traded at nearly US$100–110 per barrel before declining to approximately half of this amount (Sandalow, 2008; regarding peak oil, see Maggio and Cacciola, 2009). The economic problems in Southern Europe were triggered by trade and

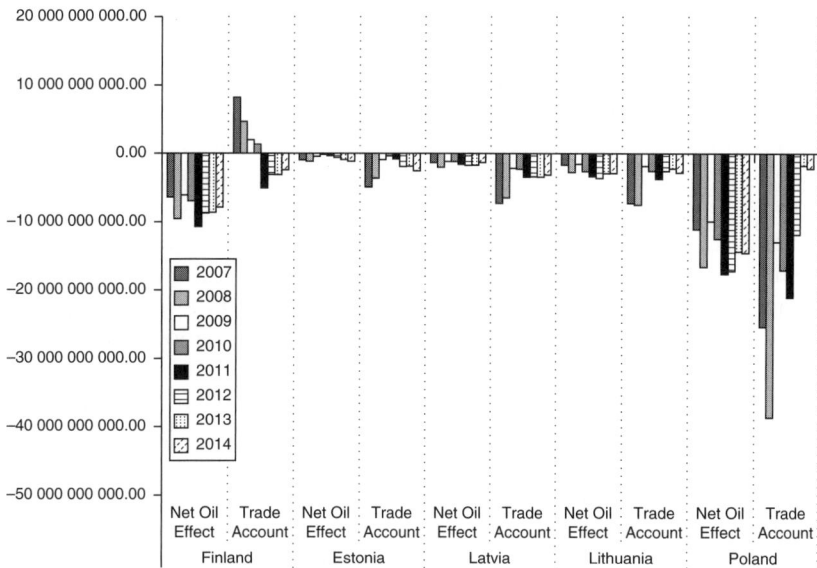

Source: UN Comtrade (2015).

Figure 8.2   *Net oil effect (export less imports), trade account performance*
              (total, surplus or deficit) in Finland, the Baltic States and
              Poland (all in USD)

current account deficits that are in part driven by the higher prices of oil in
2010–2011. While the Baltic Sea Region is typically presented in economic
reports as surviving and competitive, it has its weak side too. Much of
this is related to oil and a significant dependency on road transport (see
Hilmola, 2013).

Poland has been seen as an economic success story in recent years, but
the downside of growth is apparent in Figure 8.2. Poland has attracted
many factories (Greenfield or transfers from elsewhere), but its trade
account continues to show deficits. These are largely explained by the price
of oil and oil dependency. Polish exports increased from 2007 to 2014 by
more than 50 percent, but its trade account is still negative. Finland reflects
a similar story, except that exports are declining by 17 percent. High-tech
manufacturing has mostly been lost in Finland and old mass manufacturing still requires oil for transport.

In the Baltic States, and especially in Lithuania, the net oil effect is typically greater than the trade deficit, and this in a situation where exports
have grown since 2007 by more than 80 percent. In Estonia and Latvia,

export growth is in the range of 50–70 percent. The net oil effect explains 40–45 percent of the trade deficits in the year 2014.

If oil prices continue to increase, it is questionable whether Poland will continue its economic growth without a major recession. The same situation applies to Finland. Weakness in the Baltic States and Poland was apparent from the GDP development of these countries in the crisis of 2008/2009: all recorded declines of 14.5–20 % in Euro terms during 2009. Poland did not officially enter into recession in 2009 as the country devaluated its currency (Zloty) significantly (approximately 25 percent devaluation against the Euro). In 2009, its GDP remained mildly positive. The Baltic States maintained strong currencies and their national economies suffered as a result.

From a passenger transport perspective, road and air travel are key transport options from the Baltic States and Poland to foreign countries. In the case of expensive oil, options are fewer and the railway option is more in demand. Volcanic eruptions in Iceland during April–May 2010 resulted in a situation whereby long-distance passenger transport was blocked within the area of Rail Baltica. Without international railway transport options, it is difficult to find a substitute for a journey to Berlin or further.

5. RAILWAY SECURITY AND CONTROL

The Baltic States and Poland are lagging behind in the implementation of the common signaling and traffic control initiative, the European Rail Traffic Management System (ERTMS). This system would ease interoperability in international railway transport, increase real-time tracking and tracing and increase the efficient control of railway traffic. Even the basic communication module, the GSM-R digitalized mobile network for railways, has not received significant action in these regions (based on the situation reported in year 2012; see European Commission, 2014). In 2007, Estonia and Latvia clearly indicated that such a system would not be implemented in the near future (ERTMS, 2014). In Lithuania and Poland some plans exist for implementation, but these were long-term oriented (ERTMS, 2014). While countries realized that Rail Baltica should and would be equipped with ERTMS, this investment was not considered in near-term planning.

The failure to implement ERTMS or even GSM-R can be attributed to at least three different factors. First, railway freight transport in the Baltic States is greatly influenced by the 1520 mm Russian standard railway system – there is no need to use common, modern and European-level accepted railway communication and management standards. Countries such as Russia, Belarus and Ukraine will continue to use their own older standards in the future, with inevitable incompatibility if the system is changed on the other side of the transportation chain. Second, there is a lack of significant railway traffic on the south-north corridor, either passengers or cargo. Third, these countries do not have high-speed passenger or freight transport to accelerate implementation. Thus, from a systems perspective, railway safety and security at the national level is somewhere between the old Soviet standard and isolated new investments made to arrangement yards and railway lines (with modern automation, like mobile railway switch control, taken into use). The situation will improve incrementally as each new section of Rail Baltica is built using the European 1435 mm railway standard. This corridor will overcome all of the earlier mentioned three points that are constraining ERTMS implementation.

6.   CRIME AND THE COSTS OF BUSINESS

Several of the countries of the Rail Baltica region manifest high crime and violence costs for business. According to the World Competitiveness Report, Poland ranked lower than 90 in 2008 (Schwab and Porter, 2008). Russia was within the range of 80–100 in the same report. This means that the crime situation in Poland was not under control. A similar finding was reported in a large-scale international road transportation survey conducted during 2005–2006. Poland was ranked as high in the level of cargo crime, with Russia and Hungary (IRU, 2008). The situation has improved somewhat according to Schwab (2013). In general, the crime situation in the Baltic States and Poland is worse than in Finland, but better than in Russia (Schwab, 2011, 2013). The best performance in this area from Rail Baltica alignment countries is in Estonia.

The level of crime is not alarming, but it does suggest that complex and numerous multimodal stations for freight cannot be implemented without having proper security systems and physical surveillance in place. Typically, cargo thefts take place when rolling stock does not move and is parked for some reason (IRU, 2008). Based on an IRU (2008) survey completed during 2005–2006, Poland and its capital Warsaw together with Latvia's Riga were considered the most probable places for criminal activity directed at trucks in Europe. Based on annual statistics from the region (Eurostat, 2014), this situation still persists in Region Centralny within Poland (surrounding Warsaw). This area reported more than 4000 robberies in the most recent year, roughly 2.7 times that of Finland and slightly less than half of all robberies taking place in Sweden (the population of Region Centralny is two million inhabitants fewer than that of Sweden, but approximately two million inhabitants more than that of Finland). The actual or potential theft of cargo increases the costs of intermodality. While the situation appears to be getting better (Schwab, 2013), it is not yet clear that the long-term trend is downward, which would translate into cost savings for operating companies (lower preventive costs and actual cargo loss). The trend in robberies has not significantly declined in other possible Rail Baltica intermodal terminal sites in Poland. For example, the eastern district of Region Wschodni continues to report a high number of robberies.

It should be noted that current driving regulations in the EU restrict a single driver and truck to a maximum of 9–10 hours. Thus, a truck leaving Tallinn, Estonia, could at best reach Kaunas, Lithuania. The truck must then stop for 11 hours of free, resting time for the driver. This situation could be avoided by using two truck drivers. The maximum number of hours on the road is then raised to 20. It would then be possible to reach Warsaw, Poland, from Estonia. These of course are best-case-scenario times for transit and do not account for delays or possible crimes involving the cargo or driver.

Given the limitations on daily progress and the possibility of criminal activity, it would be feasible to place intermodal centers at the very ends of the Rail Baltica route. Of course, in many cases manufacturing sites, logistics flows, and warehousing placements have already been established, but in the north the most feasible place for an intermodal center would be in Estonia or at the southern end of Estonia and/or northern Latvia. At the southern end of Rail Baltica these loading and unloading locations should be in Lithuania (e.g. Kaunas) or northeast Poland (e.g. Bialystok). In theory, these locations would drive multimodality, improving cost-efficiency and lead time, while maximizing the railway freight journey, and limiting long-distance distribution with trucks. According to the EU project, Rail Baltica Growth Corridor Expert Group (Härkönen, 2013), the most feasible places for the intermodal terminals of Rail Baltica would be Tallinn (Estonia), Riga (Latvia) and Kaunas (Lithuania). The Polish intermodal terminal ought to be located near Warsaw.

For passenger transport, crime does not create that much of a problem. The emphasis is on high performance and short lead times between cities. Therefore, passenger terminals should be located in populated city areas (or in close proximity to these). These should have electronic and/or human surveillance to increase security (e.g. the number of robberies in some places are high). For passenger transport, the key problem is the integration of private car use; parking areas should be available for long-term parking needs. These parking places should be secured, even if the current motor vehicle theft rates in the Rail Baltica alignment are low (Eurostat,

2014). Vehicle thefts typically occur in economically more advanced countries in Western Europe such as Germany, France and the UK (Barry, 1996; Allen, 2012; *The Economist*, 2013), with vehicles transported east to Poland, Lithuania and Russia for sales and use (*The Economist*, 2013). Large transportation infrastructure investment will likely attract people from more wealthy countries to use parking facilities in the Rail Baltica alignment and could potentially increase the security threat. Connections for public transport should be available with appropriate frequency and accessibility. In Riga, Rail Baltica passes the capital on the east side and there are currently no appropriate passenger connections to support this station (AECOM, 2011a, 2011b). In Tallinn, the planned station is located some distance from the current railway station. Further, the Estonian capital does not have a centralized traveling center where all public transportation modes are integrated. Laisi et al. (2011) discuss these issues further in research into Rail Baltica and the public sector.

7.   CONCLUSIONS

As illustrated with substantial second-hand data analysis, the Rail Baltica alignment has the potential to increase security and safety in the alignment area. As noted, freight transportation and logistics as well as passenger transport have increasingly relied upon road transport. The implementation of Rail Baltica will hopefully reverse this trend and encourage the Baltic States and Poland to implement modern and standardized railway management, communication and control systems such as ERTMS and GSM-R.

Road transport makes these countries vulnerable to oil price fluctuation as well as to possible disruptions in supply. At present, oil accounts for a significant share of the trade accounts and is the primary reason for trade and current account deficits. Therefore, increasing multimodality and the greater use of railway transport is clearly beneficial for this northeast area of Europe. Currently, intermodality is seaport-railway driven in the examined countries and reaches the economies of the east and the rest of the EU through its railway corridors (Hilmola and Henttu, 2015).

A second benefit of Rail Baltica is road transport safety. While fatalities have declined in the Baltic States and Poland over the long term, they still are considerably higher than in other countries in the region (countries such as Germany, Sweden and Finland). Countries within the Rail Baltica alignment exhibit a higher rate of deaths and injuries due to road transport. The highest number of deaths and injuries occurs in the countries of Poland, Lithuania and Latvia. At present, the railway corridor stretches from Tallinn to Warsaw. If the alignment is extended to Berlin, it will have a significant effect on Polish road safety.

While crime rates and their economic impacts on business have improved in the Baltic States, there is still room for improvement. Poland has only recently shown some encouraging results in this regard. Therefore, freight terminals should be limited and journeys with freight trains should be prompt and of long distance. The current terminal infrastructure is driven by the location of capital cities within the Rail Baltica alignment, which does not necessarily serve to optimize multimodality. Problems also arise from passenger terminals in capital cities such as Tallinn and Riga that are some distance from the current public transportation terminals. Long-term and secure parking facilities for cars also require proper consideration.

ACKNOWLEDGEMENTS

The author is grateful to the reviewers of this chapter, a process which took place in three different rounds during September 2013, January 2014 and March 2014. The content of this chapter, its structure, and its general appearance has improved significantly.

The author has been part of Rail Baltica Growth Corridor (EU Baltic Sea Region Programme, 2007–2013) and Rail Baltica Growth Corridor, Russia (EuropeAid/130-934/L/ACT/RU) development projects, and without generous support from these it would have been difficult to gather and report such an in-depth study of Rail Baltica railway alignment.

REFERENCES

AECOM (2011a), *Rail Baltica Final Report: Volume I*, Chelmsford, UK: AECOM Limited.
AECOM (2011b), *Rail Baltica Final Report: Volume II*, Chelmsford, UK: AECOM Limited.
Allen, Kristen (2012), Cross border pilfering: Slow progress in battle against Polish car thieves, *Der Spiegel*, online, 3 January 2013. Available at: http://www.spiegel.de/international/europe/cross-border-pilfering-slow-progress-in-battle-against-polish-car-thieves-a-806979.html (retrieved January 2014).
Barry, James (1996), Poland, a paradise for car thieves, seeks means to fight underworld, *The New York Times*, 3 December 1996.
Blackshaw, Philip W. and Louis S. Thompson (1993), *Railway Reform in the Central and Eastern European Countries*, Policy Research Working Papers, World Bank, WPS 1137.
Bröcker, Johannes, Artem Korzhenevych and Carsten Schürmann (2010),

Assessing spatial equity and efficiency impacts of transport infrastructure projects, *Transportation Research Part B*, **44** (7), 795–811.

Buchhofer, E. (1995), Transport infrastructure in the Baltic States during the transformation to market economies, *Journal of Transport Geography*, **3** (1), 69–75.

Central Statistical Bureau of Latvia (2013), Transport – database of Latvia. Available at: http://data.csb.gov.lv/DATABASEEN/transp/databasetree. asp?lang=1 (retrieved August 2013).

ERTMS (2014), *ERTMS – European Deployment Plan and National Deployment Plans*, European Commission, Brussels, Belgium. Available at: http://ec.europa. eu/transport/modes/rail/interoperability/ertms/edp_map_en.htm (retrieved March 2014).

European Commission (2007), *Feasibility Study on Rail Baltica Railways 2007*. Available at: http://ec.europa.eu/regional_policy/sources/docgener/evaluation/ railbaltica/concl_en.PDF (retrieved December 2010).

European Commission (2014), *Commission Staff Working Document on the State of Play of the Implementation of the ERTMS Deployment Plan*, Brussels, Belgium, 14.2.2014, SWD (2014) 48 final.

European Union–Eurostat (2014), *Energy and Transport in Figures 2014*, European Union, Brussels.

Eurostat (2014), Crime and criminal justice database, Eurostat, European Union. Available at: http://epp.eurostat.ec.europa.eu/portal/page/portal/crime/data/ database (retrieved January 2014).

Härkönen, Jorma (2013), *WP6, Expert Group, Conclusions (RBGC Project Meeting, Berlin, 13.6.2013)*. Available at: http://www.rbgc.eu/media/project-meetings/project-meeting-9-berlin-06_2013/wp6.pdf (retrieved August 2013).

Henttu, Ville, Milla Laisi, Olli-Pekka Hilmola and Teemu Terävä (2012), Northern dimension of Rail Baltica, *Economics and Management*, **17** (1), 352–358.

Hilmola, Olli-Pekka (2007), European railway freight transportation and adaptation to demand decline: Efficiency and partial productivity analysis from period of 1980–2003, *International Journal of Productivity and Performance Management*, **56** (3), 205–225.

Hilmola, Olli-Pekka (2011), *Rail Baltica Influence Area: State of Operating Environment*, Lappeenranta University of Technology, Department of Industrial Management, Research Report 236, Lappeenranta, Finland.

Hilmola, Olli-Pekka (2013), From bubble to sustainable economy in Baltic States, *Journal of Transport and Telecommunication*, **14** (3), 237–249.

Hilmola, Olli-Pekka and Ville Henttu (2015), Border-crossing constraints, railways and transit transports in Estonia, *Research in Transportation Business & Management*, **14**, 72–79.

IRU (2008), *Attacks on Drivers of International Heavy Goods Vehicles*, Geneva, Switzerland: International Road Transport Union Publications.

Jonaitis, Jonas and Jonas Butkevicius (2005), Analysis of the possibilities of building the railway Rail Baltica in Lithuania, *Transport*, **20** (5), 204–213.

Karamysheva, Marina, Ville Henttu and Olli-Pekka Hilmola (2013), *Logistics of North-West Russia and Rail Baltica: Standpoints of Private Sector*, Lappeenranta University of Technology, Department of Industrial Management. LUT Scientific and Expertise Publications, Research Report 3, Lappeenranta, Finland.

Keshkamat, Sukhad S., Joan M. Looijen and Mark H. P. Zuidgeest (2009), The formulation and evaluation of transport route planning alternatives: A spatial decision support system for the Via Baltica project, Poland, *Journal of Transport Geography*, **17** (1), 54–64.

Komornicki, Tomasz and Andrzej Miszczuk (2010), Eastern Poland as the borderland of the European Union, *Quaestiones Geographicae*, **29** (2), 55–69.

Kovacs, Gyongyi and Karen M. Spens (2006), Transport infrastructure in the Baltic States post-EU succession, *Journal of Transport Geography*, **14** (6), 426–436.

Laisi, Milla and Juha Saranen (2013), Integrating the Baltic States and Europe – Rail Baltica, *International Journal of Business Excellence*, **6** (3), 251–269.

Laisi, Milla, Ville Henttu and Olli-Pekka Hilmola (2011) (eds), *Enhancing Accessibility of Rail Baltica Influence Area: Standpoints of Public Sector*, Lappeenranta University of Technology, Department of Industrial Management, Research Report 237, Lappeenranta, Finland.

Lukasiak, Marian (2001), Adapting PKP freight services to market economy, *Japan Railway & Transport Review*, February, **26**, 46–51.

Lüttmerding, Attila and Matthias Gather (2013), *Level of Service on Passenger Railway Connections Between European Metropolises*, Berichte des Instituts Verkehr und Raum (Erfurt), Band 15.

Maggio, Gaetano and G. Cacciola (2009), A variant of the Hubbert curve for oil production forecasts, *Energy Policy*, **37** (11), 4761–4770.

Marquez, Patricio V. and Anthony G. Bliss (2013), *Dangerous Roads: Russia's Safety Challenge*. Available at: http://go.worldbank.org/P4BEJK5ZB0 (retrieved August 2013).

Nežerenko, Olga, Ott Koppel and Tarmo Tuisk (2015), Cluster approach in organization of transportation in the Baltic Sea Region, *Transport* (in press, forthcoming), DOI: 10.3846/16484142.2014.994225.

Ojala, Lauri, Tapio Naula and Cesar Queiroz (2005), *Transport Sector Restructuring in the Baltic States as Members of the European Union*, Proceedings of the 3rd Seminar, Vilnius, Turku School of Economics Publications, Finland.

PKP PLK (2011), Description of the activity of PKP PLK S.A. and development perspective of Polish rail infrastructure. Presentation given in Rail Baltica Growth Corridor Workgroup Seminar in Bialystok, Poland, 10 May 2011.

Russia in Figures (2012), Number of accidents and persons suffered in rolling stock accidents. Available at: http://www.gks.ru/bgd/regl/b12_12/IssWWW.exe/stg/d02/18-09.htm (retrieved August 2013).

Sandalow, David (2008), *Freedom from Oil*, New York: McGraw-Hill.

Schwab, Klaus (2011), *The Global Competitiveness Report 2011–2012*, World Economic Forum, Switzerland.

Schwab, Klaus (2013), *The Global Competitiveness Report 2013–2014*, World Economic Forum, Switzerland.

Schwab, Klaus and Michael E. Porter (2008), *The Global Competitiveness Report 2008–2009*, World Economic Forum, Switzerland.

Statistical Office in Szczecin (2013), *Road Transport in Poland 2010–2011*, Central Statistics Office of Poland, Poland, Warsaw/Szczecin.

Statistics Estonia (2013), Transport statistics database. Available at: http://www.stat.ee/transportation (retrieved August 2013).

Statistics Estonia (2015), Last year the carriage of passengers and goods declined. New Release 36. Available at: http://www.stat.ee/90723 (retrieved April 2015).

Statistics Lithuania (2013), *Official Statistics Portal*. Available at: http://osp.stat.gov.lt/en/statistiniu-rodikliu-analize1 (retrieved August 2013).

Tanczos, K. (1999), Transition of Hungarian railway transport, *Japan Railway & Transport Review*, September, **21**, 10–13.

The Economist (2013), Crime in Germany: Car-theft epidemic at the border with Poland, *The Economist*, Charlemagne, European politics. 3 September 2013.

UN Comtrade (2015), International Merchandise Trade Statistics. Available at: http://comtrade.un.org/ (retrieved May 2015).

9. Multimodal freight transport security in Kenya

Evaristus Irandu

1. INTRODUCTION

As Diouf (2007) argues, the role of transport is very strategic in a modern economy. This is because it facilitates trade, and enhances and improves the movement of goods, people, ideas, technology and other services. Therefore, there is need to develop a transport system that is not only adequate, efficient and cheap but well planned, integrated and secure. However, according to de Bod (2008) transport infrastructure in sub-Saharan African (SSA) countries reflects the colonial legacy, which resulted in the construction of roads and railways to link the interior with the coast primarily for the extraction and export of raw materials.

Thus, historically the Kenyan transport system like that of other SSA countries, developed from the country's main port of Mombasa to take advantage of the then Ugandan railway. This linear spatial structure along a corridor remained long after road traffic took over from the railway. Today, most of the urban centres and economic activities in Kenya and the hinterland (Uganda, Rwanda, Burundi, Eastern Democratic Republic of Congo [DRC], Southern Sudan) are located or close to the Northern Corridor.

A major problem facing importers and exporters along the Northern Corridor is the high cost of freight (ILEAP and JEICP, 2004). For example, in 2001 freight costs as a proportion of import value averaged 13.9 per cent for SSA countries. This compares to an average of 8.7 per cent for developing countries overall. In landlocked countries in SSA, the transport cost factor was even higher, at 20.7 per cent. Landlocked countries face such high costs largely due to the additional costs and difficulties of transporting goods overland and through neighbouring countries. High transport costs result from a number of factors, including poor infrastructure, inefficient and unreliable transport services, coordination problems, border delays, and security and safety costs (Kenya Shippers Council, 2011). The competitiveness of SSA countries is seriously hindered by these costs, which make exports less competitive and imports more expensive. Sometimes, security problems along the entire supply chain pose challenges.

Multimodal transport services are limited in SSA where there are numerous constraints including long inland turnaround times for containers, inadequate road infrastructure, limitations on the cross-border provision of trucking services, and different national standards regarding safety requirements, vehicle sizes and railway gauges (CPCS Transcom Limited, 2010). A multimodal transport system if well developed would offer Kenya an opportunity to rethink and reorganize the transport links between production centres and storage depots and those of consumption.

The definition of multimodal transport used in this chapter is the one given by Al-Muhaisen (2005) who defines it as 'the chain that interconnects different links or modes of transport, air, sea, and land, into one complete process that ensures an efficient and cost-effective door-to-door movement of goods under the responsibility of a single transport operator, known as a multimodal transport operator (MTO), on one transport document'. Unlike the traditional unimodal transport system in which different modes operate independently and in competition, multimodal transport aims at integrating various modes and services of transport to improve the efficiency of the entire logistical supply chain. There is great need and urgency to make transport in Kenya as effective, efficient and secure as possible. This can be achieved by facilitating multimodal transport.

This chapter begins by briefly discussing the status of multimodal transport in Kenya. It then proceeds to examine the multimodal freight security in the country and along the transit corridors. The key driving factors for the evolution of freight transport security policy in the country are analysed. The chapter concludes by discussing the role of ICT in promoting multimodal freight security in the country and along the Northern Corridor. The cyber-security challenges faced in Kenya and the means of addressing them are also examined.

2.   THE STATUS OF THE MULTIMODAL TRANSPORT SYSTEM IN KENYA

Multimodal transport can be justified on the basis of irrefutable advantages associated with it, such as the reduced transport cost of door-to-door services, using a single document which permits shippers to address their problems to one person in charge of a transaction that runs through the whole transport chain, and providing a logistical platform for landlocked and transit countries.

2.1 Containerization

Kilindini Harbour, located in the city of Mombasa, is a major multimodal hub in Kenya. It is the only deep-sea port in the country and the main trade gateway to an extensive economic hinterland in the East Africa region stretching across Uganda, Rwanda and Burundi to Eastern DRC and South Sudan. It also serves the regions of northern Tanzania and Ethiopia. The main arterial cargo highway runs from the port city of Mombasa through Nairobi and Kampala to Kisangani in Eastern DRC. Distributaries branch off to Mwanza, Addis Ababa, Juba, Bujumbura and Kigali (Gekara and Chhetri, 2013). Five of the countries in the region are landlocked and rely entirely on the port as their sole trade gateway. As such, it remains the most important seaport on the east coast of Africa. The port consists of 16 deep-water berths with a total quay length of 3044 metres and a maximum dredged depth of 11 metres.

It has an important infrastructure which includes bulk oil jetties, handling facilities for coal clinker and cement, and three-berth container terminal as well as inland container terminals in Nairobi, Kisumu and Eldoret. The port has a rated capacity of 22 million tonnes annually, while the cargo handled has been on average approximately 8 million tonnes per annum, rising from 9.2 million in 2000 to 10 million in 2002, 12 million in 2003 and 13 million in 2004. The port faces many challenges such as congestion, inefficiency, cumbersome cargo clearance procedures and corruption (de Bod, 2008). It is administered by the Kenya Ports Authority (KPA) and handles all types of ships and cargo.

Despite the extensive hinterland the port commands, and recent increases in throughput, its overall performance remains significantly below international standards. The port handles under one-quarter of the container volumes handled at Durban port, and only about 2 per cent of what goes through Singapore and Hong Kong. Furthermore, it is estimated that, as a result of issues related to inefficiency, freight costs represent 35–40 per cent of import values to the region as compared to 8 per cent in European ports (AfDB, 2010; Ntamutumba, 2010).

A container terminal expansion project was completed in 2013 with the assistance of JICA. At the same time, the World Bank EATTFP is assisting port security strengthening and a cargo electronic tracking system targetting cargo transiting the Northern Transport Corridor. The JICA-assisted Mombasa Port container terminal expansion constructed four new container berths with a water depth of 11–15 m, sufficient to accommodate fourth-generation container ships with a capacity of 4600 TEU and 60 000 DWT.

The project is attracting attention from the neighbouring inland countries since it has reduced traffic congestion at Mombasa Port. In addition, the security strengthening component of the World Bank project includes capacity building and integration of monitoring and communications systems. Although efforts have been made to establish a Port Community Based Cargo Tracking System (PCBS), there has been some difficulty in sharing data and information on process and forms among KPA, Kenya Revenue Authority (KRA), logistics operators, and other agencies. Accordingly, additional efforts are required to establish an integrated information control and management system to facilitate transport along the Northern Corridor; a cargo tracking system developed by KRA will be a step in this direction.

2.2   Multimodal Transport Corridors

In their study, Limão and Venables (2001) have demonstrated that a landlocked country's transport costs can be up to 55 per cent higher than those of a comparable coastal country. They further argue that the combination of being landlocked, having a poor transport infrastructure and relying on transit countries with similarly poor transport infrastructure significantly undermines trade. To address the transport and trade needs of the landlocked countries (LLCs) within the East African Community (EAC), certain transport and trade transit corridors have been established. These are routes linking several economic centres, countries and ports. They consist of networks of transport facilities and infrastructure and their function is to promote internal and external trade using efficient transport and logistics services.

The transport corridors are also concerned with improving not only routes but also the quality of transport and other logistic services along them. Quality in this sense is defined in terms of transit time and the cost to ship goods along the corridor. Therefore, a corridor's reliability is measured in terms of transit time and flexibility and the diversity of services offered on multimodal routes.

2.2.1   The Northern Corridor

The Northern Corridor is a multimodal transport corridor served by road, rail, pipeline and inland waterways. It is the busiest and most important transport route in East and Central Africa. It provides a gateway linking Kenya's seaport of Mombasa to the landlocked countries of Uganda, Rwanda, Burundi and South Sudan. It also serves the eastern part of DRC, Northern Tanzania and Ethiopia. The total length of the main Northern Corridor arterial road is 2038 km long and links the four capitals of the original North Corridor Transit Agreement (NCTA) signatories

(Burundi, Rwanda, Uganda and Kenya). The road terminates at the Port of Mombasa on the Indian Ocean (Northern Corridor Infrastructure Master Plan, 2011).

Freight transported by rail in the Northern Corridor experiences a lot of delays at weigh bridges and border crossings. For example, moving freight by rail in a 40-ft container from Mombasa to Kampala takes five days, while to Kigali it takes seven days. In addition, the same cargo takes eight hours to cross the Kenya/Uganda border and ten hours to cross Uganda/Rwanda border. The crossing time at the weigh bridges takes 11 hours for freight destined to Kampala and 12 hours for Kigali bound freight (JICA, 2009). Weighbridges are used to control overloaded vehicles by measuring loaded weight. However, along the Northern Corridor weighbridges are installed at many points to prevent theft and diversion of goods and/or the loading of additional freight in the transit countries. Further, facilities and equipment installed at weighbridge stations are insufficient, leading to long queues of trucks.

It is observed that on average, ships take twice as long to offload at the Port of Mombasa than at Dar es Salaam. The dwell time at Mombasa Port is 51 days while at Dar es Salaam it is 25 days (JICA, 2009). The time taken to move a 40-ft container along the Northern Corridor is almost twice that of the Central Corridor. Such delays at the port or on transit are not only likely to increase transport costs but are likely to compromise the safety and security of cargo along the entire supply chain.

2.2.2   The LAPSSET Corridor

The LAPSSET Corridor aims at fostering transport linkage between Kenya, South Sudan and Ethiopia. It is also intended to promote regional socio-economic development along the transport corridor especially in the northern, eastern, northeastern and coastal parts of Kenya. The LAPSSET Corridor is currently Kenya's only economic corridor which, when completed, will contribute significantly to the growth of the country's GDP. It will accelerate the economic development of the region through enhanced cross-border trade.

The projected throughput at Lamu Port after its construction will increase from 13.5 million metric tonnes in 2020 to approximately 23.8 million metric tonnes ten years later (Lapsset Corridor Project, 2013). This will represent approximately a 57 per cent increase in throughput. This will be due to the increased volume of trade between Kenya, Southern Sudan and Ethiopia. Lamu Port will be the focal point of multimodal transport linking the three countries. Containerized cargo is expected to dominate traffic handled at the port.

2.3 Challenges of Multimodal Transport

The EAC region suffers from problems arising from inefficient transport systems. Both physical and non-physical barriers to trade are the main causes of high transport and transaction costs. Physical barriers include congestion at ports, poor rail infrastructure, police road blocks, poorly maintained roads, traffic jams, weighbridge stations and border infrastructure. Non-physical barriers include trade transactions, customs clearance, licenses, visas and immigration restrictions (Institute of Trade Development, 2012).

Some of the major challenges include an inadequate legal framework and institutional capacity, inadequate investment, inadequate capacity at the Port of Mombasa and poor infrastructure. Although the EAC is a common market, partner states continue to operate as individual states when it comes to clearing of cargo and movement along the corridor routes. This is because the legal framework and institutions have not been established. If all the legal framework and institutions were in place, the movement of cargo would be quick and easy since there would be no need for borders and customs checks, which cause delays.

Investment in infrastructure such as ports, railways, roads, waterways and airports has not kept pace with the growth of the economies in the region. This has contributed to congestion at the Port of Mombasa and on the highways. In addition, the Port of Mombasa lacks adequate capacity to handle the growing volume of cargo. Vessels reporting to the port have to wait 3–4 days before berthing. This is further compounded by congestion at the port which leads to a high cargo dwell time of 7–12 days (JICA, 2009).

Although most of the roads along the Northern Corridor are in good condition some sections require continuous maintenance. The main challenges for road transport are the delays caused by too many road blocks. In Kenya, delays from Mombasa to Malaba can total six hours per vehicle. Another challenge for road transport is the weighbridge delays along the Northern Corridor. The delays from Mombasa to Malaba can total 11 hours or more. Robbery along the highway is rampant for cargo, truck spare parts and batteries. The corruption level is also very high (Institute of Trade Development, 2012).

Railway transport is the second most important mode of transport after road transport and is critical for long-distance freight along the Northern Corridor. Due to the poor condition of tracks and ageing rolling stock and locomotives, tonnage freight volumes and passenger numbers have continued to fall year on year (from 60 per cent of port cargo in the 1970s and 1980s to 7 per cent currently) (Irandu, 2000; CPCS Transcom Limited, 2010).

3.   MULTIMODAL FREIGHT SECURITY

3.1   Vision on Security

Kenya's Vision 2030 envisages a society free from danger and fear. Security is vital in achieving and sustaining the economic growth rate that is anticipated in Vision 2030. Freedom from danger and freedom from fear provide an enabling environment for businesses to thrive. It is a key incentive for attracting investment both from within and outside the country. Today, insecurity imposes a huge burden on business in the country, with some firms spending up to 7 per cent of total sales, or 11 per cent of total costs, on security infrastructure and personnel. In addition, business firms spend an average of 4 per cent of sales on insurance against crime. Such spending not only increases the cost of business transactions but also constrains the growth of the private sector (GOK, 2012).

3.2   Sources of Insecurity

Widespread insecurity, high levels of crime, banditry and cattle rustling, inter-communal conflicts, small arms proliferation and terrorism are impacting on Kenya's development (Saferworld, 2006). Inter-ethnic conflicts and wider problems of organized crime, banditry, small arms proliferation and the insecurity associated with them seriously undermine long-term prospects for development (Saferworld, 2006). This may hinder the free flow of goods and services along the transit corridors thereby adversely affecting cross-border trade. It also makes the transport of goods within the country and along the Northern Corridor more expensive due to costs of police escort and/or the provision of private security.

3.2.1   Past terrorist attacks
Kenya is surrounded by politically unstable and strife-torn neighbouring countries such as Somalia which has become a hideout for Al-Qaeda and Al-Shabaab terrorists (Khamis and Itzhaki, 2010). This is why Kenya has experienced several terrorist attacks in the capital city of Nairobi in the recent past such as the bombing of the US Embassy in 1998 and the Westgate mall attack of 21 September 2013. Such terrorist attacks pose a serious threat to the security of freight, passengers and equipment at the Port of Mombasa and along the Northern Corridor. Therefore, there is an urgent need to secure the entire supply chain from Mombasa to Kigali and beyond.

3.2.2 Piracy attacks off the Somalia coastline

Mainly as a result of the disintegration of central government authority in Somalia since 1991, the lack of maritime security in the Horn of Africa has become an issue of grave global concern. Pirates have increasingly taken advantage of the lack of authority to ply the 2700 km coastline (Herbert-Burns, 2012). This has made it easy for them to attack foreign ships plying the Indian Ocean route, and represents one of the few cases in Africa where security problems on land have spilled over and affected maritime security severely. Due to the strategic location of Somalia and the valuable freight moved in the seas around the Horn of Africa, the lack of maritime security is worrying for the international community. Therefore, maritime security is very important to the region, both in economic and strategic terms. Kenya, together with other member states of the West Indian Ocean region, needs to enhance sea-side security (Khamis and Itzhaki, 2010).

3.3 Evolution of Multimodal Transport Security Policy

As Gagatsi (2013) observes, the security in transport has become a crucial issue internationally, especially after the terrorist attacks of September 2001. The maritime and aviation sectors are considered sensitive and high-risk transport sectors in terms of security. Today, in virtually every part of the world, attacks on supply chains are on the increase. Therefore, transport and logistics companies operating within Kenya and along the Northern Corridor will need to take security concerns into account when choosing transport routes. Given the many sources of insecurity in the country and the danger they pose to the free flow of goods in the entire supply chain, the Kenyan Government in conjunction with the international community has put up measures to address these security threats. Such measures are discussed in the sections that follow below.

3.4 Securing the Supply Chain

Security at the Port of Mombasa and along the Northern Corridor needs enhancing. A more secure transport chain will provide round-the-clock usage and will improve truck turnaround times. There will also be fewer cases of leakage and dumping. This will address issues of terrorism, counterfeits and substandard goods getting into the local markets, which are threatening the very existence of local businesses. But securing the Port of Mombasa and the freight moving along the Northern Corridor is a daunting task due to a number of challenges. These are discussed below.

3.4.1 Checkpoints

According to a survey by the Shippers Council of Eastern Africa (2013) there are eight weighbridges between Mombasa and Kampala on the Northern Corridor – seven in Kenya and one in Uganda. Besides the weighbridges, there are numerous checkpoints related to police and customs checks. The latest status on the elimination of non-tariff barriers (NTBs) in the EAC region indicates that Kenya has committed to reducing road blocks from 36 to nine, Rwanda has removed all road blocks, Uganda has nine road blocks between Malaba and Gatuna/Katuna, Tanzania has committed to reducing road blocks from 30 to 15 between Dar es Salaam and Rusumo Falls, and Burundi has committed to removing all road blocks.

As Gekara and Chhetri (2013) argue, road blocks are normally erected along the Northern Corridor ostensibly to maintain highway security and monitor illegal trade activities such as dumping and cargo diversion. However, these road blocks are, more often than not, sources of inefficiency along the corridor. A second major issue relates to safety and security for cargo and transport crews. Truck drivers operate at all hours of the day and face constant danger from highway robbers, as well as the danger of accidents resulting from unsafe conditions for large spans of the roads. This situation was described by one truck driver as follows: 'We drive day and night and there is always danger. The roads are full of potholes and trucks roll all the time . . . it is very dangerous. Sometimes people put obstacles on the road; rocks, logs and even nails . . . sharp objects to puncture our tires and steal goods. If you resist, you die . . .' (truck driver, January 2011, cited in Gekara and Chhetri, 2013).

3.4.2 Tracking and tracing shipments

The security of cargo in the logistics chain is a major concern for shippers. In order to have the security of their cargo ascertained and guaranteed at every point on the supply chain, shippers not only insure their cargo on transit but also use tracking mechanisms. The ability of importers and exporters to track and trace shipments from the point of loading to discharge therefore becomes a vital component of shipping. A study carried out by the Shippers Council of Eastern Africa in 2012 revealed that only 31.25 per cent of shippers in the region track their shipments using electronic cargo tracking, while the majority, about 67.75 per cent, use telephone to track their shipments (Shippers Council of Eastern Africa, 2013). The high cost of installation and maintenance is responsible for the low adoption and utilization of electronic cargo tracking systems. Shippers are using cell phones more to communicate with service providers as they track their cargo because this is a more readily available and cost-effective mode of communication. However, this mode of communication is doing little to promote trade in the region due to the high cross-border calling rates (Shippers Council of Eastern Africa, 2013).

3.4.3 Enhancement of sea-side security

The Port of Mombasa is secured from the sea side through the establishment of a coastal radar system. A centre for regional search and rescue has also been set up in Mombasa to deal with maritime security issues. Further, the government has stepped up sea patrols as well as coordination and cooperation between internal and international bodies.

3.4.4 Integrated security system

The Port of Mombasa is expected to be one of the most secure ports in the East Africa region hopefully after full implementation of the Integrated Security System (ISS) project which is currently in its final stages. Jointly funded by the government and the World Bank to the tune of US$21.4 million, ISS will see the automation of security in line with the International Ship and Port Facility Security (ISPS) Code requirements (Nkirote, 2012).

This also offers another advantage for the port as the system will be used to monitor cargo entering and exiting through the port's gate. The system includes Optical Character Recognition and License Plate Recognition systems for identifying containers and trucks simultaneously for documentation purposes. Also in the plan is the installation of hundreds of cameras which will be placed strategically to provide and ease surveillance around the port 24-hours a day.

3.5 Legal Frameworks for Freight Security Policy

To enable the transport sector to play its role effectively in national development, the Ministry of Transport launched the National Transport Policy Committee on 2 April 2003. Its sole mandate was to formulate an Integrated National Transport Policy (INTP). The process was conducted on a consultative basis punctuated with modelling of solutions based on international best practice to bridge the gap between local challenges and planned interventions. A sessional paper was prepared and presented to the Cabinet for approval in May 2012 but the document has not been approved by the National Assembly as yet – so what exists as of now is a draft transport policy. The country has been without a transport policy for a very long time.

3.5.1   Road transport policy framework

Road freight transport involves domestic and international movement of goods by road using heavy goods vehicles (HGVs), mainly comprising lorries, trucks, heavy vans, trailers and fuel tankers. The basic requirements for road freight transport include a high quality of service to customers, seamless multimodal operations, and optimized use of capacity and management of operations.

While all EAC member states have formulated transport policies, such policies differ in terms of their comprehensiveness, content and the extent to which they specifically address issues related to corridor performance. Thus, while most of the EAC member states have agreed to develop a common transport policy, existing policies so far contain little evidence of this as policies tend largely to reflect national preoccupations contrary to the desired Common Transport Policy as set out in Articles 89 and 90 of the East African Treaty (Ikiara, 2012). In particular, the legislative and institutional measures needed to implement regional agreements domestically are inadequate. Available literature appears to indicate that there is an inadequate policy and legal framework in the road transport sector in EAC despite road transport accounting for more than 90 per cent of all transport in the member states (Ikiara, 2012).

3.5.2   Maritime freight security policy

All of the coastal states of the Indian Ocean are members of the International Maritime Organization (IMO). The IMO is the source of international rules and guidelines governing shipping operations that flag states, port states and coastal states apply to international shipping in order to protect against vessel-source marine pollution. Several key maritime safety and security conventions have been negotiated under the auspices of the IMO. With regard to shipping, two of the most important are the Convention on Safety of Life at Sea (SOLAS) and the Convention on the Suppression of Unlawful Acts (SUA). Both are evolving agreements that have been supplemented and modified through subsequent protocols. At its Diplomatic Conference in December 2002, the IMO adopted the ISPS Code as part of an amendment to the SOLAS Convention. The objectives of this Code are to establish an international framework involving cooperation between contracting governments, government agencies, local administrations and the shipping and port industries, to detect security threats, and to take preventive measures against security incidents affecting ships or port facilities used in international trade.

The implementation of the ISPS Code is mandatory for all SOLAS contracting states irrespective of their level of development (KAM, 2007). Most recently, protocols to the SUA have been negotiated to address acts of international terrorism. The IMO also supports regional efforts to promote maritime security. In 2009, the IMO convened a meeting in which East African nations adopted a 'Code of Conduct Concerning the Repression of Piracy and Armed Robbery against Ships in the Western Indian Ocean and the Gulf of Aden' (Herbert-Burns, 2012). The Code further establishes the respective rules and responsibilities of the parties involved at the national and international levels for securing maritime security. The Code came into force on 1 July 2004.

To deal decisively with the growing threat of piracy and armed robbery in the Indian Ocean and especially off the coast of Somalia, the IMO passed Resolution A 979(24) which was adopted by the IMO Assembly on 1 January 2005. The Resolution urges governments to adopt a regional approach to combat piracy and armed robbery against ships and engage in a concerted international effort. In response to this resolution, the Kenyan Government hosted a two-day meeting of regional governments on 23–24 February 2006. The meeting was attended by delegates from the United Republic of Tanzania, Mozambique, the Transitional Federal Government of Somalia and by representatives of the UK, the USA, Australia, India, Sri Lanka, IMO and the WFP among others (Karingithu, 2008). It was agreed at the meeting that: 1) patrols by Combined Joint Task Force (CJTF) off the coast of Djibouti would be encouraged and sustained to combat incidents of piracy; 2) regional governments would hold regular meetings to review developments in combating piracy and armed robberies in the region; and 3) regional governments were to exchange and disseminate intelligence on threats by pirates on ships at sea.

The Government of Kenya enacted the Merchant Shipping (Maritime Security) Regulations in January 2005 and put up an investment of US$17 million to improve security in Kenyan seaports in compliance with the ISPS Code. A search and rescue coordination centre was set up in Mombasa to coordinate activities in the search and rescue operations of distressed ships and seafarers and also operations against piracy and armed robberies (Karingithu, 2008).

The Kenyan Government ratified the United Nations Convention on the Law of the Sea (UNCLOS) in 1989. The Convention preserves the right of innocent passage for foreign ships in territorial waters of coastal states. In addition, it provides for all ships and aircraft of all states to be allowed transit passage through straits used for international navigation. The Convention also guarantees the peace and security of oceans and seas by providing a framework for dealing with piracy, armed robbery, terrorist attacks and hijackings among other criminal activities at sea. Thus, Kenya has done its best to ensure adequate maritime security in the Indian Ocean. However, there are some challenges to be faced, such as the slow pace in domestication and implementation of relevant international conventions on maritime security, the lack of specialized maritime security personnel, and inadequate coordination between concerned agencies among others.

3.5.3 Aviation security

The importance of the aviation industry in the economic development of Africa cannot be gainsaid. In the continent, as in other regions, aviation remains the safest, fastest and most reliable form of transport. Air transport is an important facilitator of economic activity and trade. As such, airports are not just communication hubs but are the core of regional and international trade (Irandu and Rhoades, 2006). Therefore, adequate aviation security (AVSEC) is crucial to the sector's ability to deliver and sustain a sound aviation industry and vibrant economies.

Another reason why safety and security in the aviation industry should concern us more than ever arises from concerns over international terrorism. In today's world of faceless terrorists, aviation safety and security in Africa is an issue of international concern because no one knows where the next threat may come from. An aircraft travelling from any city in Africa to any other part of the world could be at high risk if adequate security is not in place at the point of departure (Institute for Security Studies, 2008).

The Civil Aviation Act (2013) defines the aviation regulatory functions to be provided by the Kenya Civil Aviation Authority (KCAA). The regulatory functions include safety and security oversight and ensuring the efficiency of all civil aviation operations in Kenya through licensing and certification of aviation technical personnel, aircraft operators, aerodrome operators and air navigation services. The aviation safety and security system in Kenya was last audited in 1999. Key among the findings was an inadequate legislative and regulatory framework, and oversight capability. The International Civil Aviation Organization (ICAO) requires states to continuously take appropriate actions to address identified deficiencies and to bring their regulatory capabilities to international standards (Obino et al., 2009; GOK, 2013).

In order to handle growth in its international and domestic air traffic and maintain its status as an important hub in the region (East and Central Africa and the Indian Ocean), Kenya needs to address some challenges. These include sustaining sufficient budgetary allocations for rehabilitation and maintenance of airport facilities; reaching international safety and security standards; and improving and strengthening airport operational and management capability (Irandu and Rhoades, 2006; Obino et al., 2009). In this regard, specific attention has to be given to airport capacity, security, and safety. If JKIA (Jomo Kenyatta International Airport) wants to stay viable as a hub it must address the problems of inadequate airport infrastructure, security and safety among other things. In order to reduce the vulnerability of airports to terrorist threats, smuggling, and illegal immigration, the major airports will be fenced. Fencing works for JKIA are complete. The government has also transferred baggage screening responsibility from the Kenya police to Kenya Airports Authority (KAA).

The aviation security measures taken by KAA to ensure adequate security for freight and passengers at airports such as JKIA are encouraging, but much needs to be done. For instance, the airport management should have direct control over the national police who provide back-up to the Authority's own security personnel. There should be adequate coordination between KCAA, KAA and central government security agencies in order to effectively counter any security threats such as terrorist attacks.

3.5.4   Pipeline transport security

The construction of a pipeline system was to ensure efficient, reliable, safe and cost-effective means of transporting petroleum products from Mombasa to the hinterland. The capacity enhancement of the pipeline was expected to significantly reduce the number of vehicles transporting petroleum products from Mombasa to Western Kenya. The real benefits of pipeline transport hinge on its ability to offer least-cost transport of fuel and its ability to attract traffic away from roads. The fact that companies still transport petroleum fuels from Mombasa by road reflects inadequate pumping capacity and a pricing discrepancy that need to be resolved.

So far, Kenya Pipeline Company (KPC) has enjoyed a considerable amount of security in its operations and of its assets, except for a few cases of vandalism where attempts have been made to puncture the pipeline leading to loss of petroleum fuels (GOK, 2010). KPC allocates substantial financial resources to enhance the security of the pipeline. The national government should collaborate with KPC to enhance the security of the pipeline installations. The KPC should also ensure that there is no human encroachment within the area reserved for the pipeline.

3.5.5   Railway safety and security

Railway transport is the second most important mode of freight transport along the Northern Corridor, after road transport (CPCS Transcom Limited, 2010). It is suitable for transporting bulky and heavy commodities over long distances. The metre-gauge railway extends from the Port of Mombasa in Kenya to Kampala, Uganda, with a series of shorter branch lines. In order to deliver services uninterrupted, there is need to develop and implement an effective safety management system which establishes and maintains safe operation, rehabilitation, and ensures the safety of railway transport. The critical and safety-related positions should be occupied by trained, qualified, and experienced people. It is necessary to ensure that all safety-related maintenance and operational information is availed to those involved with ensuring safe operations. The Government of Kenya should strengthen the Kenya Railways Corporation (KRC) so that it can monitor railway operators in terms of their state of safety. This would also ensure that infrastructure facilities and rolling stock are well maintained.

3.5.6 Multimodal transport safety and security

The multimodal transport system in Kenya consists of human porterage, pack animals, trucks, train and ship or airplane. These modes of transport are operated in an uncoordinated manner. There is a need to link port, rail, road and other forms of transport to provide a seamless transport system throughout the supply chain. Multimodal transport has been introduced by the Kenya Shipping Line (KSL) for the import of goods from foreign suppliers through the Port of Mombasa up to the dry ports in the country through one bill of lading. This has reduced the cost of delays, and has reduced transport and warehouse charges, and is able to provide prompt delivery of containerized goods. The service is expected to increase in the coming years, and would be better extended to include the transport and logistics segment from dry ports to customers. The need for more stringent security procedures in the face of the recent wave of international terrorism is becoming more and more important and poses a new and very serious challenge to customs administration as well as to operators, especially in the maritime and air transport sub-sectors. There is a growing need to find a balance between safety and security and the smooth flow of goods and services (Kenya Shippers Council, 2014).

Along the Northern Corridor, there is the risk of cargo being diverted into the Kenyan domestic market instead of intended destinations such as Uganda or Rwanda. To solve this problem, Kenya has introduced a transit monitoring system in the form of police escorts. However, transport operators in Kenya complain about delays caused by police escorts. Transport operators have also to pay for the escorts which increases their costs of doing business. Delays occur because police escorts only begin when several trucks are ready to depart. A more efficient way of preventing cargo diversion into the domestic market of transit countries could be the use of containers. A more secure transport chain would provide round-the-clock usage and improve truck turnaround times. There would also be fewer cases of leakage and dumping of counterfeit and substandard goods into the local markets, which threaten the very existence of local businesses (Ntangsi, 2014).

3.6 The Role of ICT in Multimodal Freight Transport Security in Kenya

The KRA has introduced the Electronic Cargo Tracking System (ECTS). The aim of ECTS is the development of a simplified and harmonized process which would facilitate the movement of cargo internationally, assist in the enforcement of tax laws, and maximize revenue collection. The objectives of cargo tracking systems are: 1) to know the location of the cargo consignments along the supply chain; 2) to know seal status at any given time; 3) real-time tracking management; and 4) control purposes such as the prevention of dumping or cargo diversion (Kenya Revenue Authority, 2010).

ECTS is a multi-tiered system developed to electronically monitor goods under transit, exports and KRA's control as it moves along the Kenyan supply chain from source to destination. The ECTS offers real-time cargo tracking solutions. It covers all cargo to and from customs control areas such as on transit, Export Processing Zones (EPZs), and Inland Container Depots (ICDs). It also covers all cargo to bonded warehouses, customs warehouses and all wet cargo on transit and re-exportation (Kenya Revenue Authority, 2010). The ECTS is being implemented using Radio-Frequency Identification (RFID) and GPS technology. All trucks/vehicles, tankers and containers carrying goods on transit under KRA's control are fitted with a tracking device and electronic seal which sends the seal status, truck location and any violation information to KRA on a real-time basis. ECTS is used as an anti-theft device for truck and cargo and for improving the level of cargo security.

3.7 Cyber Security

Over the past couple of years internet usage in Kenya has increased rapidly due to high levels of demand and the increase in mobile device usage. In 2012 it was estimated that there were approximately 17.4 million internet users in the country (Serianu, 2012). As internet usage increases in the country, so does the number of security threats. This is because increased dependence on ICT has exposed various organizations and institutions to premeditated security threats with possibly disastrous results. Some of the organizations that are prime targets of criminal attacks include but are not limited to the Kenya Private Sector Association (KPSA), the KRA, the KPA, the KAA, the Kenya Railways Corporation (PRC) and the Kenya Police.

Kenyan organizations are ill-equipped and unprepared to respond to ICT security threats. According to a recent Kenya Cyber Security Report (Serianu, 2012), the initiatives undertaken to address information technology security threats are not adequate. Many organizations are in the process of developing defences to deal with viruses. The country needs to improve its data protection and activity monitoring capabilities as well as developing more effective approaches to eliminating infrastructure and application security weaknesses.

4. CONCLUSIONS

As already established, Kenya does not have a policy to govern multimodal transport and also freight transport security. However, due to the threat of terrorist attacks, armed robbery and piracy along the Somalia coast, the Government of Kenya, together with other governments in the region, has adopted certain strategies to ensure adequate security along the entire supply chain. Strategies to ensure adequate aviation security at the airports in accordance to ICAO standards have been put in place, although more still needs to be done. An electronic tracking system has been developed by the KRA to monitor cargo theft and dumping in the country and along the transit corridors. It has also been argued that due to increased levels of internet use in the country threats of criminal attacks are on the rise. This calls for investments in software which can provide adequate protection to the computers used in the country, including those used in the transport sector.

REFERENCES

AfDB (African Development Bank). 2010. *Ports Logistics and Trade in Africa*. New York: Oxford University Press.

Al-Muhaisen, S. A. 2005. Overview of Trends in Multimodal Transport. IMMTA World Free Zone Convention-IZMIR Int'l Conference, 22 April.

CPCS Transcom Limited. 2010. Analytical Comparative Transport Cost Study along the Northern Corridor Region Prepared for the Northern Corridor Transit Transport Coordination Authority (NCTTCA), Mombasa.

de Bod, A. 2008. South Africa's Freight Transport Involvement Options in Sub-Saharan Africa: Declining Infrastructure and Regulatory Constraints. Unpublished master's thesis. Stellenbosch: Stellenbosch University.

Diouf, M. S. 2007. Prospects for the Integration of Transport Systems. Workshop on Multimodal Transport: Integration of Transport Systems for the Carriage of Goods. Abuja, 7–8 June.

Gagatsi, E. 2013. Review of Maritime Transport Safety and Security Practices and Compliance levels: case studies in Europe and South East Asia. Available at: https://www.google.co.ke/search?/complete/search? (accessed on 10 October 2013).

Gekara, V. O. and Chhetri, P. 2013. Upstream Transport Corridor Inefficiencies and the Implications for Port Performance: A Case Analysis of Mombasa Port and the Northern Corridor. *Maritime Policy & Management*, **40** (6), 559–573.

GOK. 2010. The Wayleaves Act, Chapter 292, Government Printer, Nairobi.

GOK. 2012. Sessional paper on Kenya Vision 2030, Office of the Prime Minister Ministry of State for Planning, National Development and Vision 2030, Government Printer, Nairobi.

GOK. 2013. Kenya Civil Aviation Act, Government Printer, Nairobi.

Herbert-Burns, R. 2012. Countering Piracy, Trafficking and Terrorism; Ensuring Maritime Security in the Indian Ocean. In Michel, D and Sticklor, R. (eds), *Indian Ocean Rising: Maritime Security and Policy Challenges*, Washington, DC: Stimson.

Ikiara, G. 2012. Training Needs Assessment (TNA) Study for Road Transport Operators in East Africa. Trade Mark, East Africa.

ILEAP and JEICP. 2004. Transportation and Trade in Sub-Saharan Africa: What Direction Should Countries Take in Doha? Available at: Dominique.njinken@ ileaiinititiave.com (accessed on 20 October 2013).

Institute for Security Studies. 2008. Africa Aviation Security: Implications for Peace and Security, Nairobi.

Institute of Trade Development. 2012. Develop a Logistics Performance Survey Index (LPI) for the Kenya Shippers Council: REF. KSC/KM/01. Final Copy.

Irandu, E. M. 2000. Improving Railway Transport in Kenya: Policy Options and Achievements to Date, Technoserve Inc, ARD-RAISE Consortium, USA.

Irandu, E. M. and Rhoades, D. 2006. The Development of Jomo Kenyatta International Airport as a Regional Aviation Hub in the *Journal of Air Transportation*, Vol. 11 No. 1: 50–64, Aviation Institute, University of Nebraska, Omaha, USA.

JICA. 2009. The Research on the Cross-border Transport Infrastructure, Phase 3, Final Report. Available at: https://www.google.co.ke/search?hl=en&noj=1&q= JICA+%282009%29 (accessed on 10 October 2013).

KAM. 2007. A Study to Analyze Kenya's Trade Facilitation Systems, Nairobi, Kenya.

Karingithu, N. 2008. Role Played by Kenya in the Fight against Piracy and Armed Robbery Against Ships off the Coast of Somalia. United Nations Open-ended Consultative Process on Oceans and the Law of the Sea, 2 June.

Kenya Revenue Authority (KRA). 2010. Implementation of Electronic Cargo Tracking System (ECTS). Presentation to WCO Technology and Innovation Forum, Smart Borders, Enabling Technologies. Cairo, Egypt, 2–4 November.

Kenya Shippers Council. 2011. Logistics Performance Index, Mombasa, Kenya.

Kenya Shippers Council. 2014. Policy Brief on the Implementation of Electronic Cargo Tracking Systems, Kenya.

Khamis, T. and Itzhaki, D. 2010. The African Homeland Security Challenges: A Strategic Approach towards Improving Security at the Main International Seaport of East Africa – Port of Mombasa, Kenya.

Limão, N. and Venables, A. J. 2001. Infrastructure, Geographical Disadvantage, Transport Costs and Trade. *The World Bank Economic Review*, **15**, 451–479.

Nkirote, M. 2012. Mombasa Port Security System to be Ready by March 2013. Kenya Construction Business Review of 11 December. Available at: http://www. constructionkenya.com/2815/mombasa-port-security-system-to-be-ready-by- march-2013 (accessed on 10 October 2013).

Northern Corridor Infrastructure Master Plan. 2011. Northern Corridor Transit and Transport Coordination Corridor, Mombasa, Kenya. Available at: http://www.ttcanc.org/documents/The%20Northern%20Corridor%20Infrastructure%20Master%20Plan.pdf (accessed on 25 September 2015).

Ntamutumba, C. 2010. Study of the Establishment of a Permanent Regional Corridor Development Working Group in PMAESA Region. PMAESA Report, Mombasa.

Ntangsi Max Memfih. 2014. Trade Facilitation: Implications for Intra-African Trade in a Globalized Economy. Available at: http://www.codesria.org/IMG/pdf/07 (accessed on 10 October 2013).

Obino, S., Chocho, T. A. and Kosgey, D. 2009. The Performance of Aviation Regulatory System in Kenya. Paper presented at the Moi University International Management and Entrepreneurship Conference, August.

Saferworld. 2006. Prioritising safety, security and conflict prevention. EU Country Strategy Paper for Kenya.

Serianu. 2012. Cyber Security Report, Edition One. Nairobi.

Shippers Council of Eastern Africa. 2013. East Africa Logistics Performance Survey 2012. Cost, Time and Complexity of the East African Logistics Chain. An Annual Publication of the Shippers Council of Eastern Africa, 2nd Edition.

10. Multimodal freight transportation security in China

Chunyan Yu and Yihong Ru

1. INTRODUCTION

China has been the fastest growing economy in the world with an average annual growth rate of 10 percent over the past 30 years. It is now the second largest economy after the United States. China is also the largest exporter and second largest importer of goods in the world. The development of the country's transportation systems has been given a high priority as they are strategically tied to the national economy and national defense. The transportation and logistics sectors have been growing at an even faster pace than the overall economy. With the world's fourth largest land area, safe and secure movements of goods and materials are critical to the rapidly expanding international and domestic trades and business. This chapter provides a brief overview of the current state of freight movements by mode and the development of transportation infrastructures, examines the issues and challenges in freight security, and provides an assessment of the security rules and regulations imposed by governments and the measures taken by various industry stakeholders to ensure the safety and security of freight transportation in China.

2. CURRENT STATUS OF FREIGHT TRANSPORTATION IN CHINA

In 2012, 41.2 billion tons of freight was transported, and total freight traffic was estimated at 17 300 billion ton-kilometers which was more than double that of 2006. Road is now the dominant mode of transporting freight, overtaking railways in 2008 in terms of freight ton-kilometers (Table 10.1).

Table 10.1   Freight traffic by mode in China

	2006	2007	2008	2009	2010	2011	2012
			Freight tons				
Road (billion tons)	14.7	16.4	19.2	21.3	24.5	28.2	32.2
Railway (billion tons)	2.9	3.1	3.3	3.3	3.6	3.9	3.9
Water (billion tons)	2.5	2.8	3.0	3.2	3.8	4.3	4.6
Air (billion tons)	3.5	4.0	4.1	4.5	5.6	5.6	5.4
Pipeline (billion tons)	0.3	0.4	0.4	0.5	0.5	0.6	0.5
			Freight ton-kilometers				
Road (billion ton-km)	965	1135	3287	3719	4339	5137	6000
Rail (billion ton-km)	2195	2380	2511	2524	2764	2947	2920
Water (billion ton-km)	5391	6428	5026	5756	6843	7542	8070
Air (billion ton-km)	9	12	12	13	18	17	16
Pipeline (billion ton-km)	132	187	194	202	220	289	310

Source: National Bureau of Statistics of China.

3.   TRANSPORTATION INFRASTRUCTURE

China's transportation network has been expanding rapidly to support its strong economic growth. According to a US Federal Highway Administration report (Cole et al., 2008), 'China is building a transportation network in 10 years comparable to what the United States did in 50 years', by investing almost 10 percent of its GDP in infrastructure.

3.1   Roads

At the end of 2012, the total *road network* reached 4.2 million kilometers, including 96 200 kilometers of expressways. National level roads account for 85.2 percent of the total road length at 3.6 million kilometers (Figure 10.1). As shown in Table 10.2, road density as measured by road kilometers per million sq km land has continuously improved. With seven radial expressways (from the capital Beijing), 11 north–south expressways[1] and 18 east–west expressways, the National Trunk Highway System (NTHS) will form the backbone of the expressway network in the country when it is completed by 2030. Mr. Dai Dongchang, chief planner of China's Ministry of Transport, claimed at a news conference on June 20, 2013 that 78.5 percent of NTHS has been completed.[2] Phase 1 of NTHS included five north–south and seven east–west national expressways.

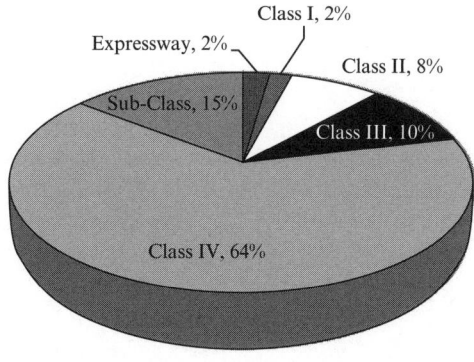

	Kilometers ('000)
Expressway	96
Class I	74
Class II	332
Class III	402
Class IV	2,706
Sub-Class	628
Total	**4,237**

Source: Ministry of Transport, China.

Figure 10.1   China's road network in 2012

Table 10.2   Road network in China

	2008	2009	2010	2011	2012
Road network length (million km)	3.7	3.9	4.0	4.1	4.2
Road density (road km per million sq km)	38.9	40.2	41.8	42.8	44.1

Source: Ministry of Transport, China.

3.2   Railways

China has the second largest rail network in the world. At the end of 2012, the conventional rail network covered a total length of 98 000 km and the high speed rail network was 9356 km (Figure 10.2). China's railway network has long been connected to the Trans-Siberian Railway via northeastern China and Mongolia, which forms the Eurasian Land Bridge (also known as the New Silk Road) moving freight and passengers overland from Pacific seaports to European seaports. In addition to this original link, the New Eurasian Land Bridge, also known as the New Eurasian Continental Bridge (NECB) runs from Lianyungang port in China to Rotterdam with a total distance of 11 870 km (Novikova and Kennedy, 2012).

China has also been making steady progress to connect its rail network with its neighbors in Southeast Asia. Three lines that link Yunnan Province to Southeast Asian nations have been included in China's medium- and

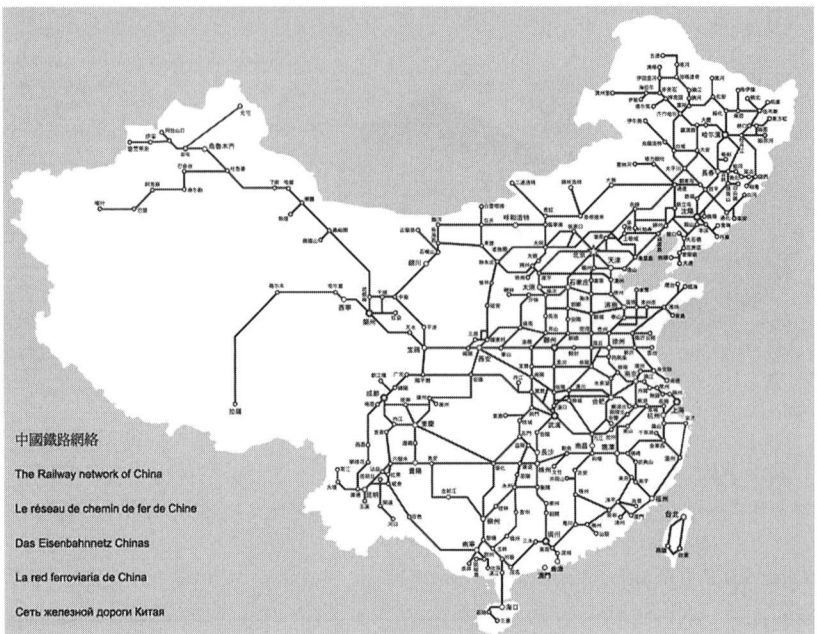

Source: http://en.wikipedia.org/wiki/File:ChinaRailwayNetwork.png.

Figure 10.2   Railway network in China

long-term railway network plan and preliminary work has begun. These lines will connect Kunming (capital city of Yunnan Province) to Laos, Vietnam, Cambodia, Myanmar, Thailand, Malaysia and Singapore, with the ultimate goal being to provide a continuous 14 000-kilometer rail link between Singapore and Istanbul in Turkey, with possible onward connections to Europe and Africa (Zhao, 2013).

3.3   Seaports

There are a total of 31 862 shipping berths in operation in China, of which 5623 are located at coastal ports, and 1517 can serve ships of 10 000 tons and over. Table 10.3 shows that 997 of the 1517 deep water berths are for specialized cargo, 379 are for bulk cargo, and 340 are for general cargo. China now has seven of the top ten container ports in the world.

Table 10.3   Deep water berths in China

	2012	2011	Change %
Specialized berth	997	942	55
Container	309	302	7
Coal	189	178	11
Metal and mineral	60	52	8
Crude oil	68	68	0
Refined oil	114	111	3
Liquid	141	123	18
Grain	34	33	1
Bulk cargo	379	338	41
General cargo	340	322	18

Note: These berths can serve ships of 10 000 tons and over.

Source: Ministry of Transport, China.

Table 10.4   Airports certified to serve airlines

	Number of airports	Percentage (%)
Total	183	100
Northeast region	20	20
Eastern region	47	26
Western region	91	50
Central region	25	14

Source: CAAC, 2012 Civil Aviation Development Statistics Bulletin.

3.4   Airports

There are a total of 183 airports which were certified to provide services to airlines in 2012 (Table 10.4); 57 served at least 1 million passengers, and 49 airports handled at least 10 000 tons of cargo (Figure 10.3).

China continues to expand its transportation networks. A Chinese official announced at the 6th Annual US-China Transportation Forum that over the next five years China is planning to develop 500 000 km of highway/expressway (4.2 million km currently) and 108 000 km of motorway; increase the number of civil airports to 230; and invest US$82–98 billion annually[3] in a new railway fund to expand the network to 272 000 km by 2050.

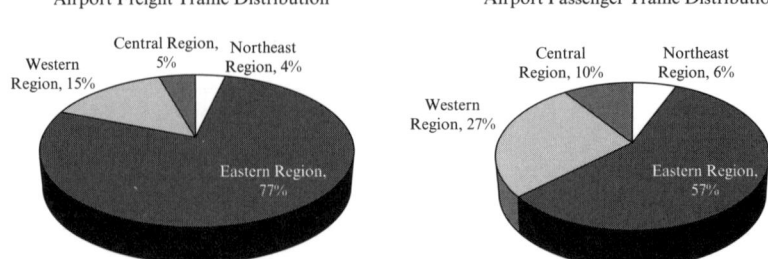

Source: CAAC, 2012 Civil Aviation Development Statistics Bulletin.

Figure 10.3   Regional distribution of airport traffic in China

4.   FREIGHT SECURITY: ISSUES AND PROBLEMS

There is no reported case of implanting explosives with cargo shipments in any mode in China. However, small-scale theft and pilferage of cargo is considered rampant. As domestic consumption among China's growing middle class increases demand for all kinds of consumer goods in the coming years, cargo thieves would have more incentives to fully exploit the opportunities.

4.1   Roads

Armed robberies of valuable goods worth millions of dollars as they are transported across China's vast network of expressways have become a very serious problem. The authors failed to obtain any systematic statistics on the number of incidents or the value of merchandise lost due to highway robberies.[4] However, anecdotal examples may provide some indications about the severity of the problems.

A 2009 news report[5] estimated that US$14.6 million of cargo was lost to robberies on the Guangdong–Jiangxi expressway and the Beijing-to-Zhuhai expressway over 2007–2009. A recent news article[6] describes the capture of a band of highway pirates who committed more than 50 robberies of trucks from June to October 2013 on the TongGuan section (in Shaanxi Province) of the Lianyungang–Khorgas expressway. They generally acted during the night, armed with bludgeons, cudgels, metal pipes, some garden tools or rocks. Although their 'weapons' are primitive, they were rather efficacious. There are numerous similar stories reported in the Chinese news media. Most of the reported cases involved the use of primitive 'tools', but the robbers appear to be well organized. Some reports mentioned that some bands even provide 'training' for new members.

Liu and Li (2007) identified two main reasons for the widespread highway robberies: lack of effective policing on the highway and lack of liability by highway operators for damages resulting from robberies. First, highway patrol officers do not have the authority to investigate criminal activities. Their mandate is to keep highway traffic moving smoothly. When they receive robbery reports, they need to forward the reports to local police. The local police have the authority to investigate criminal activities in their jurisdiction. Highways/expressways generally cross multiple police jurisdictions, but the local police are reluctant to go beyond their own jurisdiction to investigate or chase robbers. Consequently, highways become a blind or vacuum zone in terms of policing. Second, there is no 'freeway' in China. All highways and expressways are tolled. Although users have to pay to use the highway, the highway operators do not seem to have any legal obligation nor liability for the security of the users, and thus do not have a strong incentive or motivation to actively take steps to prevent or deter criminal activities. The highway operators often refuse to issue free passes for police officers to conduct criminal investigations, and the local police officers do not want to pay highway tolls to investigate robberies along the highway. Subsequently, highway patrol and local police are more interested in issuing traffic tickets than in capturing robbers.

4.2   Railways

Freight trains are also often targeted by thieves and robbers. According to Lu and Mu (2008), there were 13 973 reported cases of freight train theft and robberies with an estimated value of ¥33.7 million (about US$5.5 million) in 2005, and 11 711 reported cases with an estimated value of ¥41.7 million (about US$6.8 million) in 2006.

While highway robberies are almost always carried out by force and truck drivers are often the direct victims, railway thieves try to avoid direct confrontation with train operators. However, freight train robberies often result in damages beyond the value of the stolen goods. For example, in one case, a band of eight robbers were stealing steel sheets from a moving train, and falling sheets damaged power line poles, resulting in a key rail line being closed for five hours.[7] In another case, the robbers pushed giant pallets of cotton off a moving train in a tunnel causing multiple cars to derail in the tunnel. The rail line was shut down for more than 69 hours, causing ¥3 million (about US$491 000) in direct costs and more than ¥10 million (about US$1.6 million) in indirect costs.[8]

Railway police are responsible for preventing and investigating train robberies, and the burglars are often tried in railway courts. In one reported case, a farmer stole a total of 4.2 tons of soy bean, corn, flour, and fertilizer, worth ¥13 948[9] (about US$2300) over seven attempts. He was convicted in a railway court and sentenced to three years and two months in prison and a ¥7000 fine.[10] In another case, a band of four attempted to steal coal from a slow moving train, and were discovered by a single railway police officer. They fought off the police officer and stole 800 kg of coal worth ¥488 (about US$80). They were later captured. They were tried in a railway court for both the robberies and assault on the police officer, and were all sentenced to five years in prison and a ¥2000 fine.[11] These two reported cases show that the penalty for train robbery is severe.

4.3   Air Transport

Theft and pilferage of air cargo are often internal 'jobs'. For example, an airline cargo handler and logistics company employee conspired to steal some electronics at Beijing Capital International Airport.[12] In another reported case, three airline employees stole a shipment of gold chains weighted at 2445.75 grams with an estimated value of ¥970 000 (about US$159 000). They were caught and sentenced to ten years, three years, and three years, respectively.[13] Despite such news reports, historically China has been considered as low risk for air cargo theft (FreightWatch International, 2013).

4.4   Port and Beyond

While trucks and freight trains are subject to 'traditional' robberies and burglaries, ports, shipping companies and shippers increasingly become victims of 'modern' trickery, the so-called 'logistics crimes'.[14] These criminals take advantages of the gaps and holes in the port logistics systems, and use modern technology to steal whole loads of trucks or shipping containers. They often form their own 'supply chain' starting with fraudulent access to the cargo to selling off the stolen merchandise. These crimes have received the attention of all levels of government, and governments have established special task forces to attack the problems.

5.   TRANSPORT SECURITY RULES AND REGULATIONS

Transport security and safety are not clearly defined and distinguished in China. In fact, the term An Quan (安全) is often used for both safety and security. Therefore, some rules and regulations apply to both security and safety. This section focuses on security-related rules and regulations.

5.1 Air Transport

Air transport security is subject to the Public Air Transport Enterprise Security Code (Airline Code) and the Civil Aviation Airports Security Code (Airport Code). The Airline Code applies to all air transport companies (Chinese owned and foreign) that provide public air transport services in China, as well as other organizations, agencies and personnel related to public air transport. The Airport Code applies to all civil aviation airports including combined military and civil use airports.

Both the Airline Code and the Airport Code were signed by the director of Civil Aviation Administration of China (CAAC) on July 16, 2013 and became effective on September 1, 2013. The Codes are developed based on the Civil Aviation Security Regulations of People's Republic of China which was enacted on May 10, 2006.

Air cargo security is further subject to Air Cargo Security Regulations issued by CAAC on September 27, 2012. The Regulations cover four aspects: (1) responsibilities of and requirements for shippers, shippers' agents (or freight forwarders) and air carriers; (2) inspection of cargo; (3) secured cargo handling area; and (4) loading and unloading of air cargo.

5.2 Port and Ocean Shipping

Ocean shipping security is subject to the International Ship Security Code of People's Republic of China (Ship Code) and the Port Facility Security Code of the People's Republic of China (Port Code). The Ship Code was announced by the Ministry of Communication[15] on March 12, 2007 and took effect on July 1, 2007. It applies to ships (Chinese owned or foreign) on international voyages, including passenger ships, cargo ships of 500 GT and upwards, and mobile offshore drilling units. The Port Code was announced on November 30, 2007 and went into effect on March 1, 2008. It applies to port facilities serving passenger ships, cargo ships of 500 GT and upwards, and mobile offshore drilling units.

Both the Ship Code and the Port Code were developed based on the International Convention for the Safety of Life at Sea (SOLAS), 1974 and the International Ship and Port Facility Security Code (ISPS Code). The Ministry of Transport provides the leadership for ship and port facility security in the nation under both Codes. The Maritime Safety Administration (MSA) is responsible for SOLAS compliance and ISPS compliance. Regional maritime administrations are responsible for training and certifying ship security personnel and security firms, supervising and monitoring ship security personnel and company security guards, and implementing and enforcing ship security measures and related duties. The transport department of the city or county where the port is located is responsible for providing oversight of port security.

The 2008 Port Code replaced the 2003 Port Code. Under the 2003 Port Code, ports were required to conduct security assessments and to develop port facility security plans. By August 1, 2007, 748 ports received certification that they had met the security requirements. China conducted the first port security courses, and has since provided various port security-related training for thousands of trainees, both domestic and foreign.

The Port of Shanghai and the Port of Shengzhen participate (since 2005) in the Container Security Initiative (CSI) program. CSI consists of four core elements: (1) using intelligence and automated information to identify and target containers that pose a risk for terrorism; (2) pre-screening those containers that pose a risk at the port of departure before they arrive at U.S. ports; (3) using detection technology to quickly pre-screen containers that pose a risk; and (4) using smarter, tamper-evident containers.

5.3   Railways

There are no specific rules or regulations on railway security. However, the Chinese railway system has always had its own police force, and courts, and Procuratorate. As of August, 2013, there were more than 80 000 railway police officers[16] with responsibility for the security of passengers and freight on the trains, at train stations and along the rail tracks. Following the elimination of the Ministry of Railways, railway police now report to both the Ministry of Public Security and the newly established China Railway Corporation.

5.4   Roads

The Traffic Management Bureau under the Ministry of Public Security oversees the highway and expressway security in the country. Each province has its own traffic police force under the Provincial Public Security Bureau. The main responsibility of the traffic police (highway patrol) is to ensure road safety. They investigate and report traffic incidents and accidents, and enforce the rules of the roads through fines, driver license suspension and other legal penalties. As discussed in the previous section, however, traffic police are not authorized to investigate criminal activities, such as highway robberies, that often pose dangers to the users of the roads. Investigation of criminal activities is the responsibility of local police. Lack of coordination and cooperation between the two police forces has been cited as one of the main reasons for having highways and expressways rife with armed robberies (Liu and Li, 2007).

6. PRACTICES AND TECHNOLOGY

This section provides a number of examples of what freight carriers (of all modes) have done to ensure the safety of cargo, people and equipment.

6.1 Railways

In 2006 Shengyang Railway Bureau initiated a series of actions to counter-attack freight burglary within its jurisdiction (Ding, 2008). It set up six surveillance points at the junctions with the two neighboring bureaus: Harbin Bureau to the north and Beijing Bureau to the south. In addition, it installed 18 surveillance points within its own region at the boundary points among the sub-sections. It also set up observation towers and stake-out points at major stations and marshalling yards, and integrated the train dispatching system (DIMS) and freight dispatching system (TIMS) into the police information systems. This integrated information platform allows security personnel to monitor and track the movements of the trains and to pinpoint the location of the incidents. Instead of relying on security personnel only, the Bureau promotes community participation in fighting crimes. Train attendants, station agents, rail track maintenance workers, and citizens along the rail lines are all encouraged to be vigilant and to report suspicious activities.

Millions of laptop computers and accessories are manufactured in China each year, and bound for customers in European cities such as London, Paris, Berlin and Rome. Hewlett-Packard, the Silicon Valley electronics company, has pioneered the revival of the famous Silk Road, shipping laptops and accessories by express freight train over the New Eurasian Land Bridge. The merchandise are placed in sealed shipping containers and armed guards are deployed on the train to ensure the safety of the train and its freight. When the train travels across desolate Eurasian steppes, guards toting AK-47 military assault rifles board the locomotive to keep watch for bandits who might try to drive alongside and rob the train. Sometimes the guards would even sit on top of the steel shipping containers (Bradsher, 2013).

Anti-theft doors and electronic surveillance systems have been installed on freight trains. Surveillance cameras are installed at various locations, which allow the train attendants to monitor the trains in motion. There is also some application of DTMF-based wired or wireless monitoring systems.[17] Trains are moving constantly, and are frequently loaded and unloaded at various stations or terminals, which sometimes may affect the effectiveness of the monitoring and surveillance systems.

Freight train security issues have received considerable attention in terms of R&D activities. A number of patent applications have been filed for newly developed freight train anti-theft alarming and monitoring systems,[18] including freight train anti-theft systems based on wireless protocol ZigBee. The technology has been applied in the high speed rail monitoring systems as one of China's IoT[19] pilot projects. The monitoring systems include wind speed monitoring, anti-intrusion, vibration monitoring, and geological disasters monitoring (Huang, 2012). A number of patent applications have also been filed for ZigBee based rail container tracking systems, rail crossing alarm systems, and other safety management applications. ZigBee technology has been applied in train anti-collision systems in other countries (Arun et al., 2013).

6.2   Port and Ocean Shipping

Seaports comprise a complex range of operations – highly fragmented infrastructure, very diverse tenants, multiple modes of transports, and just the sheer volume of people, equipment, vehicles, cargo and vast land area – which makes ports vulnerable to criminal activities and terrorist attacks. Ports have established various procedures and adopted advanced technologies to ensure the safety and security of cargo and passengers.

The Port of Shanghai, the largest port in China (and in the world), has implemented multiple security measures. The following describes some of these measures:[20]

1. 24-hour security guards and reinforced berth patrol. Contracts with security firms include clauses on rewards and penalties. Penalties will be imposed on the security firm or related personnel if goods are stolen or damaged by criminal activities within the area for which they are responsible. If the security personnel are able to successfully prevent theft or other criminal activities, they will be rewarded.
2. The port employs five canine teams to provide 24-hour patrols (12-hour shift for each team).
3. Surveillance cameras are installed throughout the port.
4. Boats and ships not directly related to port operation are not allowed to dock at port facilities.
5. A special police force was formed to prevent more sophisticated 'logistics crimes'.[21]

Advanced technology has been applied to enhance port security. For example, Rizhao Port[22] (in Shangdong Province) has implemented an intelligent security system which includes GPS location monitoring, electronic eye target surveillance, motion detector alarms, and digital imaging and facial recognition.

The Port of Shengzhen has installed x-ray machines, human life detector systems, micro-vibration sensors, and infrared intrusion prevention systems on perimeter walls. Companies that move freight to/from the port have installed carbon dioxide detectors (preventing human smuggling), metal detectors, electronic entry controls, CCTV security monitors, etc. The Port has signed security agreements with barge operators, harbor pilots, ship lines, and other related companies, in terms of coordinating security plans and procedures, providing security training, and conducting security response drills.

Containers are an important component of port operations. Albeit without specific guidelines for container security, China is rather more advanced in terms of container detection technology. Mobile cargo and container scanner systems have been developed and implemented at various ports. Electronic locks with radio-frequency identification (RFID) technology have been implemented at Yangshan Port, Luchao Port, and Gaoqiao Port (part of the Ports of Shanghai). All container vehicles to and from these ports are now equipped with RFID tags.

Ship security in general is lacking. Ships are not equipped with explosive detection systems. Crews are often not clear about the difference between security and safety, and thus may neglect the security implications of their procedures and actions. For example, crews would want to keep doors, windows, stairs, and other access points free of barriers for reasons of safety, ignoring the fact that entry or access to the ship needs to be controlled for reasons of security.

6.3 Air Cargo and Airports

The security of air cargo lies mostly with shippers, freight forwarders, airlines, and cargo handling companies. Airport operators' direct involvement in air cargo security is often through their cargo handling subsidiaries. Airlines and cargo handling agents have established various security procedures and have adopted different technologies.

Shanghai Pudong Int'l Airport Cargo Terminal Co., Ltd. (PACTL) is a Sino-German joint venture,[23] founded in 1999. It is based at Shanghai Pudong International Airport and provides cargo handling and warehousing services to 44 airlines. PACTL handles 25000–30000 tons of cargo each week.

In addition to a sophisticated closed circuit TV (CCTV) system, an entry and exit control system, PACTL owns 16 x-ray machines operated by trained professionals from an independent security company. They require all cargo to undergo an x-ray scan before being loaded onto aircraft. Oversized items that could not fit into the x-ray machines need to undergo special tests for explosives, and are required to stay in the warehouse for 24 hours before being loaded into the aircraft. For shipments with oversized items, the entire shipment has to stay in the warehouse for 24 hours.

Xiamen Airlines,[24] a member of SkyTeam, has a security department that is responsible for both passenger and cargo security. The airlines have both x-ray machines and explosive detection devices. All freight and mail are required to undergo x-ray scan before being allowed to be in the warehouse and loaded onto the aircraft. Suspicious items will be opened for a manual check and explosive tests. Security personnel must undertake required training and accumulate sufficient experience before being certified to operate x-ray machines.

Heilongjiang Airport Company Ltd. is a holding company under the Capital Airports Holding Company. It operates four airports in Heilongjiang Province that collectively handled 92 000 tons of cargo in 2012. The company has developed freight security handbooks for its cargo handling stations at each airport. The following summarizes some key points of the freight security handbook at Qiqihar Airport:

- Lines of succession of operational responsibilities of the security personnel which specify each individual by name and his/her responsibility.
- Responsibilities include:
    1) implementing and enforcing freight safety and security rules and procedures, and providing feedback on the effectiveness of these rules and regulations;
    2) establishing emergency response procedures, organizing and conducting emergency response drills;
    3) facilitating safety and security information exchanges between government agencies, airport security committee and various freight handling agents;
    4) implementing decisions by the airport security committee, and providing regular reports to the security committee including risk analysis, evaluation of equipment and devices, recommendation of how to improve security rules and procedures;
    5) developing training programs for related personnel, including training record keeping and training timetables;

6)   security background check of related personnel;
7)   entry and exit control of secured areas;
8)   enforcing security check procedures for both outbound and inbound cargo shipments.

- Detailed descriptions of security check procedures and loading procedures for outbound cargo.
- Detailed description of response procedures if explosives are found, bomb threats, and some other potential safety and security incident scenarios.
- Equipment and devices:
  1)   closed circuit TV monitoring systems;
  2)   x-ray machines.

It should be noted that the freight security handbook includes not only security rules and procedures but also aspects of safety procedures.

7.   SUMMARY AND CONCLUDING REMARKS

The vast land area and rapidly expanding international and domestic trades pose tremendous challenges to the safe and secure transport of goods and materials. Although there is no reported incident involving explosives with cargo shipments by any mode in China, theft and pilferage of cargo are considered rampant and appear to have increased in recent years. While trucks and freight trains are often victims of 'traditional' robberies and burglaries, air cargo theft is more likely to be an internal 'job' involving employees, and ports and shipping companies increasingly become victims of the so-called 'logistics crimes' involving the use of modern technology.

Because of the nature of their international operation, air transport and ocean shipping are subject to clearly defined safety and security rules and regulations that are generally based on international conventions. The implementation and enforcement of these rules and regulations tend to put more emphasis on safety rather than security. This is consistent with the general belief that China is a fairly stable country with a relatively low security risk. However, the continuing efforts of various international agencies – such as the International Civil Aviation Organization (ICAO), the International Maritime Organization (IMO) and the World Customs Organization (WCO) – to heighten awareness of various freight security risks, will help to prompt policy makers and stakeholders to re-examine current regulations and general practices to further strengthen transport safety and security while facilitating the flow of cargo.

There are no specific regulations on road and railway security. Railway police officers are responsible for the security of passengers and freight in the trains, at train stations and along the rail tracks. The Traffic Management Bureau under the Ministry of Public Security oversees the highway and expressway security in the country. The main responsibility of the traffic police, however, is to ensure road safety rather than security. The investigation and prevention of criminal activities on highways and roads are the responsibility of local police. Lack of coordination and cooperation between the two police forces has been cited as one of the main reasons for rampant highway robberies.

Railway, road, and ocean shipping companies have invested significant efforts in preventing theft and pilferage, including technologies such as electronic surveillance systems, anti-theft doors, GPS location monitoring, electronic locks with RFID technology, etc. Air cargo security procedures and practices focus more on the detection of explosives and illegal items (and dangerous goods), generally employing x-ray machines and explosive detection devices. Overall, all modes of transporting freight have increasingly adopted advanced technology and new operational procedures to improve the safety and security of cargo, equipment, and people. China is generally considered as a low-risk country for cargo security.

NOTES

1. The initial plan calls for nine north–south expressways, but has since been increased to 11. It was referred to as 7911 network, and is now referred to as 71118 network.
2. See http://www.china.com.cn/news/2013-06/20/content_29176110.htm
3. US$105.9 billion was budgeted for railway investment in 2013.
4. It should be noted that many of the reported robberies were targeting truck drivers for their cash.
5. 'Highway robbers plague China, Chinese truckers lose goods to gangs of sword-wielding robbers', October 28, 2009, available at: http://www.rfa.org/english/news/china/highway-robbers-10282009110050.html
6. See http://www.chinanews.com/fz/2013/11-08/5481739.shtml
7. See http://www.lw58.com/html/boshilunwen/2011/0901/98677.html
8. See http://www.lw58.com/html/boshilunwen/2011/0901/98677.html
9. He only received ¥1950 (about US$320) cash after selling his loot.
10. See http://news.enorth.com.cn/system/2010/01/06/004405040.shtml
11. See http://china.findlaw.cn/bianhu/zhuanti/daoqiezuidingxing/41046.html
12. See http://www.airnews.cn/air/16721.shtml
13. See http://news.gxnews.com.cn/staticpages/20130730/newgx51f78d33-8160673.shtml
14. Note that in many 'logistics crime' cases, truck drivers are involved.
15. It has now been renamed as the Ministry of Transport.
16. See http://finance.sina.com.cn/china/20130831/013216623084.shtml
17. Dual-tone multi-frequency signaling.
18. See http://ip.com/patfam/en/40826532
19. 'Internet of Things'.
20. See http://www.shgk.org.cn/gkzz_text2.asp?id=134
21. Similar special police forces are also formed at other major ports in China.

22. See http://d.wanfangdata.com.cn/periodical_gkkjdt201205022.aspx
23. Shanghai Airport (Group) Co., Ltd. (51 percent), Lufthansa Cargo AG (29 percent) and JHJ Logistics Management Co., Ltd. (20 percent).
24. China Southern Airlines (51 percent), Xiamen Construction and Development Group (34 percent), and Jizhong Energy Group (15 percent).

REFERENCES

Arun, P., Sabarinath, G., Madhukumar, S. and Careena, P. (2013), 'Implementaion of ZigBee Based Train Anti-Collision And Level Crossing Protection System for Indian Railways', *International Journal of Latest Trends in Engineering and Technology*, Vol. 2, Issue 1, 12–18.
Bradsher, K. (2013), 'Hauling New Treasure Along the Silk Road', *New York Times*, July 20, 2013.
Civil Aviation Administration of China (CAAC) (2012), Civil Aviation Development Statistics Bulletin, Beijing, P.R. China.
Cole, D., Furst, T., Daboin, S., Hoemann, D., Meyer, M., Nordahl, R., Parker, M., Penne, L., Stoner, N. and Tang, T. (2008), Freight Mobility and Intermodal Connectivity in China, Office of International Programs, Federal Highway Administration, Washington, DC, Publication No. FHWA-PL-08-020.
Ding, J. (2008), 'Analysis of Freight Train Theft', *Journal of Railway Police College*, Serial 73, Vol. 18, No. 1, 20–26.
FreightWatch International (2013), 2013 Global Cargo Theft Threat Assessment: Executive Summary, FWAPAC Sdn Bhd, Penang, Malaysia, May.
Huang, J. (2012), 'ZigBee Overview, Internet of Things Enabler, and the Development in China', ZigBee Alliance, Presentation on March 13, 2012, available at: http://www.zbsigj.org/wp/wp-content/uploads/2012/03/20120313_keynote.pdf
Liu, X. and Li, N. (2007), 'Study and Thought about Robbery on Highway', *Journal of Hebei Youth Administrative Cadres College*, Vol. 74, No. 2, 71–74.
Lu, P. and Mu, X. (2008), 'Current Status and Analysis of Railway Freight Robberies', *Journal of Railway Police College*, Serial 74, Vol. 18, No. 2, 87–91.
Novikova, K. K. A. and Kennedy, O. R. (2012), 'New Eurasian Land Bridge: An Evaluation of Efficiency Characteristics', *Global Journal of Business, Management and Accounting*, Vol. 2, No. 1, 028–040.
Zhao, L. (2013), 'China on Track to Rail Link with Neighbors', *China Daily USA*, October 13.

11. Multimodal freight transportation security in Brazil

Michael J. Williams

INTRODUCTION

Brazil, formally known as the Federal Republic of Brazil, is the largest and most populated country in South America. Bordered by the Atlantic Ocean, and every other country in South America except Ecuador and Chile, Brazil faces a variety of cultures and neighboring governments. Claimed by Portugal in 1500, Brazil gained its independence in 1822 after three centuries of Portuguese rule and was then governed by a monarchical system until the military proclaimed it a republic in 1889. There were several military and populist governments until the military peacefully relinquished power to civilian rulers in 1985 (Fausto, 1999; CIA Factbook, 2013). Organized into 26 states and a federal district, Brazil has a network of 5564 municipalities connected by a myriad of roads, rail lines, airports and waterways.

Brazil's GDP makes it the seventh largest economy in the world as well as one of the fastest growing, and as such it has been grouped with three other emerging countries referred to as the BRIC (Brazil, Russia, India and China). The BRICs are among the fastest-growing economies in the world and are attractive to companies looking for new markets of supply as well as in which to sell. Accounting for nearly 33 percent of the country's GDP, Brazil's industries are very diverse and include textiles, machinery and equipment, shoes, computers, automobiles and parts, aircraft, and consumer durables. Brazil is also a major world supplier of natural resources that include iron ore and other minerals, lumber, and petrochemicals (Rother, 2012; Purtell and Rice, 2013).

CHALLENGES

As a result of its size, Brazil faces some unique challenges with its transportation system due to diverse geography, considerable natural resources, poverty with the resulting high crime rate, and a sizeable but underutilized labor pool. In recent years, the country has emerged as South America's economic leader and has made considerable effort to develop its transportation system. Brazil's declining birth rate over the past 50 years has resulted in reduced population growth and an aging population that will reach a critical stage in the mid-2020s. The large working-age population is under-educated and -trained, with crucial social and educational programs being underfunded. Adding unique challenges to its development and transportation efforts, Brazil has a 4655 mile (7491 km) coastline along the Atlantic Ocean and river system with nearly 30 000 miles (48 000 km) of navigable waterways that include the Amazon Basin (Pires, 2011b; CIA Factbook, 2013). The Brazilian land mass is also very diverse and includes mountains, hills, plains, lowlands, and tropical rainforest. The climate within the country ranges from tropical to temperate. All of these factors affect the movement of raw materials, produce and other goods throughout the country (Ellicott, 2011).

INFRASTRUCTURE OVERVIEW

Highways

Over the past 30 years the Brazilian government has implemented a systematic approach to managing its transportation infrastructure that is eventually expected to lead to an integrated national surface transportation system that includes water, road, and rail. Throughout the country, the majority of freight is transported by roadways, which have recently received planning and funding priority due to public demand as well as to two major upcoming sporting events: the 2014 World Cup and the 2016 Summer Olympics. This emphasis has resulted in a 300 percent increase in highway mileage which today exceeds 1.5 million miles. Although Brazil has one of the world's largest road systems, approximately 90 percent of it is unpaved and even many of the paved roadways are in various states of disrepair. Despite these conditions, 85 percent of goods and people are transported by road and virtually all of Brazil's state capitals are linked by paved roads. Most large cities have state-of-the-art metropolitan expressways but there are few modern high-capacity highways away from the large population centers. In 2010, a record of over 5.4 million vehicles was sold in Brazil and that demand is expected to increase in coming years (Pires, 2011a). Since such a small percentage of Brazil's highways are paved, the majority of road travel is complicated by congestion, potholes which drastically limit speeds, crime, and high accident rates. Rural highways

Table 11.1   Brazil's commercial fleet by vehicle type, January 2010

Type	Number
Light trucks	3 861 622
Medium/heavy trucks	2 422 465
Buses	676 537

Source: Blower and Woodrooffe, 2010.

leading to mining or farming sites are often clogged with large trucks which can create a veritable standstill when inclement weather turns these unpaved roads into muddy 'parking lots'. A major factor in the wear and tear effects on Brazil's road system is that there were nearly 7 million registered commercial trucks and buses at the beginning of 2010. According to Jose Carlos Silvano, president of the Union of Freight and Logistics Companies of Rio Grande du Sul, approximately 1 million additional trucks will be put into service on Brazil's roadways through 2019, and 'we need infrastructure projects to prepare for future demand' (Pires, 2011a). Table 11.1 shows the distribution of commercial vehicles in Brazil as of January, 2010. Inter-city roads in Brazil are recognized as among the most dangerous due to congestion, poor driving skills, and poor roads. There are also no laws which require mandatory rest stops for truck drivers, who often drive for long periods of time without rest, creating accidents which in turn increase congestion.

Unlike the Interstate Highway System in the United States, controlled-access highways are virtually non-existent outside of the aforementioned areas, requiring movement of freight over two lane paved highways at best and unpaved poorly maintained roads at worst. The accident rate is high as cars share the right-of-way with large heavily-laden trucks, aggressive drivers, and even corrupt police officers. Poor maintenance has resulted in a serious pothole problem which exacerbates the congestion problem by keeping speeds below 50 km/h (35 mph) on many of the busiest routes.

Water Transport

As previously mentioned, Brazil has a lengthy coastline and many miles of inland waterways that offer potential for the economic use of water transport; however, due to funding constraints it is a resource that has yet to be appropriately exploited. Although slow and primitive by modern standards, transportation by water is an economical way to move the significant mineral and agricultural resources located within Brazil's interior.

Table 11.2   Brazilian merchant marine fleet

Type	Number
Bulk carrier	18
Cargo	16
Chemical tanker	7
Container	13
Liquefied gas	11
Petroleum tanker	39
Roll on-Roll off	5
Total	109

Source: CIA Factbook, 2013.

Each year, over 350 million tons of raw materials and goods are transported by water. As expected from such movements, the Brazilian government is showing an increased interest in water transport and has pledged significant resources to the construction of waterways and ports. Brazil's merchant marine continues to increase and as of July 2013 totaled slightly over 100 ships of various types, with over 50 percent of those vessels either foreign-owned or -registered. Table 11.2 lists Brazil's merchant marine fleet which are commercial vessels exceeding 1000 gross register tonnage (GRT). Of the 109 ships listed in Brazil's merchant fleet, 27 are foreign-owned and 36 are registered in other countries.

Despite the fact that Brazil has over 15 fully-equipped harbors, the movement of goods by water is greatly underutilized. Often the only mode to reach many remote communities, only around 13 percent of freight is shipped by water. Ideal for moving large amounts of low-value products such as fuels, grains and minerals, water transportation has a potential that is not likely to be realized from road or rail transport of such shipments within the foreseeable future. Only Brazil's oil and gas industry seems to have made significant investments in moving products by water with state-owned Petrobras investing heavily in terminals across several costal states and also maintaining its own fleet of cargo vessels. Across the entire country only the Amazon Basin fully utilizes the capabilities of shipping by water, and although the country is one of the most productive with regards to agriculture and mining, the lack of infrastructure in other parts of Brazil has resulted in higher transportation costs and some abandonment of water transport (Pires, 2011b). With a complex and abundant inland network of waterways, the dominant issue affecting water transportation of cargo in Brazil is its underutilization. Tremendous potential exists to access remote parts of the country where raw materials and agricultural assets are plentiful, and the 7000 km coastline offers opportunities for international trade. Although a slow method of transport, Brazil's rivers and their tributaries allow for the cost-effective exploitation of large amounts of minerals, fuels, and grains from the interior. Current shipping costs are excessive given that the product must be loaded onto relatively low-capacity trucks and make its way slowly over fairly primitive roads to either production facilities or shipping ports. While naturally highly navigable, the majority of Brazil's inland water system requires maintenance and upgrading such as charting, dredging, and navigational improvements. Despite the potential advantages, recent years have seen a greater focus on using water resources for hydroelectric facilities in lieu of making accommodations for water transport. Significant investment as well as a policy shift will be needed to realize the true potential of water-based commerce (Pires, 2011b).

Rail Transport

The movement of people and goods by rail began in the 1800s and evolved from many different railroad companies into a nationalized line (Rede Ferroviaria Federal, Sociedade Anomima or RFFSA) in 1957. RFFSA was privatized into a number of private organizations which agreed to 30-year concessions to operate specific routes between 1999 through 2007 and today service is covered by a number of public and private operators. Brazil's rail system consists of nearly 30 000 km (18 500 miles) of track and is considerably less dense than its global peers. For example, Brazil has only 3.4 km of track per 1000 square kilometers as compared to 130 km for Germany, 21 km for the United States, and 7 km for China. There is also some need for standardization of Brazil's railroads given there are currently four different track gauges currently in use. Table 11.3 lists Brazil's railroad track by distance and gauge.

As of late 2010, Brazil's railroads transported only about 25 percent of the country's freight movements and the country continues to depend heavily on truck transport which threatens both further development and national competitiveness. This percentage is slowly increasing with a major governmental effort currently underway to lengthen, standardize, and increase the capacity of Brazil's rail system. Also under development is a high-speed rail project intended to connect Rio de Janeiro, Sao Paulo, and Campinas (da Costa, 2009; OSEC, 2010). The biggest disadvantage of Brazil's railway network is simply the lack of track to both the sources of its abundant resources, namely agricultural, mining, and manufacturing locations, and to the consumption or international transfer points. Rail is

Table 11.3   Brazilian rail infrastructure by distance and gauge

Gauge	Gauge		Distance	
	mm	ft/in	km	miles
Broad	1600 mm	5ft 3in	4057	25
Narrow	1000 mm	3ft 3–3/8in	23 489	41
Dual	1000 mm and 1600 mm	3ft 3–3/8in and 5ft 3in	336	43
Standard	1435 mm	5ft 8–1/2 in	202	25

Source: SCI, 2011.

both cheaper and more efficient than trucking, with a single railcar capable of taking approximately ten trucks off the roads. Expanding Brazil's railroads would serve well to reduce the logistical bottlenecks on the highways and at various export points (Oliveira, 2011). Movement of cargo by train is also less prone to hijacking, pilferage, or damage than trucks and can be made even more secure with basic improvements in security.

Air Transport

Due to its size, unimproved ground transportation, and need for rapid economic growth, Brazil has a natural need for air transportation, particularly for high-value or time-sensitive goods. The transport of low-cost or bulk goods by air is cost prohibitive, which will likely limit the extent to which air cargo transport will develop in Brazil. Despite some disrepair, the Brazilian aviation infrastructure is fairly well-developed with service to every state capital and most major cities. As of 2012, Brazil has over 4100 airports, of which less than 20 percent have paved runways (CIA Factbook, 2013). Recent airline deregulation has increased the popularity of air travel and in some cases makes it as cheap as taking a bus. This efficiency has turned to concern as Brazil's airports have not been able to handle the increase in demand. Although most passenger airlines offer a cargo service, there are several cargo-focused airlines. Table 11.4 lists examples of cargo carriers that were in service as of November, 2013.

In addition to problems of capacity, especially at the major airports, the overall infrastructure is in need of maintenance and upgrading. Budgetary issues have impeded improvements of runways, radar equipment, and other vital systems (MercoPress, 2010). While passenger air travel has increased in popularity, so too has the movement of cargo by air, which has undergone significant growth in recent years.

Table 11.4   A sample of cargo airlines in Brazil

Name	Founded	Headquarters	Fleet size	Aircraft type(s)
ABSA Cargo Airline	1995	Campinas	4	Boeing 767-300F
Air Brazil	2005	Sao Paulo	2	Boeing 727-200F
Rio Linhas Aereas	2007	Curitiba	7	Boeing 727-200F
			2	Boeing 767-200F
Skymaster Airlines	1995	Manaus	3	Boeing 707-300C/F
			1	Douglas DC-8-62F
			2	Douglas DC-8-63F
Total Linhas Aereas	1988	Belo Horizonte	6	Boeing 727-200F*

Note: * also has one ATR-42-500 aircraft for charter service.

Source: AirlineUpdate.com

Pipeline Transport

As Brazil's geography is diverse, so is the placement of various pipelines. Mountains, rainforests, deep water, and major cities are all locations for the nearly 24 000 km (14 900 miles) of pipes currently in use. Pipelines are ideal for transporting gaseous- or liquid-based products in a relatively safe and secure environment and are an ideal mode given the nature of Brazil's road and rail systems. Throughout Brazil, industry transports a number of different products by pipeline, with most being petrochemicals. Table 11.5 shows a breakdown of Brazil's pipelines by product.

A breakdown by product lines includes: condensate, gas, liquid petroleum gas, crude oil, and refined products. In addition to transporting chemicals by pipeline, Brazil has a network of slurry pipelines in operation that transport various ores such as phosphate, iron ore, and bauxite. In addition, a 525 km (326 mile) iron ore slurry pipeline is planned between the Minas-Rio mine to a port at Açu (Renno, 2009; CIA Factbook, 2013). Brazil has both the natural resources as well as the demand for gas and petroleum, both of which are efficiently transported by pipeline. What it does not currently have is the infrastructure to properly exploit those resources and satisfy demand. There is a shortage of both drilling equipment and pipelines to the point where some companies are hesitant to bid on gas and oil rights offered by the government. During a recent auction by the Brazilian government, less than 33 percent of the areas offered for sale were purchased amid both equipment shortages and ecological concerns (Blount and Lorenzi, 2013). Another factor negatively affecting the expansion of gas and oil production throughout

Table 11.5   Brazil's pipeline system by product

Product	Total length	
	km	miles
Condensate	38	38
Gas	13 514	8397
Liquid petroleum gas	352	218
Oil	3729	2317
Refined products	4684	2911
Slurry	1500	932

Sources: Renno, 2009; CIA Factbook, 2013.

Brazil is corruption and violence against those who threaten to impede such expansion.

GOVERNMENT POLICY AND INITIATIVES

As previously mentioned, Brazil has significant challenges affecting the movement and security of freight within the country as well as through various points where raw materials and products leave the country. The vast majority of freight is moved by truck over an inadequate road system. Railroads are insufficient and what do exist are grossly underutilized. And, although Brazil has an extensive network of waterways, only the Amazon River region is sufficiently improved and utilized, and that only out of necessity due to the large number of remote villages where water is the only practical means of access. As a result of these challenges, a National Logistics and Transport Plan (PNLT) was announced in April 2007. Essentially the PNLT calls for investing as much as US$180 billion between 2010 and 2025 (Raso, 2012). Table 11.6 gives details by transportation mode for a portion of the planned investment.

Given the nature of Brazil's transportation woes, the major use of available funding will go towards reducing regional bottlenecks and providing interconnections between the north–south regions and the southeast. In addition to enhancing the infrastructure for upcoming major sporting events, Brazil is a leading producer of soybeans and along with the United States is a principal exporter, which also necessitates significant investment in transportation (Friend and da Silva Lima, 2011). Ports, ferries, expansion of highway capacities, lengthening the railroad network, integration of water with road and rail networks, and an increase in

Table 11.6   Brazilian projected transportation investments

Projected investments 2010–2015	(US$ billion)
Highways	22.6
Railways	48.5
Waterways and ports	17.8

Source: Raso, 2012.

oversight of all modes to ensure safety, security, and proper use of the infrastructure, are all objectives of the infrastructure plan (Raso, 2012).

In August 2012, Brazilian President Dilma Rousseff announced the implementation of an investment package totaling nearly US$66 billion for road and rail systems that are in dire need of improvement and crucial for solving Brazil's serious transportation woes. There is also hope that such investment will revive a floundering economy. Improvements will include constructing or improving over 4600 miles of federal highways and building over 6000 miles of track. In addition, funding will be provided to build or upgrade seaports, waterways, and airports. These plans come as Brazil is preparing to host the 2014 World Cup and the 2016 Summer Olympics, which has created a sense of urgency as the dates of those events approach. A directional shift in transportation includes the movement of cargo away from the heavily congested road system and towards more sustainable modes such as rail and water. Planned expenditures support this strategy with emphasis on the most efficient transmodal movement of freight. The overall aim is to shift freight transport from the highways to more sustainable modes, especially rail transport. The development of the rail infrastructure network will support this strategy. The PNLT has concise, measurable objectives that have the overall modal shift occurring by 2015 with the added intent of achieving specific environmental objectives as well.

FACTORS AFFECTING THE MOVEMENT AND SECURITY OF FREIGHT

Cargo Crimes

A major impetus behind cargo theft and hijacking is the black market. For centuries, goods stolen during transport have been redirected from legitimate logistical chains into a marketplace not subject to taxation, regulation, or safety practices. With the advent of the global economy, raw materials, manufacturing, warehousing, and end users are dispersed throughout the world. This requires a sophisticated transportation network typically spanning thousands of miles, a network where materials and goods can be stolen at virtually any point from source to consumer. A unique twist to the issue is that goods are often stolen in developing nations such as the United States and Europe, repackaged into shipping containers and then transported to countries with sophisticated black market systems, such as Brazil (Palmer, 2010).

Often regarded as one of the most dangerous countries regarding crimes involving cargo, Brazil maintained that reputation in 2012 according to the National Association of Cargo Transport and Logistics (Associação Nacional do Transporte de Cargas e Logística). Along with Mexico and South Africa, Brazil is one of three countries in the world at greatest risk of cargo loss due to criminal activity. High crime rates and a congested and ailing infrastructure make for a perfect storm of cargo theft, with the state of Sao Paulo registering more than half of all cargo crime in the entire country (Queiroz, 2012). As the economy continues to struggle, cargo thieves have become ruthless with very little regard for the safety of their victims. The most targeted cargo, due to the ease with which they can be sold, are pharmaceuticals, food, tobacco, and electronics. Thieves have become so brazen that they do not hesitate to engage with law enforcement officers, often with superior firepower and technology that is restricted to use only by the military or elite police agencies. Also occurring more frequently is the use of electronic jammers which thwart security monitoring and location tracking equipment. One interesting point is that most of the products stolen still become available to the consumer, either on the black market or through legitimate stores. Pharmaceuticals on the black market can be a lucrative trade, with sale prices ranging from double to ten or more times retail prices. To sell stolen prescription drugs 'legally' requires documentation, including invoices, and is often an 'inside job' where an employee is a part of the scheme and of course will receive a portion of the profit. Such operations are usually very well organized and often involve cooperation between different groups of thieves (Queiroz, 2012).

Rio de Janeiro and Sao Paulo appear to be the leading states for cargo theft in the entire country, and are where a combined total of 84 percent of all reported incidents occur. The most common crime committed against cargo shipments is hijacking, with gunfights between police or armed escorts being common. Parked and unoccupied trucks are also common targets, with thieves typically using legally registered trucks to haul away the stolen goods. In an effort to combat the high rate of hijackings and other cargo-related crime, the government has allocated significant resources both to increase the number of police personnel and provide better weapons and surveillance equipment (FreightWatch International, 2012). The thieves also use electronic equipment, especially jammers, to prevent tracking of the stolen vehicles. And they often kidnap the drivers as well (Utsumi, 2014). The rate of highway-based crime involving cargo theft has reached such a critical level that some shippers are turning to much slower water transport in order to safeguard their shipments. Although tripling the time in transit, the more secure water movement of cargo often shows savings of over 20 percent when factoring in cargo losses due to theft using roads or rail (Spinetto and Sciaudone, 2013).

In 2013, more than BRL1 billion in cargo was stolen, according to the National Association of Cargo Transport and Logistics (NTC&Logistica) in over 15000 incidences. The southeast region of Brazil saw over 80 percent of these crimes with the state of Sao Paolo alone accounting for more than half. With urban areas accounting for almost 70 percent of the thefts, loading and unloading operations were the phase of transport most often targeted. Once stolen, cargo is often taken to smaller cities where it is split into smaller portions and sold to distributors who will make it available either on the black market or sell it to a legitimate business. While robberies involving aircraft and ocean/river vessels do occur, the overwhelming majority involve trucks on highways and in warehouses. This has resulted in some criticism of the reliance on highway transportation over the other modes, especially given the lower capacity and vulnerability when compared to the other modes (Utsumi, 2014).

Besides crimes against trucking, air and water modes are also targeted. Chartered planes are stolen, usually from large cities, and are taken to remote airfields for dissemination of their cargo which also ends up either on the black market or in legitimate businesses. Stealing aircraft does not come without significant risks due to airspace surveillance and onboard tracking equipment. Due to high crime rates and concerns about the safety of a shipment, insurance companies have begun to refuse coverage on the transportation of pharmaceuticals, electronics, alcoholic beverages, and cigarettes. Loss has been so great in recent years that if a company is willing to cover the shipment, insurance premiums significantly increase the cost of moving the products. Some technological products may increase the final transportation cost by nearly 30 percent due to insurance costs (Puin, 2012).

Security Issues and Measures

Brazil is attractive to foreign investors and companies not only because of its abundance of minerals and agriculture products, but also due to a number of other factors such as the strength of its economy, political stability, and a growing domestic market of consumers (Mello, 2012). When considering entering the Brazilian market, companies must understand the risks of establishing product supply lines and conduct a transportation risk assessment. Such a study should include: business location studies, existing trucking operations, third-party transportation service providers, container loading processes, and supporting export locations such as airports, seaports, and border crossings. In early 2013, the security management company, First Advantage, conducted a study of 45 nations worldwide that assessed the overall safety and security of international cargo movements both within and to/from those countries. Specific discrepancies identified within the study included: no background checks for employees of shipping companies; a lack of shipping container inspections; insufficient or no transportation threat awareness or security training for employees; and shipping containers arriving at terminals without seals. The U.S. Customs and Border Protection's Customs-Trade Partnership Against Terrorism (C-TPAT) program is an objective-based standard used to assess transportation security risks. Brazil is among the highest risk nations in relation to supply chain theft. However, when considering C-TPAT data, Brazil has a 'low' threat rating due to the amicable relationship with the United States and western culture (Purtell and Rice, 2013).

In addition to measures taken by governments and transportation authorities, there are also steps individual companies can take to reduce losses due to criminal acts. While the thieves are becoming more sophisticated, so too are the companies moving the cargo. Trucking companies, for example, are taking a number of different steps designed to prevent or discourage theft. They are training their drivers to avoid potentially hazardous situations such as leaving the trailer unattended, to avoid truck stops and rest areas, to recognize and avoid road blockages which could conceal a possible ambush by thieves, and, finally, how to react if they are actually hijacked. Companies are often employing two-driver teams, hiding tracking devices within the cargo, and even restricting shipments to days that statistically have lower incident rates. Statistically, cargo thefts may involve company insiders nearly 80 percent of the time, which is causing increased monitoring of cargo as well as employees with access to large quantities of cargo (Germond, 2012).

TRANSPORTATION SECURITY CHALLENGES AND OUTLOOK

As this chapter has discussed, Brazil faces challenges regarding the safety and security concerning the movement of freight within the country. Crime remains a significant issue as does over-capacity and a crumbling transportation infrastructure. Despite these challenges, Brazil is growing economically and continuing to increase its presence in regional and world markets. The Brazilian government has realized the importance of transportation to its financial outlook and has begun taking steps towards planning and improvement for the long term. Two huge tests loom on the horizon regarding Brazil's ability to move people and goods efficiently around the country and to its exporting ports: the 2014 World Cup and the 2016 Summer Olympics. A record soybean harvest in early 2013 highlighted some of the shortcomings and bottlenecks with the Brazilian transportation network and also highlighted the importance of its capabilities. As the result of a commodities boom in Brazil beginning in 2011, money became available to the government for improvements to infrastructure. While critics say the spending lacks direction and clear objectives, progress is being made, although with apparent priority towards projects that are intended to make a positive impression on visitors to the upcoming major sporting events (UPI, 2013). Brazil is an emerging regional and world leader with both complex problems and great potential, and it is acutely aware that changes to transportation infrastructure and security are needed.

REFERENCES

AirlineUpdate.com (2013), International Airline Industry Directories. Available at: http://www.airlineupdate.com/content_public/airlines/south_america/brazil.htm (accessed October 2, 2013).

Blount, Jeb and Lorenzi, Sabrina (2013), 'Ecological Doubts, Pipeline Shortage, Undercut Brazil Natgas Bid', *Reuters* – UK Digital Edition, November 28, 2013. Available at: http://uk.reuters.com/article/2013/11/28/uk-brazil-oilauction-idUKBRE9AR0P420131128 (accessed November 30, 2013).

Blower, Daniel and Woodrooffe, John (2010), 'Survey of the Status of Truck Safety: Brazil, China, Australia, and the United States', The University of Michigan Transportation Research Institute Ann Arbor, Michigan 48109-2150, U.S.A., Report No. UMTRI-2012-13, May 2012. Available at: http://deepblue.lib.umich.edu/bitstream/handle/2027.42/90952/102856.pdf (accessed November 12, 2013).

CIA Factbook (2013), 'The World Factbook: Brazil'. Available at: https://www.cia.gov/library/publications/the-world-factbook/geos/br.html (accessed August 6, 2013).

da Costa, Francisco Luiz Babtista (2009), 'Rail Network Expansion Program: Rio de Janeiro – São Paulo – Campinas High Speed Train'. Available at: http://www.brasemb.or.jp/economy/pdf/PAC%20Seminar/08FranciscoLuizBdaCosta.pdf (accessed November 2, 2013).

Ellicott, Karen (ed.) (2011), *Countries of the World and Their Leaders Yearbook 2012*, Vol. 1, Detroit: Gale, pp. 306–323.

Fausto, Boris (1999), *A Concise History of Brazil*, Cambridge, UK: Cambridge University Press.

FreightWatch International (2012), '2013 Global Cargo Theft Threat Assessment'. Prepared by FreightWatch International – Supply Chain Intelligence Center. Available at: http://www.freightwatchintl.com/sites/default/files/attachments/FreightWatch%202013%20Global%20Cargo%20Theft%20Threat%20Assesment%20Full_0.pdf (accessed November 21, 2013).

Friend, J. Daniel and da Silva Lima, Renato (2011), 'Impact of Transportation Policies on Competitiveness of Brazilian and U.S. Soybeans', *Transportation Research Record: Journal of the Transportation Research Board, No. 2238*, Transportation Research Board of the National Academies, Washington, DC, pp. 61–67. Available at: http://www.rslima.unifei.edu.br/download1/ppm 2011/2238-008.pdf (accessed November 2, 2013).

Germond, Nancy (2012), 'Managing Cargo Theft: The "New Normal" for Transportation Firms', All Business: Your Small Business Advantage. Available at: http://www.allbusiness.com/print/16641264-1-9a0bs.html (accessed May 3, 2014).

Mello, Juliana (2012), 'The Ultimate Guide to Why You Should Do Business in Brazil', *The Brazil Business*. Available at: http://thebrazilbusiness.com/article/the-ultimate-guide-to-why-you-should-do-business-in-brazil (accessed August 1, 2013).

MercoPress (2010), 'Brazil's Air Transport Infrastructure is a "Growing Disaster" says IATA', MercoPress, South Atlantic News Agency. Available at: http://en.mercopress.com/2010/11/23/brazil-s-air-transport-infrastructure-is-a-growing-disaster-says-iata (accessed September 12, 2013).

Oliveira, Nelza (2011), 'Railroads Poised to Reduce Logistical Bottlenecks in Brazil'. Infosurhoy.com, 22 February 2011. Available at: http://infosurhoy.com/en_GB/articles/saii/features/economy/2011/02/22/feature-02 (accessed October 2, 2013).

OSEC (2010), 'The Brazilian Market for Railway Technologies', OSEC, Business Network Switzerland. Available at: http://www.s-ge.com/de/filefield-private/files/1672/field_blog_public_files/7918 (accessed September 19, 2013).

Palmer, Jared S. (2010), 'The Cargo Theft Threat', Inbound Logistics, January 2010. Available at: http://www.inboundlogistics.com/cms/article/the-cargo-theft-threat/ (accessed May 2, 2014).

Pires, Cristine (2011a), 'Brazilian Highways Taking Opposite Direction Than Economic Growth'. Infosurhoy.com, 15 February 2011. Available at: http://infosurhoy.com/en_GB/articles/saii/features/main/2011/02/15/feature-02 (accessed October 2, 2013).

Pires, Cristine (2011b), 'Brazil: Waterways Gain Prominence in 2011'. Infosurhoy.com. Available at: http://infosurhoy.com/en_GB/articles/saii/features/economy/2011/03/01/feature-03 (accessed October 16, 2013).

Puin, Karolina (2012), 'Cargo Transportation Costs in Brazil'. The Brazil Business. Available at: http://thebrazilbusiness.com/article/cargo-transportation-costs-in-brazil (accessed March 14, 2014).

Purtell, Dan and Rice, Jr., James B. (2013), 'Assessing Cargo Supply Risk'. Published on Security Managed at http://www.securitymanagement.com. Available at: http://www.securitymanagement.com/article/assessing-cargo-supply-risk (accessed October 12, 2013).

Queiroz, Acacio (2012), 'Brazil's Carnival of Cargo Theft', *Risk Management* – Digital

Edition, August. Available at: http://www.rmmagazine.com/2012/08/01/brazils-carnival-of-cargo-theft/ (accessed October 2, 2013).

Raso, Ebe (2012), 'Transportation (Other than Aviation)'. Report found on export.org website. Available at: http://export.gov/brazil/static/CC_BR_DoingBusiness_CCG_PDF_Chap4_Transportation_Latest_eg_br_063770.pdf (accessed November 15, 2013).

Renno, Marcelo (2009), 'Overview of the Pipeline Industry in Brazil: Capturing Pipeline Opportunities', Brazilian Petroleum, Gas and Biofuels Institute. Available at: http://www.braziltexas.org/attachments/contentmanagers/767/Capturing-Pipeline-Opps-in-Brazil.pdf (accessed November 2, 2013).

Rother, Larry (2012), *Brazil on the Rise: The Story of a Country Transformed*, New York: Palgrave Macmillan.

SCI (2011), 'The Brazilian Railway Market: Facts, Figures, Players and Trends'. Report by SCI Verkehr GmbH. Available at: http://www.sci.de/uploads/tx_edocuments/MC_Brazil_Product_Information.pdf (accessed October 28, 2013).

Spinetto, Juan Pablo and Sciaudone, Christiana (2013), 'In Brazil, Road Bandits Force Switch to Sea Shipping', *Bloomberg Businessweek*, June 20, 2013. Available at: http://www.businessweek.com/articles/2013-06-20/in-brazil-road-bandits-force-switch-to-sea-shipping (accessed October 12, 2013).

UPI (2013), 'Price Gouging, Random Violence Blight Run-up to Brazil World Cup'. Available at: http://www.upi.com/Top_News/Special/2013/11/06/Price-gouging-random-violence-blight-run-up-to-Brazil-World-Cup/97331383781042/ (accessed May 5, 2014).

Utsumi, Igor (2014), 'Stolen Cargo in Brazil', *The Brazil Business*. Available at: http://thebrazilbusiness.com/article/stolen-cargo-in-brazil (accessed May 5, 2014).

PART III

Multimodal passenger transportation security: themes and frameworks

12. Challenges for multimodal passenger transport

Monika Bak and Jan Burnewicz

1. INTRODUCTION – CONCEPTS, TERMS AND DEFINITIONS FOR MULTIMODAL PASSENGER TRANSPORT

The forms of passenger transport analysed in publications and research reports are most frequently described by two notions – as multimodal transport and intermodal transport. It should be determined if there is any difference and what the difference is between these two terms. As far as the transport of goods is concerned the essence of these terms has already been set while in case of passenger transport quite substantial freedom of interpretation has been observed. The view that these terms are synonyms cannot be accepted (see Bockstael-Blok, 2001), nor can the idea that one notion is more popular in use in the US while the other in Europe. The majority of publications and Internet sources contain the statement underlying the difference in the essence of the two analysed modes of transport. The observation that the difference between these two terms lies in the fact that the multimodal term refers to passenger transport while intermodality refers to freight transport is a moot point (Sitran et al., 2011). In the case of freight transport *Glossary for Transport Statistics* confirms clearly that intermodal transport is a special type of multimodal transport.[1] Although there is no similar official interpretation referring to passenger transport one can assume that also in this case the relationship between these two terms is similar.

Many authors of publications and reports point to the lack of definitions of passenger multimodal and intermodal transport (Bak et al., 2012). In fact, the attempts to define them are limited to very succinct terms. The efforts in defining them are limited to the statement that both types of transport include at least two different modes which can be used in a door-to-door transport chain in the integrated way. In the literature, multimodal transport was defined as a combination of two or more modes of movement of goods or passengers such as air, road, rail or maritime. This combination does not require interoperability between the modes, they simply exist parallel to each other (Kozak and Szendro, 2011). Quite an accurate differentiation of both forms of transport is included in the final report of the SUTRANET research project:

> Multimodality implies that there is more than one modal option on a particular route or in a particular transport corridor. This also implies that there is a choice between at least two different modes of transport. Intermodality is characteristic of such transport system that allows at least two different modes to be used in an integrated manner in a door-to-door transport. (Kristiansen and Johannsen, 2005–2007, pp. 1–2 [5–6])

The difference between multimodality and intermodality is not only limited to the fact that in a multimodal system transport modes are in parallel relations while in an intermodal system they are in relay order. Multimodality is a more complex system because there are both monomodal and intermodal options as alternative solutions. In the case of multimodality its chief feature is a great freedom in the choice of modes and transport systems, in the case of intermodality there may be only one option in a given transport corridor.

It is obvious that direct transport is most convenient for the user. Creating intermodal transport systems is justified in reducing inconveniencies connected with the change of transport means and not in replacing direct movement by one means of transport. However, there is a difference in the degree of technological and organizational maturity of the forms of multimodal transport of goods and passengers existing at present.

In practice, multimodal systems of movement of goods are more mature as their efficiency has been provided by a number of technical and organizational innovations. The concept of multimodal passenger transport is still developing and it will never be as strictly integrated as multimodal freight transport. The passenger is able to cover a certain distance from one means of transport to another going on foot, whereas a load requires movement even on the smallest distance. Not long ago discussions about multimodal transport were mainly focused on freight movements. More attention was devoted to this form of transport in the US than in Europe (Button, 2003).

The idea of creating intermodal systems is only sensible when they gain advantage over monomodal systems as far as economical, functional, ecological, social reasons and security are taken into account. Intermodality focuses on connecting a few various modes in a seamless transport system by efficient intermodal interchange terminals. Intermodal terminals of transport nodes are probably the most significant part of an intermodal transport network. If intermodal interchanges are slow or inconvenient for users they will look at a monomodal system as more efficient. To use intermodal transport means in the best way that coordination and cooperation of all monomodal bodies is required while planning all intermodal interchange terminals (Anderson et al., 1995).

Passenger intermodality is a policy and planning principle that aims to provide a passenger using different modes of transport in a combined trip chain with a seamless journey (Müller et al., 2004a). In the European Union's (EU) transport policy the notion of co-modal transport was formed, which is characterized by optimal structure of multimodal forms. Co-modality is the notion which was used for the first time in the EU in 2006 and it refers to the intelligent use of two or more modes of transport to obtain the greatest benefit from each of them to make the whole journey most sustainable. Optimalization means the balance in the use of sources in the context of economical, environmental and social benefits.

2. MULTIMODAL PASSENGER TRANSPORT NEEDS

2.1 Physical Infrastructure

Physical infrastructure plays a key role in the development of interconnections. It is impossible to provide well-functioning multimodal passenger transport with non-provision or with an inadequate standard of infrastructure. Additionally, the identification of basic problems of interconnections proves that beside inadequate provision of services and information, actually poor design, maintenance and the operation of physical infrastructure are the crucial barriers for multimodal transport integration.

The starting point for the evaluation of potential infrastructure should be its classification. The physical elements of the multimodal passenger journey can be classified into three types of journey stages, each one part of the overall, multimodal, door-to-door trip from the origin to the destination points (Enei et al., 2011, p. 10):

- The short-distance (first/last mile) feeder/distributor journey stage that can be situated at the origin or destination of the intermodal journey.
- The interchange or transport node journey stage, in which the traveller has access to a distribution system or to transhipment/ intermediary locations within the transport network. With reference to the passenger transport this function is mainly serviced by stations, transport terminals, airports and ports, where the transport flows originate, end or are being transhipped from one mode to the other.

- The main trip journey stage, representing the lengthier segment of the trip that can be made by road (coach, bus, car), rail (train), air (airplane) or ship.

The network design as a background for multimodal infrastructure provision is fundamental then both for transport links (feeder journey stage and main trip stage) and nodes. Reducing congestion and travel time, as well as providing efficient infrastructure for safe and comfortable journeys are crucial challenges. At the EU level there is even the need expressed in the official document (Directive 2010/40) for so called open-system architecture[2] which defines the functionalities and interfaces necessary for the interoperability/interconnection with infrastructure systems and facilities.

As for *transport links* all modes are involved, and beyond the traditional meaning of infrastructure connections some special solutions can be developed aiming at improving multimodality. Examples of specific solutions of potential links involved in a multimodal journey can be classified as (Enei et al., 2011; Sammer et al., 2009):

- Availability of long-distance modes and quality of connections, e.g. Maglev link as in Shanghai Pudong Airport.
- Availability of public transport for access to and egress from the terminal, e.g. metro/s-Bahn links in many airports or railways and ferry terminals, or tram links used in connecting railway stations but also in airports, e.g. in Sydney etc.
- Provision of direct access to the major road network (e.g. motorway), which is already a universal solution in many airports.
- Supply of car parks or garages and park and ride facilities.
- Availability of taxis in a central location.
- Existence of cycle lanes leading to/from the interchange point or availability of cycle stands.

Efficient infrastructure for multimodality also requires the provision of well-designed *interchanges*. The current status of existing interchanges reveals many shortcomings, e.g. designing nodes is often seemingly treated in a superficial manner. In some cases the function of interchange becomes subsidiary to the form (for example, an architecturally superb station that is really difficult for travellers to use). In other cases the concept of interchange seems stunningly absent (with a town's bus, coach and rail stations located well away from each other).[3] As an example, the survey evidence in Korea shows that the major impediments to the use of high-speed trains are poor access to stations and inconvenient transfers from trains to local transport modes. Better access to and from terminals, as well as convenient transfer design and operation between modes can boost passenger use (International Transport Forum, 2012). On the other hand, one can also give some examples of good practice access and transfer design and operation, e.g. in Swiss cities, where the routes and timetables of trains and buses are coordinated. There are many examples of solutions which can improve interchange infrastructure (Bonsall et al., 2010), e.g. moving walkways, elevators and escalators, level access to trains and buses, visibility axis between modes, direct, uninterrupted, logical paths, provision of assistance for travellers with reduced mobility, tactile guidance systems for the disabled, multilingual or pictogram information, provision of monitoring cameras, cycle facilities at modal interchanges, and multimodal information and ticketing booths.

2.2 Technology Facilitating Passenger Intermodality

Technological development contributes to transport development in many ways, including improvement of passenger intermodality. It was presented most clearly at the EU level, where in the policy paper (EC, 2011a) it was indicated that infrastructure technological upgrading, e.g. to be obtained through a full deployment of many applications of ICT (information and communication technology), is considered to play an important role in improving:

- Modal transport efficiency, by making vehicles and infrastructure more intelligent.
- Market integration, since technological upgrading is essential to transport operations and the lack of interoperability creates the barrier between borders.
- The simplification and harmonization of administrative procedures, thus reducing the cost associated with trans-border operations.

It should be stressed that technological solutions, both ICT and ITS (intelligent transportation systems), may improve the main or long-distance leg, as well as the local links of the intermodal journey, but may also favour integration among modes, supporting in such a way the development of co-modal and intermodal solutions as well. ICT solutions improving co-modality can be classified into the following five categories (Bielefeldt et al., 2013):

- Transportation management systems – covering ICTs, the aim of which is to help in planning and running the transport system in an efficient manner.

- Traveller information systems – solutions designed in order to provide travellers with information (travel time, routes, traffic conditions, etc.).
- Smart ticketing and tolling applications – ICTs addressing ways to get tickets and to pay for using transport services.
- Smart vehicles and infrastructure – including:
  - ICTs aimed at improving vehicle operation;
  - vehicle-to-vehicle (V2V);
  - vehicle-to-infrastructure (V2I) communications.
- Demand-responsive transport (DRT) and shared mobility systems – covering ICTs fostering transport services adjusted to demand.

The review of programmes and implementations of technology facilitating passenger intermodality highlights differentiated approaches and advancements in specific regions all over the world.

In Japan a lot of effort was made to improve integration in passenger transport through technological improvements at the level of the Ministry of Land, Infrastructure, Transport and Tourism (Yamamoto, 2011). Some examples already developed in Japan can be mentioned in line with improving the accessibility and safety of pedestrians, interactive communication between bus on-board units and roadside beacons, control of traffic signals, and arrival times displayed at bus stops. New approaches are developed aiming at the integration of land use planning and transport (e.g. transit-oriented development plan in Toyama city), as well as a demand-responsive transport service (e.g. on demand bus in Nakamura City).

Similarly, in China technology developments improving passenger inter-modality are treated as a priority of the national transport policy, which means subsequently the realization of investment projects. Among China's major objectives are the following: intelligent public transport management and service, multimodal passenger transit centres' management and service, and traveller information service and electronic payments for the use of infrastructure (Wang, 2013).

In many regions of the US ICT has been developed extensively in transport for multimodality improvements. In the transport strategy for Virginia, for example, mobility, connectivity and accessibility are treated as a priority to facilitate the easy movement of people, to improve the interconnectivity of regions and activity centres, and to provide access to different modes of transportation. Implementation of new technologies is promoted in the transportation policy plan for 2035 (VTrans, 2012).

In Russia too the objectives of efficient and technologically advanced multimodal passenger transport have started to play an increasingly important role in transport policy. As an example of recent investments, the Lastochka express train linking the city of Adler with Sochi's airport, constructed for Sochi 2014, can be mentioned. Also worthy of mention is one of the biggest transport infrastructure projects in Europe aiming at multimodality improvement – a high-tech multipurpose passenger transport interchange complex – Kalanchevskiy – which will link three Moscow airports (Vnukovo, Domodedovo and Sheremetyevo) with the railway station and metro and public transport in general.

2.3 Transferability of Best Practices

One of the most important questions for multimodal passenger transport is whether best practice examples can be introduced easily in other places and in other contexts (e.g. transfer from urban area to rural area, from high to low GDP area etc.). Good transferability results would improve the global picture of multimodality in the transport sector.

Starting from general conceptual frameworks adopted in previous research projects, an effort was made in the COMPASS project (optimized co-modal passenger transport for reducing carbon emissions) to enrich the framework with other potential aspects of interest for the evaluation of transferability. Three main aspects are considered for the transferability assessment of ICT solutions improving co-modality (Bak et al., 2013):

- Applicability of the solution – the spatial area and the demand segment addressed by the solution; co-modality refers to solutions that can be implemented in an urban area, in a rural area or at a regional or corridor level, and that can intercept different demand segments (i.e. short-distance or long-distance, the latter being also national or international).
- Interest in the solution – three different groups of stakeholders are considered: the traveller, the operator and the government.
- Feasibility of the solution – investigated in relation to the following set of stakeholders: financier, regulator, technology supplier and non-users.

Based on the cross-cutting analysis for solutions investigated by COMPASS case studies the conclusion can be drawn that transferability assessment is considered a delicate matter which is strongly influenced by the subjective perceptions and experiences of all stakeholders involved, and that these might differ quite a lot from country to country and from zone to zone, making it very complex to reach an indisputable point of view. When taking into account different transferability dimensions, different types of barriers are more or less important in given situations. Yet, it was possible to identify the strongest influences – the most significant and difficult to overcome barriers resulting from low interest for operators and low feasibility for financiers. In addition, the lack of interest for travellers generates implementation barriers. Other factors, like low interest for government or low feasibility for regulators, technology suppliers or non-users seem to be easier to overcome.

The applicability of the ICT solutions tested shows that it is usually high regardless of the region and context. ICTs bundled together, while more complex than single-use solutions, offer more benefits to the users due to the synergy effects and are still well transferable. Interest for travellers is varied and is solution-dependent rather than location-dependent. The level of interest of travellers for ICTs is strongly related to the perceived benefits deriving from their exploitation: most of these are related to the quality level and to the timing of information delivered to final users.

The interest of operators towards the diffusion of applications to transport is strongly influenced by the benefits achievable from their implementation and by the balance between the costs (financial and organizational on the operator side) and the operator's expected benefits. Organizational and institutional aspects are another condition of transferability success. Issues such as obtaining interest and support from major stakeholders, most typically at national and local government, are the most significant.

The interest of governments is conditioned on the role of ICT in fulfilling policy objectives. Governments are more likely to promote and support those ICTs which contribute to the achievement of specific policy goals (e.g. reduction of CO_2 emissions) as compared to ICTs which only contribute to the user's wellness (i.e. those only increasing the user's comfort). Then, of course, the financial side of ICTs is a challenging issue in their development. Profitability – evaluated in terms of additional revenues compared with the overall magnitude of costs for the implementation of the solution – is generally low and is further accompanied by a generally low likelihood of benefiting from international and also national funding. The scale of investment is often unclear but is required to meet the capital costs of design, planning and implementation.

As far as technology supply is concerned, the analysis revealed that the level of technology to be made available by the end-user for investigated solutions varies. For some solutions it is only a matter of the development of non-resource consuming applications for existing technologies (e.g. applications for smartphones); for others, investment in transport technology and/or an increase in the capacity of telecommunication networks is needed. In general terms, higher transferability potential can be expected for those solutions requiring no or limited provision of technology equipment by the operator and/or end-users. Technology can be a barrier only if it indicates a lack of technical capacity or when given solutions are not transferable.

Finally, it has to be added that from the travellers' perspective the major problems would be the lack of full realization of possible benefits, unspecified user needs, or the difficult measurement of benefits for the user. Additionally, as is emphasized by Preston (2012), behavioural barriers should be treated very seriously. There is a general difficulty that has been faced in defining the integration concept. It is argued that the ladder of integration can be a useful tool in the framing policy. Another behavioural barrier relates to difficulties in 'operationalizing' the concept and then the lack of practical evidence on the success of integrated policies. The behavioural change that the integration requires, both for individuals and institutions, can also be a barrier. Additionally, for non-users externalities, mainly environmental impacts, can be mentioned as a potential constraint in developing multimodal solutions.

3. POTENTIAL FOR THE IMPROVEMENT OF REGIONAL ACCESSIBILITY

The integration of passenger transport systems can bring positive effects in the form of increased transport accessibility to regions. It is difficult to dispute the thesis that creating coherent transport chains connected with multimodal hubs, which shorten travellers' interchange times, brings a similar effect as increasing the speed of means of transport on transport routes. Regional development can be stimulated by increasing passenger and goods transport accessibility, but there may be dilemmas and conflicts when determining the improvement priorities of these two kinds of accessibility.

Improving the passenger transport accessibility of all centres of a region is not possible by creating direct monomodal connections for each of them with the capital of the region or important centres outside the region. The network of such connections would be too dense and too expensive. Thus, in practice, a network of common connections of lower density is created in such a way that the chosen bigger centres play the role of hubs and interchange points. These hubs are serviced efficiently by public transport only when their passengers are offered intermodal transport with the smallest number of changes (the best option being when only one is necessary). When there are too many changes passengers give up the intermodal offer, even when the hubs are equipped with integrating infrastructure, when travellers are provided with up-to-date online information, and when there are intermodal ticketing, rate and scheduling systems. Investing only in the linear infrastructure of the region, particularly in the road infrastructure, can speed up the process of turning passengers away from intermodal transport. Congestion appears on a smaller scale in regional road transport than in urban transport, and traffic congestion, though less great, does not encourage travellers to be interested in intermodal transport.

In many cases infrastructural investment cannot bring absolute advantages, but only capital relocation among regions. Advantages for one region or town may be accompanied by losses for others; thus, the final effect can be neutral or even negative. So when assessing the effects of implementation of transport infrastructure investment it is necessary to identify the effects of distributional and generative character (Koźlak, 2012).

Depending on the geographical location, as well as economic and social specificity, passenger mobility in the given region can have a various structure: in one case interregional transport can dominate, in another case transport in relations outside the region can dominate. In the latter, improvement of the domestic and international accessibility of the region generally requires development of intermodal systems, because neither air nor rail transport is possible without complementary feeders to airports and rail stations by other means. Regions located peripherally on the continent, which are economically and socially troublesome for regions located centrally, are doomed in terms of the benefits of intermodal systems. In Europe the travel time from the most peripherally located regions to the centrally located areas is sometimes several hours (Péraldi, 2004). Improving their accessibility requires undertakings not only in the linear infrastructure, and means of transport, but also in integrating the means and streamlined transport chains as far as significant reductions in travel time are concerned.

The reliability of passenger transport systems is another important attribute in both urban and long-distance transport. A multimodal system offers a greater guarantee of reliability, as when there are traffic disruptions to one mode there is an available alternative. In an intermodal chain, failure in any one link causes the whole system to stop. When providing satisfactory transport accessibility to regions there is always a dilemma of whether to choose a multimodal or an intermodal solution. The solution to such a dilemma must be based on many criteria, including financial, functional and social criteria.

4. POLICY AND LEGAL FRAMEWORKS FACILITATING INTERMODAL COOPERATION

The main reason for the current poor progress in the development of intermodal systems of passenger transport is the monomodal character of carriers' activities and the concentration of attention in transport policy on the problems of individual transport modes. Users of passenger transport services do not exert distinct pressure for setting up intermodal systems, valuing most highly direct monomodal transport (mainly individual motor cars). This means that without an active and efficient transport policy the acceleration of intermodal system development processes is not possible.

In recent years in many countries and integration groupings the necessity of promoting the development of intermodal passenger systems has, at least formally, been underlined. The policy supporting the development of these systems must be based on comprehensible premises and objectives acceptable by the society. This is not a simple task taking into consideration the fact that there are various expectations in urban and long-distance intermodal transport. Politicians consider intermodality chiefly from the point of view of sustainable transport development; transport users expect mostly greater efficiency and lower costs.

Notes on passenger intermodality can be found in documents dealing with the transport policy of some states. In contrast to the policy of supporting intermodality in freight transport there are only vague declarations in the case of passenger transport. As was noted by Müller et al., intermodality is generally observed in political documents, but its practical implementation is still invisible in many fields (Müller et al., 2004b).

The integration of passenger transport in the common transport policy carried out in the EU between 1962 and 2013 achieved a limited range of political, regulatory and financial solutions. Considerably more precise integration concepts were presented in the Green Papers from 1995 and 2007 than in the more decision-making-type White Papers on Transport of 2001 and 2011 (Burnewicz, 2012). One of the first official EU references to the problem of passenger transport integration was found in the European Commission's Announcement from 1992, in which the significance of public transport integrity as a condition of making passenger transport integration more attractive than the alternative private motor transport was underlined (Commission of the European Communities, 1992). Nevertheless, none of the ideas formulated in the announcement was implemented in practice by any form of legal act (directive or order) or any community programme. In 1995, in the Green Paper 'The Citizens' Network', an in-depth survey of technical, organizational, information and ticketing solutions – which were possible for practical application and which were integrating urban passenger transport – were presented (Commission of the European Communities, 1995), but the solutions are still to be implemented by means of appropriate political decisions and legal regulations. The issues of passenger transport integration in common transport policy appeared also in the text of the White Paper on Transport in 2001, where emphasis was placed on providing journey continuity in towns and in long-distance transport, including via the integration of high-speed trains with air transport (Commission of the European Communities, 2001). Yet the recommendations of this document have not been implemented. In the Commission's Communication announcement from 2006, referring to the White Paper from 2001, the introduction of the notion of passenger transport co-modality is a novelty; the term is understood as the optimalization of resources necessary for transport's operation (Commission of the European Communities, 2006). In the Green Paper 'Towards a New Culture for Urban Mobility', the proposals included in the Green Paper from 1995 were updated, stressing the necessity of the development of ITS systems and the integration of urban transport with pedestrian and bicycle traffic (Commission of the European Communities, 2007). In the Green Paper from 2009 the need for the reorientation of TEN-T development was underlined, so that due to co-modality it became more efficient and more environmentally-friendly for both the movement of goods and passengers (European Commission, 2011). The latest EU White Paper on Transport from 2011 contains new ideas and recommendations referring to intermodality and passenger transport integration. Attention was focused on determining which technical, organizational and financial means were necessary for further integration of various means of passenger transport to provide undisturbed door-to-door journeys. The following factors were underlined as significant: the development and application of intelligence systems; interoperability and multimodal scheduling; journey and traffic information in real time; Internet booking and intelligent tickets; the setting up of international multimodal operators; and the means of providing continuity of service in case of traffic disruption. Great emphasis was placed on innovations which allow faster integration of passenger transport processes (European Commission, 2011). The Commission also presented the concept of passenger rights in all means of transport; rights which constitute a complementary issue in relation to the idea of providing a continuous door-to-door journey.

As observed by Christiaens et al., passenger intermodality is implemented in the whole of Europe and the following activities are of special significance: a) door-to-door information and ticketing; b) intermodal networks and interchanges; and c) integration of long-distance travel with the last urban mile. Long-distance passenger intermodality must become a central pillar of the new EU transport policy and this policy priority must be well promoted at the national and European political level and backed up by European tools to implement the policy (Christiaens et al., 2011). Similarly, as in the US, European specialists and politicians must pay special attention to air and rail transport integration (Button, 2003).

The practical implementation of supporting passenger intermodality in the EU is based not only on the ideas worked out in academic circles, but also on the legal acts introduced and the available funds. Up until now the following issues have been covered by legal regulations: public passenger transport services by rail and by road; the introduction of more market forces in the provision of public transport services (Regulation (EC) 1370/2007); the rights of air passengers (Regulation (EC) 261/2004 and Council Regulation (EC) 2027/97); the rights of passengers travelling by sea and inland waterway (Regulation (EU) 1177/2010); the rights of passengers in bus and coach transport (Regulation (EU) 181/2011); rail passengers' rights (Regulation (EC) 1371/2007); the rights of people with reduced mobility in air transport (Regulation (EC) 1107/2006); and telematics applications for passenger services of the trans-European rail system (Commission Regulations (EU) 454/2011 and 665/2012).

The technical and organizational solutions regarding setting up multimodal nodes, online electronic information systems, electronic tickets and other intermodality elements require additional financial means from public and non-public sources. However, in the EU there have been no special programmes for financing passenger intermodality, as PACT and Marco Polo programmes refer to freight intermodality. In practice, public funding structures rarely fit well with complicated multi-player, multimodal projects with a long preparation time, uncertain timelines and no simple categorization of measures. European funding programmes in particular have almost no compatibility with door-to-door, long-distance intermodal projects (Müller et al., 2004a).

In the US, the policy supporting passenger intermodality had its beginnings in the 1990s. Intermodal connections, the links that allow passengers to switch from one mode to another to complete a trip, have been an important element of federal transportation policy since the passage of the Intermodal Surface Transportation Efficiency Act of 1991 (ISTEA). There is a general consensus that the US passenger transportation system has become more intermodally linked since the passage of ISTEA, but the degree of that connectivity has never been measured. The Intermodal Passenger Connectivity Database (IPCD) was developed to provide a baseline connectivity measurement against which to measure future progress. According to Lockwood, federal and state support for intermodal transportation has concentrated on four areas: 1) encouraging intermodal facilities in state-wide and regional plans, focused on expanding hub terminals and intermodal access to them; 2) support for coordinated planning for interregional freight and passenger corridors of regional and national significance, including ad hoc state and regional entities; 3) eligibility for financial support in overcoming major bottlenecks – typically intermodal access to ports, airports and terminals – through new types of federal loans and credit support; and 4) research to support improved systems of operations and management, including improved trucker and traveller information systems (Lockwood, 2003). On the other hand, Buehler and Hamre maintain that multimodality is gaining recognition as a potential strategy for reducing automobile reliance and increasing the efficiency and sustainability of transportation systems (Buehler and Hamre, 2013).

Thus far in the EU, more attention has been paid by politicians to promoting urban transport multimodality and intermodality, while in US greater pressure is put on transport integration over long-distance journeys. The weakness of American multimodality in these trips is the low-quality rail services and the lack of such solutions as European high-speed rails. According to the parameters of the FAA Modernization and Reform Act of 2012, Congress decided to commission research into the conditions for increasing integration of passenger air transport with rail services. The research task, defined as 'Air-Rail Code Sharing Study', was to explain, among other things, 'the potential costs to taxpayers and other parties and benefits of the implementation of more integrated scheduling between airlines and Amtrak or other intercity passenger rail carriers achieved through code sharing arrangements' (FAA Modernization and Reform Act of 2012).

The policy of supporting intermodal integration in passenger transport is more and more visible in other countries in the world, especially in Japan, China, Indonesia, Latin American countries, Russia and others.

As Perkins noted, the interconnected Japanese rail and bus service networks serving the metropolitan areas located along the spine of the high speed Shinkansen rail lines act as the largest seamless public transport system in the world (Perkins, 2012). With airports, Shinkansen, metro-rail and tollways optimized for more electric-powered vehicles, Japan will seamlessly interconnect a balanced intermodal passenger transport network, with minimal dependence on fossil fuels (Dorsey, 2013).

In China the policy of supporting passenger intermodality is a new one, caused by increasing congestion, a rise in energy consumption and the increasing negative impact of the transport sector on the environment. As outlined by Wan and Liu, in order to address the problem of its sparse infrastructure, China plans to construct more than 12 000 kilometres of new high-speed tracks for passenger transportation and plans to separate the passenger transportation line from the freight line (Wan and Liu, 2008). The construction of many multimodal hubs is planned, which would facilitate passengers' access to high-speed rail journeys.

In Russia's transport policy the need for intermodal integration is observed in both long-distance traffic and urban transport. Passenger rail is also essential to economic growth – not just for travel and tourism, but also for the mobility of the labour force. For urban development in particular, integrated intermodal transport systems are necessary to relieve Moscow's notorious congestion. According to Donchenko, one of the principal problems of urban transport in Russia is the inefficiency of UPT management at city level: a lack of clear strategies for UPT development and management; frequently inefficient managing structures; poor interfacing of different kinds of UPT; and the practical absence of multimodal urban passenger transport, and so on (Donchenko, 2004).

5. CONCLUSIONS

The major challenge for multimodal passenger transport is how to achieve greater efficiency and reduce the environmental impact of passenger transport by judicious encouragement of integration, cooperation and, where appropriate, competition in the provision of multimodal passenger transport. Then it is necessary to solve the major problems associated with multimodality. These concern the physical infrastructure and include the non-provision of local and main links – or the inadequate standard of the infrastructure for these – but also include the poor design, maintenance or operation of modal interchange points. But it should be remembered that there is great potential for technological applications – such as ICT and ITS solutions – to be implemented in order to make multimodal transport more efficient, quicker, and more environmentally and passenger friendly.

The best practice examples of applications improving multimodality in specific contexts have already been analysed well. But their transferability is not always feasible. Therefore, there is a need to disseminate the effects of specific solutions and implementations, as well as to suggest a transferability approach including the assessment of the applicability of the solution in different contexts, the interest in the solution, and the feasibility of the solution.

The integration of passenger transport systems can bring positive effects to regions in the form of increased transport accessibility. Improving passenger transport accessibility in all centres of a region is not possible by creating direct monomodal connections from each of them to the capital of the region or important centres outside the region. Thus, in practice a network of common connections of lower density is created in such a way that the chosen bigger centres play the role of hubs and interchange points. These hubs are serviced efficiently by public transport only when its passengers are offered intermodal transport with the smallest number of changes (the best being when only one journey is necessary).

Users of passenger transport services do not exert a particular pressure to set up intermodal systems, and value direct monomodal transport most highly (mainly individual motor cars). This means that without an active and efficient transport policy the acceleration of intermodal system development processes is not possible. Intermodality is generally observed in political documents, but its practical implementation is still invisible in many fields. Thus far, in the EU greater attention has been paid by politicians to promoting urban transport multimodality and intermodality, while in the US greater pressure is put on transport integration for long-distance journeys. The policy of supporting intermodal integration in passenger transport is more and more visible in other countries in the world, especially in Japan, China, Indonesia, Latin American countries, Russia, and others.

NOTES

1. See Convention on International Multimodal Transport of Goods, United Nations, Geneva, 24 May 1980, Article 1 – Definitions (Convention failed to come into effect); *Glossary for Transport Statistics*. Document prepared by the Intersecretariat Working Group on Transport Statistics, European Communities, United Nations Economic Commission for Europe, European Conference of Ministers of Transport, 2003. Third edition available at: http://epp.eurostat.ec.europa.eu/cache/ITY_OFFPUB/KS-BI-03-002/EN/KS-BI-03-002-EN.PDF, p. 103.
2. This term appeared in the Directive 2010/40 (EC, 2011c) of the European Parliament and of the Council of 7 July 2010 on the framework for the deployment of Intelligent Transport Systems in the field of road transport and for interfaces with other modes of transport, OJ L 207/1.
3. Here also sometimes the term 'transport integration' is used simply to mean a well-designed interchange. For more, see Stephen (2010).

REFERENCES

Anderson, S. E. et al. (1995), 'Towards the Future: The Promise of Intermodal and Multimodal Transportation Systems', Center for Transportation Research University of Texas at Austin. Available at: http://library.ctr.utexas.edu/digitized/swutc/60017_71249-3.pdf (accessed 27 September 2015).

Bak, M., Borkowski, P., Pawlowska, B. (2012), 'Passenger Transport Interconnectivity as a Stimulator of Sustainable Transport Development in the European Union', in P. Golinska and M. Hajdul (eds) *Sustainable Transport. New Trends and Business Practices*. Berlin: Springer. Available at: http://link.springer.com/chapter/10.1007%2F978-3-642-23550-4_2#page-1 (accessed 27 September 2015).

Bak, M., Borkowski, P., de Stasio, C., Di Bartolo, C., Brambilla, M., Maffii, S. (2013), 'Transferability of Solutions', Working Paper of COMPASS, co-funded by FP7. TRI, Edinburgh Napier University, Edinburgh, November 2013.

Bielefeldt, C., Bak, M., Carreno, M., Matthews, B., Stewart, K., Caramanico, G., Cooper, J., Enei, R., Biosca, O., Shibayama, T., De Stasio, C., Schnell, O. (2013), 'COMPASS – Final Results and Conclusions', Deliverable 2.1 of COMPASS, co-funded by FP7. TRI, Edinburgh Napier University, Edinburgh, November 2013.

Bockstael-Blok, W. (2001), *Chains and Networks in Multimodal Passenger Transport: Exploring a Design Approach*, Delft University Press, January 2001.

Bonsall, P., Abrantes, P., Bak, M., Bielefeldt, C., Borkowski, P., Maffii, S., Mandel, B., Matthews, B., Shires, J., Pawlowska, B., Schnell, O., de Stasio, C. (2010), 'An Analysis of Potential Solutions for Improving Interconnectivity of Passenger Networks', Deliverable 3.1, INTERCONNECT, co-funded by FP7. TRI, Edinburgh Napier University, Edinburgh, May 2010.

Buehler, R. and Hamre, A. (2013), 'Trends and Determinants of Multimodal Travel in the USA', Virginia Tech. Washington DC. Available at: http://ntl.bts. gov/lib/48000/48500/48583/VT-2012-09.pdf (accessed 12 November 2013).

Burnewicz, J. (2012), 'Transport Policy Towards Integration of Passenger Transport', in M. Bak (ed.) *Integration of Passenger Transport in European Union*. Zeszyty Naukowe Ekonomika Transportu i Logistyka (in Polish). University of Gdansk.

Button, K. (2003), 'The European Market for Airline Transportation and Multimodalism', *Airports as Multimodal Interchange Nodes*. Report of the One Hundred And Twenty Sixth Round Table on Transport Economics. European Conference of Ministers of Transport. Held in Paris on 20–21 March 2003.

Christiaens, J. et al. (2011), 'Intermodal Passenger Transport in Europe. Passenger Intermodality from A to Z', The European Forum on Intermodal Passenger Travel. Available at: http://www.mobiel21.be/sites/default/files/publications/ Brochure%20link%20kleiner.pdf (accessed 20 November 2013).

Commission of the European Communities (1992), 'The Future Development of the Common Transport Policy. A Global Approach to the Construction of a Community Framework for Sustainable Mobility', Communication from the Commission. Document drawn up on the basis of COM(92) 494 final, 2 December 1992. White Paper. Available at: http://aei.pitt.edu/1116/1/future_ transport_policy_wp_COM_92_494.pdf (accessed 19 November 2013).

Commission of the European Communities (1995), 'The Citizens' Network. Fulfilling the Potential of Public Passenger Transport in Europe', European Commission Green Paper. Commission of the European Communities. COM(95) 601 final, Brussels, 29 November 1995. Available at: http://eur-lex.europa.eu/LexUriServ/LexUriServ.do?uri=COM:1995:0601:FIN:EN:PDF (accessed 5 December 2013).

Commission of the European Communities (2001), 'White Paper. European Transport Policy for 2010: Time to Decide', COM(2001) 370 final, Brussels, 12 September 2001. Available at: http://ec.europa.eu/transport/themes/strategies/ doc/2001_white_paper/lb_com_2001_0370_en.pdf (accessed 15 December 2013).

Commission of the European Communities (2006), 'Keep Europe Moving – Sustainable Mobility for Our Continent. Mid-term Review of the European Commission's 2001 Transport White Paper', Communication from the Commission to the Council and the European Parliament. COM(2006) 314 final, Brussels, 22 June 2006. Available at: http://eur-lex.europa.eu/LexUriServ/ LexUriServ.do?uri=COM:2006:0314:FIN:EN:PDF (accessed 27 September 2015).

Commission of the European Communities (2007), 'Green Paper. Towards a New Culture for Urban Mobility', COM(2007) 551 final, Brussels, 25 September 2007. Available at: http://eur-lex.europa.eu/LexUriServ/site/en/com/2007/com2007_0551en01.pdf (accessed 20 November 2013).

Donchenko, V. (2004), Policies Ensuring the Sustainable Development of Urban Transport Systems in Russia. Conference on Implementing Sustainable Urban Travel Policies in Russia and Other CIS Countries. Moscow, 30 September–1 October 2004. Available at: http://www.internationaltransportforum.org/IntOrg/ecmt/urban/Moscow04/Donchenko.pdf (accessed 27 September 2015).

Dorsey, T. (2013), 'Interstate High Speed Rail Progress', SoulOfAmerica. Available at: http://soulofamerica.com/interact/soulofamerica-travel-blog/interstate-hsr-network-part-2/ (accessed 28 November 2013).

Enei, R., Bak, M., Baird, A., Matthews, B., Schnell, O. (2011), 'Analysis of System Requirements for Co- and Intermodality in Long-Distance Passenger Travel', Deliverable 4.2 of ORIGAMI, co-funded by FP7. TRI, Edinburgh Napier University, Edinburgh, July 2011.

European Commission (2011a), 'White Paper. Roadmap to a Single European Transport Area – Towards a Competitive and Resource Efficient Transport System', European Commission, Brussels, 28 March 2011. COM(2011) 144 final. Available at: http://eur-lex.europa.eu/LexUriServ/LexUriServ.do?uri=COM:2011:0144:FIN:EN:PDF

European Commission (2011b), 'A European Vision for Passengers: Communication on Passenger Rights in all Transport Modes', COM(2011) 898 final, Brussels, 19 December 2011. Available at: http://ec.europa.eu/transport/themes/passengers/doc/comm-2011-898-european-vision-passengers_en.pdf (accessed 25 November 2013).

European Commission (2011c), 'Directive 2010/40 of the European Parliament and of the Council of 7 July 2010 on the Framework for the Deployment of Intelligent Transport Systems in the Field of Road Transport and for Interfaces with Other Modes of Transport', OJ L 207/1, Brussels. Available at: http://eur-lex.europa.eu/legal-content/EN/TXT/?uri=CELEX:32010L0040 (accessed 27 September 2015).

International Transport Forum (2012), 'Towards Seamless Public Transport', Policy Brief, October 2012.

Kozak, B. and Szendro, G. (2011), 'Possibilities of Intermodality in Passenger Transport. Tested Methodologies and Results from Europe', PRESS4TRANSPORT. Available at: http://www.press4transport.eu/vpo/tem-athic_fiches/PossibilitiesIntermodalityPassengerTransport.pdf (accessed 27 September 2015).

Koźlak, A. (2012), *Nowoczesny system transportowy jako czynnik rozwoju regionów w Polsce*. Wydawnictwo Uniwersytetu Gdańskiego, Gdańsk. Available at: http://libra.ibuk.pl/book/67338 (accessed 10 November 2013).

Kristiansen, J. and Johannsen, H. W. (2005/2007), 'Transport Systems Concepts and Definitions', SUTRANET – A project within the Interreg IIIB North Sea Programme, Annex 1.2.1 to the Final Report, Aalborg University June 2005/2007. Available at: http://sutranet.plan.aau.dk/pub/wp1%20publications/1.2.1_Systems%20Definitions.pdf (accessed 27 September 2015).

Lockwood, S. (2003), 'Multimodal Transportation vs. Intermodal Transportation', Second James L. Oberstar Forum on Transportation Policy and Technology – Intermodal Transportation: The Potential and the Challenge, University of

Minnesota. Available at: http://www.cts.umn.edu/events/oberstar/2003/documents/lockwoodpaper.pdf (accessed 20 December 2013).

Müller, G. et al. (2004a), 'Towards Passenger Intermodality in the EU. Report 1'. Analysis of the Key Issues for Passenger Intermodality. Dortmund, July 2004. Available at: http://www.tfl.gov.uk/microsites/interchange/documents/report_1_en.pdf (accessed 26 November 2013).

Müller, G. et al. (2004b), 'Towards Passenger Intermodality in the EU. Report 3' (Final Version). Recommendations for Advancing Passenger Intermodality in the EU for the European Commission DG Energy and Transport Unit G 3 Motorways of the Sea and Intermodality. Dortmund, December 2004. Available at: http://www.ils-forschung.de/down/towards-pass-3.pdf (accessed 23 November 2013).

Péraldi, X. (2004), 'Accessibilité des régions périphériques de l'Union européenne et politiques publiques de transport', *Revue Région et Développement*, 15–2002. Available at: http://region-developpement.univ-tln.fr/en/pdf/R15/R15_Peraldi. pdf (accessed 30 November 2013).

Perkins, S. (2012), 'Seamless Transport Policy: Institutional and Regulatory Aspects of Inter-Modal Coordination', *Discussion Paper No. 2012-5*. OECD/ITF. Available at: http://www.internationaltransportforum.org/jtrc/DiscussionPapers/DP201205.pdf (accessed 10 November 2013).

Preston, J. (2012), 'Integration for Seamless Transport', *Discussion Paper No. 2012-01*, International Transport Forum, Southampton, April 2012.

Sammer, G., Stark, J., Uhlmann, T. (2009), 'Guidelines for Seamless Intermodal Interchanges', Deliverable D14 of KITE 4.2, co-funded by FP6, STRATA GmbH, Karlsruhe, April 2009.

Sitran, A., Maffii, S., de Stasio, C. (2011), 'Impacts of Improved Interconnectivity on a European Scale', Deliverable D5.1 of INTERCONNECT, co-funded by FP7. TRI, Edinburgh Napier University, Edinburgh, May 2011.

Stephen, P. (2010), 'Transport Integration – An Impossible Dream?', Universities Transport Studies, Group Annual Conference, 5–7 January 2010, University of Plymouth, 2010.

VTrans Safe, Strategic, Seamless 2025 update (2012), 'An Update to Virginia's Statewide Multimodal Long-range Transportation Policy Plan', Office of Intermodal Planning and Investment, Virginia 2012. Available at: http://www.vtrans.org/resources/VTransUpdateDraft_for_PC_112712_FINAL.pdf (accessed 27 November 2013).

Wan, Z. and Liu, X. (2008), 'Chinese Railway Transportation: Opportunity and Challenge', Illinois Center for Transportation. Available at: http://ict.uiuc.edu/railroad/CEE/pdf/Events/TRB09/Xiang-TRB%20Paper.pdf (accessed 22 November 2013).

Wang, X. (2013), 'China ITS Update', 10th AASHTO International Day, 14 October 2013, Tokyo. Available at: http://ssom.transportation.org/Documents/5-Xiaojing_China.pdf (accessed 15 November 2013).

Yamamoto, T. (2011), 'Intermodal Passenger Transport in Japan, Road Authorities' Approach to Delivering Integrated Transport Services to Customers – Our Experiences and Lessons Learned', XXIV World Road Congress Mexico 2011.

13. Economic and policy issues in multimodal passenger transport security

Luca Zamparini

1. INTRODUCTION

The years following the events of 9/11 have been marked by a raised interest in transportation security from both researchers and public administrations. Several programs and initiatives have tackled the security dimension of transportation for virtually all modes. However, it must be emphasized that fewer analyses have been devoted to multimodal passenger transport with respect to freight transport. This has happened despite the fact that multimodal passenger transport systems may be a likely target for potential terrorists, given that their hubs normally concentrate a large amount of people on predictable days and at predictable times, as became tragically clear in March 2004 at the Madrid railway stations of Atocha, El Pozo del Tio Raimundo, Santa Eugenia and Calle Telez where concurrent terrorist bombings killed 191 people and wounded almost 1800. Moreover, the intermodal nature of these hubs may generate weaknesses due to the different security protocols that are deployed in the various transport modes (i.e. the degree of security that characterizes the railway or metro stations that adjoin an airport may be different, and, most probably, lower to that arranged within the airport).

It must also be considered that multimodal systems emerge as economically feasible only if there is the possibility to take advantage of a critical mass and thus to move many people on the same vector in the main arcs of the system. Consequently, multimodal passenger transport systems represent an attractive target for a series of reasons (Transport and Infrastructure Senior Officials' Committee, 2013): they present a high potential for mass casualties and are open to the public, very accessible and vulnerable; they cause havoc to more than one transport mode at the same time; they generate public fear and anxiety and resonate highly in the targeted communities; lastly, they may cause a relevant economic impact. The following sections will discuss the economic issues in multimodal passenger transport security, two specific initiatives that have been developed by the International Road Transport Union and by the Transit Cooperative Research Program of the Transportation Research Board, and the multimodal passenger security policies of the European Union (EU) and of Australia. The aim of this chapter is to highlight some relevant issues that will be discussed thoroughly in the country-specific chapters that constitute Part IV of this book.

2.   ECONOMIC ISSUES IN MULTIMODAL PASSENGER TRANSPORT SECURITY

From a simple quantitative viewpoint, security risk can be computed according to the following simple formula (Polzin, 2002):

Security Risk = Probability   of   Incident   Attempt   ×   Vulnerability   × Damage

In the decades that preceded the 9/11 attacks, the probability of an incident attempt was estimated to be very close to zero (non-existing) while the degree of vulnerability of a transport vector or infrastructure and the momentous damage that may be caused by a terrorist attack were deemed as relatively unimportant. Consequently, security protocols and issues were considered as operational and not as strategic/planning priorities. This perception has drastically changed since the attacks of September 11th 2011 in New York, since the above-mentioned Madrid episode on March 11th 2004, and since July 7th 2005 in London, given that they have demonstrated that the probability of an incident attempt may sensibly be different from zero. Coherently, investments aimed at improving the degree of security for passenger transport systems have become an important issue of policy makers. These investments need to take into account the above-mentioned security risk but they also need to estimate the effects that they will generate on the overall efficiency of the multimodal transport system. Once security becomes one objective of transport related investments, an analysis should be performed in order to assess how these investments can optimize the transport networks with respect to vulnerability of the system, incident attempts and resilience in case of damages to the infrastructure and services. Such an analysis should also take into account the medium- to long-term effects of (lack of) security related episodes, given that their costs are in most of the cases higher than those related to the immediate aftermath of the event (Zamparini, 2014).

A paper by Tarr et al. (2005) has listed the main solutions envisaged to improve the security of multimodal transport for both freight and passenger transport. The options directly related to passenger transport were the following: a) employee training; b) inspection of priority tracks, tunnels and bridges; c) increased security for subways and buses; d) awareness education and training; and e) new performance technologies. For all of these options, an important role is played by technology and by new security devices such as: electronic employee ID targets and vehicular gates at metro stations, metro-rail fiber optic networks, programmable intrusion equipment, closed-circuit TV and motion detection alarms, personal protection equipment for employees, chemical emergency sensor programs, bomb-resistant containers at intermodal hubs, and so on. It must be considered that technology can in most cases provide an increase in security but also the threats emerging from the adoption of innovative technology must be taken into account. Therefore, economic estimation techniques aiming at analyzing the economic feasibility and efficiency of the implementation of these new devices, such as Cost Benefit Analysis and Multi-criteria Analysis, should be carried out before investing in these new technologies. On the other hand, most of these devices can be subject to a series of possible attacks by terrorists, as discussed by Rotter (2009), and are summarized in Table 13.1.

It is therefore important to bear in mind all possible effects and threats that may emerge from the implementation of a particular security strategy. The measures may be related to personnel's training and behavior or to the adoption of new technologies and devices. The next sections will discuss two different documents (IRU, 2006; TCRP, 2007) that deal with both aspects of security protocols and strategies.

3.   THE INTERNATIONAL ROAD TRANSPORT UNION PASSENGER TRANSPORT SECURITY GUIDELINES

In 2006 the International Road Transport Union (IRU) released a document that contained the guidelines that should be followed by bus, coach and taxi operators and drivers in order to increase the degree of security in passenger transport. The objective of these guidelines is to raise the awareness and assist managers of bus and coach companies to implement effective and appropriate measures to maximize the degree of security. The emphasis is on the adoption by these firms of the approved security guidelines, codes of conduct and schemes provided by public or private organizations. Moreover, firms are required to appoint a responsible person for

Table 13.1   Threats to RFID security and possible countermeasures

Threat	Possible countermeasure
Rogue scanning of confidential data from personal documents	Using short-range tags, shielding, authentication of the reader, moving sensitive information to a protected database, activation of tag by the user
Rogue scanning of data of items carried by a person	Permanent deactivation, RFID privacy management devices like RFID Guardian
Eavesdropping of confidential data from personal documents	Data encryption, using short-range tags, shielding tags with reader during information exchange
Rogue scanning or eavesdropping of other non-public data	Data encryption, using short-range tags, shielding, authentication of the reader, moving sensitive information to a protected database, restricted physical access
Relay attack	Using short-range tags, shielding, distance bounding protocols
Tag cloning and replay attack	Tag authentication with challenge-response protocol, tag design which counters reverse engineering
People tracking	Reader authentication, random identifiers in anti-collision protocol, changing pseudonyms, using short-range tags, shielding
Change of tag content	Limited use of rewritable memory in tags, disabling writing features
Physical tag destruction	Adequate physical location of tags on objects in retail
Blocking and jamming	Facilities for detection and localization of jamming devices
Reverse engineering and side channel attacks	Protective layers, dummy structures, memory and bus scrambling, encryption of memory content

Source: Rotter, 2009.

all security strategies and protocols and to carry out firm-specific risk assessment by using past records and experiences. The result of this risk assessment should consist of the identification of the weakest links in the transportation chain. The result of the security assessment should be the issuance of a security policy statement and of a security plan and checklist of the basic security protocols that should be followed by the personnel. Moreover, emphasis is placed on the training of staff in order to manage in the most appropriate way all the situations that may be related to a breach in security. This should include both preventive measures and the strategies to minimize the effects of a security threat.

The security protocols should be continuously checked and re-evaluated both by the internal staff and by external experts. Security training should consider what are the security risks, how to recognize them, the strategies to reduce such risks and the response to a security breach. Moreover, they should consider the awareness of the security plans by the appointed individuals and their role in their implementation.

An important chapter of this document is related to the management of a bomb threat by the managers and/or security personnel of a transport firm. All the protocols that should be followed are listed, and the possible strategies to extract as much information as possible from terrorists jointly with the way in which to deal with (probably) shocked personnel are summarized. A clear emphasis is placed on the necessity to cooperate with the police and other public officers in dealing with this kind of security emergency.

4. THE TRANSIT COOPERATIVE RESEARCH PROGRAM ON PUBLIC TRANSPORTATION PASSENGER SECURITY INSPECTIONS

The Transit Cooperative Research Program report (TCRP, 2007) on public transportation passenger security inspections (PSI) was issued in 2007 on behalf of the Transportation Research Board in the United States. The aim of this study was to guide policy makers in the implementation of PSIs. The steps that are suggested are the following: a) conduct a risk assessment; b) establish a security plan; c) understand legal and liability issues; d) understand customer perceptions; e) conduct costumer and community outreach; and f) collaborate with local law enforcement and first responders. The first phase (risk assessment) is necessary in order to understand whether there are the appropriate circumstances that justify the use of a PSI by a transit agency in order to safeguard a critical infrastructure. There should be a positive correlation between the degree of risk and the intensity of a PSI. The use of a cost-benefit analysis should guide the decision in this respect. For a low risk, only passive measures should be implemented. For an intermediate degree of risk, passive measures, low level of PSI and a contingency plan should be put in place. In case of a high degree of risk, all possible PSIs (both manual and with the use of technology) should be implemented.

The security plan should aim at eliminating or, at least, mitigating the security risk for the transport system. Even in those cases where no actual risk appears to be present, the mass transit operators/agencies should envisage a contingency plan for the cases in which the security environment may suddenly change due to unexpected circumstances. In case a cost-benefit analysis does not justify the implementation of a PSI, the reasons or the rationale should be elicited clearly.

The legal and liability issues that may arise in case a PSI is implemented may be related to a large number of causes. Among them, it is worthwhile mentioning the racial profiling, searches, use of radiating technology, standards related to civil liability for unauthorized searches, and injuries caused by a PSI. The standards and protocols of the PSI should be fixed in accordance with the existing laws in a determined territory. Moreover, personnel should be trained specifically in order to avoid unnecessary harm to people and protocols and actions that may lead to legal charges. Lastly, personnel should also be trained to identify the cases that deserve further and more accurate inspection.

In the circumstances and environment in which there is a difference in risk perceptions between mass transit agencies and operators on the one hand and the general public on the other, the agencies and the security personnel should try and justify their behavior by clearly explaining to passengers the specific risks and threats that the transport system is facing without generating excessive alarm and tension. Moreover, the diffusion of this information should not jeopardize security.

The provision of information about the reasons why a PSI is implemented and the necessary timing may be very useful to obtain the collaboration of customers and to help them schedule their trips for the access or egress legs to a multimodal transport hub.

The collaboration with local law enforcement organizations and with first response agencies represents a very important necessary condition in order to mitigate the outcomes of a security related accident and to coordinate the efforts in order to have an optimal security strategy. The interchange of information with these organizations is another important issue that should be considered when planning and implementing a PSI.

The preceding and the current sections have analyzed two specific initiatives aimed at increasing the degree of security in multimodal transport systems. The next two sections will provide a general description of the multimodal passenger transport security policies that have been implemented in the EU and in Australia. The aim is twofold. On the one hand, common strategies and issues will be ascertained. Moreover, these next sections will provide a first discussion of country policies that will be complemented by the chapters that constitute the last part – Part IV – of this book.

5. THE EU SECURITY POLICY FOR MULTIMODAL PASSENGER TRANSPORT SECURITY

An EU Commission Staff Document issued in 2012, following the Commission's 2011 White Paper on Transport that had identified the land transport security advisory committee as one of the top priorities, has summarized the main issues related to transport security and the strategies that should mostly be pursued in order to strengthen multimodal passenger transport security. The document starts by mentioning the fact that transport security is not normally considered as a positive feature by transport operators given that it is normally perceived as a negative cost, the return and effectiveness of which is normally very difficult to measure. Another difficult issue is represented by the creation of a single market and by the Schengen rules that have removed border controls within the EU. This causes concern given the heterogeneous attitudes towards terrorist attacks among the EU countries which are characterized by varying degrees of risk of terrorist attacks. Countries with low levels of security may represent palatable entry points for terrorists and security threats. Consequently, the economic importance of actions and strategies against threats to security of multimodal passenger transport systems should not be estimated at the country level but on an EU-wide basis. Moreover, the role of private stakeholders (transport operators, transport infrastructure managers, equipment manufacturers and transport users' organizations) in the implementation of security measures is considered as an important prerequisite for the success of the overall strategy.

The document stresses the fact that a key feature for multimodal passenger transport security is represented by the heterogeneity of modal security protocols that are present in multimodal hubs. An example is related to airports. The EU legislation on aviation security does not include the provision of measures for airport car parks, airport railway stations and the check-in areas of airports. All these infrastructures are considered as 'landside'. Therefore, better and more integrated security at these multimodal transport interchange facilities and at similar ones adjoining railway or bus stations and mass transit systems should be implemented.

Furthermore, the document emphasizes the lack of security exercise in international railway security and the need to foster the implementation of EU-wide security standards for the high-speed railway network. Moreover, security features should be fundamental requirements in the design of rail and subway rolling stock and infrastructure. The importance of training staff is also highlighted.

Another important domain of multimodal transport security is constituted by the planning of the aftermath of an accident given that perfect transport security is impossible to achieve. Contingency plans need to be tested by means of regular exercises whose cost can be justified on the grounds of the number of lives that can be saved by a prompt response to a security accident. Contingency plans should also include the possibility of restoring the functionality of the transport system as quickly as possible in order to minimize the medium- to long-term costs of security accidents that in most cases are more cumbersome than the short-term ones.

One final issue that is considered in the EU document and that can also be related to multimodal passenger security is the importance of research. The following sub-section will provide an overview of the EU-funded projects for multimodal passenger transport security within the 7th Framework Program.

5.1   The EU-funded Projects for Multimodal Passenger Transport Security within the 7th Framework Program

Within the 7th Framework Program of the EU, several projects have addressed the security of multimodal passenger transport. Table 13.2 presents a brief summary of these projects.

The DEMASST (Demo for Mass Transportation Security: Roadmapping Study) project was aimed at developing adequate and well-accepted security for mass transportation in Europe with a comprehensive approach. DEMASST was based on a structured approach to the demonstration program that should identify the main security gaps and the related integrated solutions. From an economic viewpoint, DEMASST took into account the vast variance in mass transportation systems and tried to create synergies between demo tasks and the use of less costly methods.

The ISTIMES (Integrated System for Transport Infrastructure

Table 13.2   EU-funded projects for research in multimodal passenger security

Project acronym	Project start date	Project end date	EU financial contribution (€)	Total cost of project (€)
DEMASST	January 12th 2009	May 11th 2011	956 558	1 840 549
ISTIMES	July 1st 2009	June 30th 2012	3 113 460	4 367 950
STAR–TRANS	November 1st 2009	April 30th 2012	2 105 588	3 195 188
SECUR-ED	April 1st 2011	September 30th 2014	25 468 072	40 187 354

Source: European Commission, 2012.

Surveillance and Monitoring by Electromagnetic Sensing) project was conceived in order to design, assess and promote ICT-based systems that would provide real-time and detailed information and images of the infrastructures in order to allow decision support for emergency and disaster situations.

The STAR–TRANS (Strategic Risk Assessment and Contingency Planning in Interconnected Transport Networks) project was intended to develop a risk assessment methodology for critical infrastructures and to apply it to several infrastructures in order to ascertain common risks, threats and vulnerabilities and to identify the impact of failures on multimodal transport infrastructures.

The most comprehensive EU 7th Framework project for multimodal passenger transport security was the SECUR-ED (Secured Urban Transportation) project. Its main aim was to provide the means to increase urban transportation security to transport operators of medium and large European cities. The project was intended to tackle all societal, cultural and legal issues related to multimodal urban transport. It was based on three interrelated elements: 1) security organization; 2) security risk management plans; and 3) security risk mitigation safeguards.

6. THE AUSTRALIAN SECURITY POLICY FOR MULTIMODAL PASSENGER TRANSPORT SECURITY

As for many other countries, the strategy for the enhancement of security in multimodal passenger transport emerged as a response to the events of 9/11. A first agreement was reached in 2004 with the Australian National Transport Security Strategy document that was then amended following the Special Council of the Australian Governments meeting on Counter-Terrorism that was held in 2005 (Transport and Infrastructure Senior Officials' Committee, 2013). Further agreements at all levels of government led to the National Surface Transport Security Strategy in 2009, which is reviewed every three years. The driving principles of the Australian Security Strategy are that regulatory responsibility rests with the states and territory governments and that transport firms and operators have responsibility for the arrangements related to security that need to be developed in their facilities, assets and networks. The guiding principles of the Australian strategy are the following:

- intelligence-led risk management to multimodal transport security;
- a need to develop consistent approaches in all Australian regions;

- avoiding necessary duplications by sharing information and materials;
- cooperation between public and private stakeholders;
- to increase the confidence of operators and consumers on the security of the multimodal transport systems;
- identifying the vulnerabilities of the systems and utilizing appropriate risk management techniques and best practices principles;
- using a multimodal and inter-jurisdictional approach in order to understand all possible threats and to achieve a seamless movement of people across modes.

It thus emerges that this strategy is based on the need to balance efficient security and cost-effective practices and protocols (by avoiding duplications and relying on best practices). Moreover, the collaboration among private and public stakeholders is also deemed as a very important prerequisite in order to achieve the maximum degree of security.

The pursuit of all the above-mentioned guiding principles should lead to the achievement of a series of strategic objectives:

- promoting best practice risk management;
- allowing operators to access guidance materials in order to implement nationally consistent measures;
- making private stakeholders aware of the benefits that emerge from security measures. Such benefits may more than compensate the costs incurred by the private firms;
- promoting scalability in order to have security levels that are proportionate to the incurred threats;
- enhancing the development of accident response plans;
- promoting appropriate incident and suspicious activity reporting arrangements in order to maximize the prevention of acts of terrorism;
- developing multimodal transport systems resilience by means of sharing lessons learned from security exercises conducted on an ongoing basis and on the oversight of risk management, business and service continuity.

The main issues that emerge from this list of objectives are the necessity to obtain standards that should be applied in the various areas of the country, the importance of cooperation among public agencies and private stakeholders, and the need to constantly improve the security standards, protocols and strategies on the basis of the evolution of the threats posed by criminals and terrorists.

7. CONCLUSIONS

This chapter has highlighted that an important prerequisite for the development of policies, strategies and protocols aimed at maximizing the degree of security of a multimodal passenger transport system is a consideration of the risk that such a system is exposed to. This risk is a function of the probability of the incident attempt, of the vulnerability of the system, and of the damage resulting from a breach in security. Policies aimed at countering this risk should be based on cost-benefit or multi-criteria analyses that should help when choosing the most appropriate options. The investment in multimodal transport security can either be related to the training of personnel, to the use of new technologies, or to a combination of both. Moreover, the description of two specific initiatives and of the general framework of the multimodal transport security policies in the EU and in Australia has allowed us to elicit some common patterns and relevant features. The most important of these are: the need to identify consistent standards that should be adapted and applied in all possible contexts; the importance of cooperation among public agencies and with private stakeholders; and the constant improvement of the security standards, protocols and strategies. The chapters that constitute the next section of this book will provide a detailed description of several other countries. This will allow us to draw some general conclusions and to underline the commonalities and heterogeneities among different regions of the world.

REFERENCES

European Commission (2012), *Commission Staff Working Document on Transport Security*, EU Commission.

IRU (2006), *IRU Road Passenger Transport Security Guidelines*, Geneva: IRU.

Polzin, S. E. (2002), *Security Considerations in Transportation Planning: A White Paper*, STC White Paper, available at: http://www.planning.dot.gov/documents/SecurityPapers/SecurityConsiderations_Polzin.pdf (last accessed 19th February 2015).

Rotter, P. (2009), 'Security and privacy in RFID applications', in C. Turcu (ed.) *Development and Implementation of RFID Technology*, Intech, pp. 237–260.

Tarr, R. W., V. McGurk and C. Jones (2005), 'Intermodal transportation safety and security issues: training against terrorism', *Journal of Public Transportation*, **8** (4), 87–102.

TCRP (2007), *Public Transportation Passenger Security Inspections: A Guide for Policy Decision Makers*, Washington, DC: Transportation Research Board.

Transport and Infrastructure Senior Officials' Committee (2013), *National Surface Transport Security Strategy*, available at: http://www.infrastructure.

gov.au/transport/security/pdf/National_Surface_Transport_Security_Strategy_
September_2013.pdf (last accessed February 21st 2015).
Zamparini, L. (2014), 'Economic issues in maritime transport security', in
K. Bichou, J. Szyliowicz and L. Zamparini (eds.), *Maritime Transport Security.
Issues, Challenges and National Policies*, Cheltenham, UK and Northampton,
MA, USA: Edward Elgar.

PART IV

Multimodal passenger transportation
security: policy applications

14. Multimodal passenger transportation security in the United States

Joseph S. Szyliowicz

INTRODUCTION

The U.S., like every other country, developed its transportation system along modal lines. First came roads and canals and ports, then the railroads and finally aviation. In recent decades, it became increasingly apparent that these systems could not cope with the increasing demands placed upon them by people and businesses, and that the existing system had created new problems of urban sprawl, pollution, and bottlenecks in cities and elsewhere that impeded individual mobility and economic development. Planners and others seeking to resolve these problems came to understand that a new paradigm for transportation was necessary, that the individual modes (road, rail, air, water) could no longer be managed separately and that transportation had to be viewed from a holistic perspective that recognized the interrelatedness of the modes and aimed to implement policies and projects that integrate the modes into a coherent system.

Such an approach would have many potential benefits. It would minimize the negative aspects of the modal approach, including the dominance of the automobile, and the high social, environmental, and economic costs involved in running an un-integrated system. An integrative approach could minimize environmental impacts and the use of energy, offer more choices for personal and freight mobility, and promote sustainable development. In the U.S. this approach is known as intermodalism, elsewhere the term 'multimodal' is often used. Although there are many definitions of intermodalism, suffice it to say that an intermodal system has two qualities. First, the individual modes are integrated into a seamless system; second, each mode within that system is used for the purposes for which it is best suited.[1]

The U.S. has been striving to achieve that new vision since 1991 when Congress passed the landmark Intermodal Surface Transportation

Efficiency Act (ISTEA), legislation that explicitly called for a new approach to transportation policy and planning. Its explicit use of the word 'inter-modal' in the title reflected the understanding that transportation policy in the U.S. had entered a new era. Such a vision could obviously not be achieved easily or quickly for there were many barriers to overcome ranging from the continuing power of the well-established modal systems to the nature of the U.S. political system wherein the states implement transportation policies and projects.

The State of Intermodalism

Nevertheless, linkages between modes have increased significantly, thus creating a variety of terminals whose security is of national importance. The most intermodally oriented is the commuter rail system for con-nections to other modes are available at 812 of the 1160 stations served by commuter trains utilizing the tracks of the national rail network. Of these, 734 (90 percent) connect to one other mode, primarily transit bus, 75 stations have two modal connections, and three have three. In addi-tion, a further 79 stations have 'near connections', that is another mode is available a short distance away.[2] Airports are much less connected. Although the U.S. possesses a very large number of airports – over 13 500 of one sort or another – only 376 have regularly scheduled flights and less than half of these, 150, have a connecting mode. The most common is the transit bus, only 23 airports have a rail connection. Forty-six airports have an intercity bus service.[3] More than 12 million people travel by rail daily and rail stations have similar connectivity patterns. Of the 274 mainland rail stations with intermodal connections, 232 are served by transit bus. Cruise ship ports too are well connected. In many cities, passenger vessel terminals have been relocated from the cargo handling areas of the port to new terminals in or near the city center. As a result, these terminals are well connected to bus, rail, and ferry stations. Fifteen ports account for 9.7 million of the 10.4 million passengers that embark on sea journeys. Of these, two-thirds have a bus, rail, and/or ferry connection, four-fifths have dedicated transportation.[4] Ferries are also a popular mode of transport, carrying, in 2007, over 100 million passengers, almost all of whom transfer to bus or rail at one end of the journey at least. Finally, 190 companies operate about 700 ships from almost 500 terminals in 37 states.[5]

Security Issues and Policies

The emergence of intermodalism has created a large number of targets with great appeal to terrorists who, in recent decades, have changed their policy and seek to inflict as large a number of casualties as possible when they attack. Large intermodal terminals also have symbolic value which further enhances their attraction.

Securing these intermodal facilities is a challenging task due to their characteristics. They are very large facilities both in terms of the area they cover and the large numbers of people who flow through daily. To function effectively they must be accessible, thus presenting a difficult trade-off between security and convenience. Obviously, the higher the level of security, the less convenient and accessible the facility will be, thus endangering its *raison d'être*. Furthermore, a wide range of public and private actors are involved in their operations. Coordinating the security practices of numerous organizations and agencies, is always a challenging and difficult task. Adding to the security challenge is the very nature of these facilities which are designed to explicitly bring together two or more modes, each of which has its own culture, organization, and operating procedures. Thus, intermodalism, through the creation of new nodes that enhance mobility also creates new vulnerabilities. In order to secure these nodes a modal focus is necessary but inadequate, though there is a strong tendency to think of security in intramodal terms due to the strong historical and organizational power of the various modes. Still, intermodal security requires an intermodal perspective as well. In the U.S., as elsewhere, this task is further complicated by the tendency to continue to think of security in modal terms, so that following an attack upon that mode, the concern is with the adoption of measures that would further secure that specific mode – usually to prevent a recurrence of a particular type of attack – not with the security of other critical elements within the system or of the entire system.

Furthermore, numerous weapons are available to an attacker, each of which poses particular issues and problems for transportation security planners and managers. To date the most common weapon is explosives, but terrorists are innovative and they have attempted to use them in novel forms. From bombs hidden in suitcases on planes, they have come to rely on powerful plastic explosives (PBX, RDX, and HMX) which are difficult for x-ray machines to detect, and terrorists have tried to smuggle them past screening devices in novel forms as in the case of the notorious 'underwear bomber' who had hidden them in his underwear and tried to destroy a Northwest Airlines Flight on Christmas Day, 2009.

Terrorists are also known to seek other means of attack. One of these is to target information technologies. Intermodal facilities are highly dependent upon information and data processing technologies, technologies that are vulnerable to cyber-attacks. This threat is difficult to prevent and contain, as evidenced by the large number of successful attacks that are known to have been visited upon private and public data systems across the U.S. Although the Department of Homeland Security (DHS) is the lead agency for cyber security of critical infrastructure, by mid-2005 it still had not developed threat and vulnerability assessments or recovery plans. Recognizing the need for more action, the new U.S. Homeland Security Secretary, Michael Chertoff, announced in July 2005, as part of the reorganization of the DHS, the establishment of a new office – Assistant Secretary for Cyber Security and Telecommunications. However, cyber security is still viewed as one of three major challenges confronting the Department of Transportation (DOT). As a recent report noted: 'The GAO and others have found that DOT has not consistently implemented effective controls to ensure that financial and sensitive information is adequately protected from unauthorized access and other risks.'[6]

Another weapon that can wreak havoc with intermodal facilities is nuclear and bio-chemical weapons. It takes only 50 kg of Highly Enriched Uranium (HEU) to assemble a primitive bomb, but doing so is no easy matter. A radiological attack using a radiological dispersal device (RDD) such as a 'dirty bomb' that disseminates radioactive materials in inter-modal facilities is more probable since the necessary materials are widely available and RDDs are relatively easy to build. Chemical and biological weapons also pose a serious threat, for relatively small amounts could spread such diseases as plague, botulism, and smallpox.

The potential effectiveness of such weapons was demonstrated in Tokyo in 1995 when five terrorists punctured bags of sarin (a deadly nerve agent) in the subway during the morning rush hour, and fled. The chemical agent spread quickly over large distances affecting fifteen different subway sta-tions. Even though the attack was badly planned, 12 people died and 1600 were seriously injured. This attack revealed not only the lethality of such a weapon but also the issues that responders face in dealing with an attack. An efficient response requires communications and information flows between the relevant agencies, rapid diagnosis and reaction times, staff preparedness, public information, and adequate medical facilities. The lessons learned have been widely disseminated and, hopefully, effectively integrated into the intermodal passenger security practices in the U.S.

ADMINISTRATION

The lead agency in the effort to safeguard intermodal transportation is the Transportation Security Administration's (TSA) Office of Security Policy and Industry Engagement (OSPIE). This is but one of the many branches of the TSA, itself a part of the DHS which was established after the 9/11 disaster in 2001 and is responsible for all aspects of homeland security.

The TSA is responsible for safeguarding all passenger and freight systems. The DOT plays a supportive role (as established by the September 2004 Memorandum of Understanding) by providing various forms of technical assistance such as helping to develop and implement security standards.

To achieve intermodal security, OSPIE has designed a strategy to ensure the security of the modes and their interactions. It has been summarized as follows: 1) completion of industry threat, vulnerability, and consequence assessment; 2) development of baseline security standards; 3) assessment of operator security status versus existing standards; 4) development of plan to close gaps in security standards; and 5) enhancement of systems of security. The specifics on how this is to be achieved for specific sectors are contained in the Transportation Systems Sector-Specific Plan. In the sections that follow we will consider the security procedures and their effectiveness for the major intermodal nodes.

Achieving these goals is obviously a challenging task. One major difficulty, as noted above, is the very nature of intermodal facilities whose operations involve a large number of public and private stakeholders. The TSA website recognizes this issue, noting that intermodal security requires the active participation of 'all sector partners, including government (federal, state, regional, local, and tribal) and private industry stakeholders'. Thus, OSPIE 'will ensure the safe movement of passengers and promote the free flow of commerce by building a resilient, robust, and sustainable network with our public and private sector partners'.[7] Achieving effective coordination among all these entities, however, is a complex and difficult challenge that has not always been effectively met.

The Intermodal Nodes

Airports
Airports have two primary characteristics that create security problems. First, they cover large areas for they need space for runways and hangars and for their terminal facilities (including parking) and concourses. Thus they require a secure perimeter. Second, they are complex systems that possess many of the attributes of a modern city such as hotels, restaurants and coffee shops, and a rich variety of retail stores. Millions of people flow through their landside spaces, disembarking, checking in, shopping, checking luggage, boarding and the like. Large numbers of managers and employees are required to provide these services and they represent a rich variety of stakeholders including airport operators, airline officials, retailers, and many government agencies. Thus the issue of the security of the workforce is an important one.

The concern with airport security developed in the 1960s due to a number of airplane hijackings. The screening of passengers and their luggage began in the early 1970s but 9/11 was the decisive event that transformed the U.S. approach to homeland security. Heretofore, airport security was not tightly enforced due to airline concern with alienating customers and with costs as well as weaknesses within the Federal Aviation Administration, the responsible government overseer.[8] Passenger screening was contracted out to private companies whose standards varied greatly.

Significant changes were then enacted that have profoundly affected millions of people. The most visible and far-reaching change involved the replacement of private screeners by a force of federal workers employed by the TSA, part of the Department of Homeland Security, with tougher regulations concerning identification and carry-on luggage enforced. These regulations have changed over time in response to specific events such as the failed 'shoe bomber' incident which led to all passengers having to remove their shoes, or the subsequent ban on liquids following the attempt by terrorists to detonate a liquid bomb on board a plane. In order to deal with the coordination and related issues, a new position was created, Federal Security Director. Directors are responsible for supervising and coordinating all security activities at major airports. They are expected to establish and implement screening standards for passengers and employees, carry out risk assessments, provide security training for employees, and establish close coordinated interactions with all law enforcement and emergency response agencies.[9]

Technology has also come to play an increasing role in passenger screening. Machines of various types are used to screen baggage for explosives and other forbidden items. These range from x-ray units for luggage to full body scanner machines (Advanced Imaging Technology (AIT) machines) that screen passengers for both metallic and non-metallic weapons and which have largely replaced metal detectors. Since 2008 over 740 AIT units have been deployed at almost 160 airports nationwide. These machines aroused considerable privacy concerns when they were first deployed because they take pictures of the body but, according to the TSA, these machines have been modified so as to provide only a generic human outline.[10] Even so, they are not viewed favorably by many passengers because of nuisance factor involved – having to totally empty one's pockets and stand with raised hands. The deployment of these four machines also provides an example of the rather flexible ways in which the TSA has dealt with technology for it failed to fully follow the DHS's acquisition policies, a failure which led to the DHS 'approving nationwide AIT deployment without full knowledge of TSA's revised specifications'.[11]

Administrative shortcomings are but one of the TSA's weaknesses in its attempts to look to technology to ease what many travelers consider a burdensome experience, for it has even deployed technologies that had to be withdrawn. Perhaps the most notorious example involves the Explosive Trace Portals (ETPs) 'puffer' machines which were designed to simply let passengers pass through a portal that would discharge a blast of air thus loosening particles which could be analyzed promptly for explosives. The TSA eagerly purchased 200 units and began to deploy them in 2004. At the height of this program 94 units had been placed in 37 airports but by 2006 it was clear that these machines 'took too long to screen passengers . . . often broke or were unreliable . . . (and) created clouds of particles which would often contaminate other passengers, thus increasing the list of suspects requiring additional examination'.[12] By 2008 the TSA, realizing that the technology's many problems could not be fixed, had abandoned the project, having spent about US$30 million. Some ETPs are, however, still in use at 15 airports as part of the layered approach to security.[13]

Although the TSA drew some important lessons from this episode, opening the TSA Systems Integration Facility (TSIF) in early 2009, the ETP failure was symptomatic of the TSA's strategic approach to technology, an approach that contains significant shortcomings. In October 2009, the Government Accountability Office (GAO) reported that the TSA:

> had not completed a cost-benefit analysis to prioritize and fund the Passenger Screening Program's (PSP) priorities for investing in checkpoint technologies, as required by the National Infrastructure Protection Plan's (NIPP) risk management framework. At the time of our report, TSA had not developed life-cycle cost estimates of each screening technology the PSP is developing, procuring, or deploying, and could not provide us with information on their priorities for the research and development of checkpoint screening technologies or the processes they followed to develop these priorities.[14]

The deployment of the body scanner machines provides another example of the TSA's lack of foresight. Originally there were two types of AIT machines, one that utilized radio waves, the other x-rays. The latter aroused significant health concerns and was finally taken out of service owing to pressure from many quarters, including Congress.

Though improvements have been made in developing and in assessing technologies – the GAO politely noted, in 2013, that 'challenges remain'[15] – the DHS and the TSA remain fixated on the development of new technologies. These include liquid detection equipment whose use would permit passengers to carry liquids onboard planes and credential authentication technology (CAT) that would rapidly identify fake boarding passes and other documents. It is also working on a smaller version of the whole body scanner, the AIT-2 at a cost of US$245 million even though it is also adopting policies to facilitate the screening process, thus reducing the need for such equipment.[16]

Even if these 'challenges' can be overcome, technology is not a panacea that will safeguard airports from attack. While technology has an important role to play in enhancing security, it is important to bear in mind that specific technologies are expensive to develop and maintain and do not always achieve the goals that have been anticipated, as the case of the 'puffer machines' revealed only too vividly. Moreover, technologies are not neutral artifacts, they yield important social, cultural, and economic consequences as is indicated by the controversy over privacy aroused by the full body scanner machines. Thus, any accurate calculation of risks and benefits, an important prerequisite to a deployment decision, should include a consideration of those non-technical or economic factors.

Moreover, technologies should be regarded only as elements that can be used to achieve a larger strategic vision. The TSA recognizes this and plans to 'take steps to further enhance its layered approach to security through new state-of-the-art technologies, expanded use of existing and proven technologies, better passenger identification techniques and other developments that will continue to strengthen the agency's capabilities to keep terrorists off commercial aircraft'.[17]

The 'better passenger identification techniques' reflect the recognition that it is necessary to change the basic approach that has guided the screening effort – looking for weapons and treating all passengers equally in terms of risk. Such an approach has yielded thousands of scissors, pocket knives, and other such objects, as well as some that are truly dangerous, but even Tom Ridge, who introduced many of these protocols, has stated 'We need to move from looking for weapons to paying attention to people who are or could be terrorists.'[18] However, doing so means moving away from an orientation that views every passenger as an equal threat with a risk based approach.

Beginning in 2011, the TSA has taken some preliminary steps in that direction by implementing new procedures for passengers 12 and under, 75 and older, and active military personnel. Though the airlines and the travel industry as well as many government officials favor an approach that differentiates passengers according to the potential risk they pose, the major issue that has agitated many is the ways in which travelers will be assigned to various risk categories. Many people are concerned that large amounts of private data will be required, thus raising important civil liberty issues.[19] This concern led to the abandonment of an earlier attempt to categorize passengers, the CAPPS II system which was designed to identify people who fit a particular profile. Though it was tested in 2003, it was abandoned in July 2004 because of the privacy concerns that stemmed from the use of private data bases. Still, the TSA's PreCheck program that enables 'trusted' passengers to keep their shoes and coats on and to avoid having the full body scanners is considered a success and will be expanded.[20]

While it is relaxing the passenger screening protocols, the TSA wants to continue and expand its use of the Visible Intermodal Prevention and Response (VIPR) teams. These teams patrol airports looking for suspicious behavior and stopping and questioning people whom they judge worthy of additional attention. Then they talk to the suspect to determine if he or she indeed poses a threat. Altogether 3000 officers are located in 170 airports, at a cost, to date, of over US$1 billion.[21] This program, known as SPOT (Screening of Passengers by Observation Techniques), has aroused significant privacy concerns. Moreover, it was recently evaluated and found to be of questionable validity. Although the DHS had carried out its own evaluation in April 2011 which validated the program, that 'study does not demonstrate effectiveness of the SPOT behavioral indicators because of methodological weaknesses'. And, meta-analyses found the program's accuracy to be 'the same as or slightly better than chance (54 percent)'.[22] John S. Pistole, the TSA's administrator, has responded to these findings by implementing changes designed to improve the substance and administration of the program and arguing that it was an integral part of its 'layered' approach that also utilizes intelligence, technology, and various unpredictable activities and should therefore be continued.[23] As we shall see below, this project has been expanded to intermodal surface facilities where it has aroused even more controversy over its effectiveness as well as its impact on civil liberties.

But passengers are not the only potential threat. As noted above, airports house thousands of workers ranging from administrators to retail clerks. Accordingly, a program of background checks of airport workers and staff has been instituted, as well as restricting access to various critical airport areas such as the runways. The entire airport perimeter is also supposed to be inviolate. Yet despite such measures there have been cases of individuals accessing runways.[24]

Such issues, as well as the other weaknesses discussed above, reflect the degree to which airport security has been a very costly activity that remains a work in progress. Indeed, a noted expert on terrorism, Brian Jenkins, has recently argued that it is necessary to take a completely fresh look at how the U.S. approaches airport security:

> After 40 years of focus on tactical measures, it is time for a sweeping review of aviation security. Instead of forming the usual federal commission to undertake this task, several non-government research institutions could be selected to independently design an optimal aviation security system, beginning not with the four decades of accumulated security measures currently in place but with

a clean slate. The competing models would be reviewed and the best ideas or combination of ideas would be put forward. Even if the results turn out to resemble what is already in place, at least the process offers some comfort that we are pretty close to getting it right.[25]

Surface transportation terminals

The security procedures that have been implemented at airports have not been and obviously cannot be applied to surface intermodal facilities because the number of passengers, operators, and employees involved in surface transportation is far greater than the numbers involved in aviation. There are, for example, over 6000 local transit providers involved with bus, light rail, subway, and commuter rail operations though only a fraction of these involve urban intermodal facilities. Still, an essential characteristic of an intermodal passenger terminal if it is to operate efficiently is open access through numerous entrances. All major terminals fit this pattern for they have to accommodate a tremendous volume of passengers, especially during morning and evening rush hours. In the U.S. more than 10 million trips are taken every day on metro and commuter rail systems.[26] Moreover, in order to move large numbers of passengers efficiently all stations have clear signs of their schedules and transit patterns. Thus, by their very nature these nodes are attractive targets since they are difficult to secure, and provide numerous easy avenues of escape. For these reasons they represent easier targets than airports which are well guarded and where numerous other security measures have lessened their vulnerabilities. Still, like airports they represent attractive targets for their symbolism, the potential for mass casualties, and their role as critical nodes in the transportation system, the devastation of which would create major economic disruptions. It should not be surprising, therefore, that terrorists have attacked such facilities in many cities including Tokyo, London, Madrid, and Mumbai, or that since 9/11 there have been many more assaults on surface transport than aviation – 800 attacks on surface transport, with nearly 4000 people killed, compared with 75 assaults on airliners, with 157 fatalities.[27]

Despite the greater vulnerabilities of surface terminals, the TSA, for obvious reasons, following the 9/11 attacks, focused primarily on aviation. That focus covered all aspects of security including not only the amounts spent or the people deployed but also such basic security elements as mandates. It provided specific security mandates for aviation but it failed to do so for intermodal facilities or for rail and mass transit generally.[28] Even as recently as 2006 it had not developed appropriate security guidelines and standards or goals and indicators to measure its success in establishing security measures for surface transportation – even though the GAO had made such recommendations in 2002.[29] Congress, recognizing the

TSA's lack of progress in developing a security strategy for all modes of transportation, had mandated the development of a National Strategy for Transportation Security in the 9/11 Act. Though due April 1, 2005 this document was not completed until five months later, September 2005. One key factor behind the DHS's failure to act was the Department's inability to define the TSA's relationship with other offices (such as the Federal Transit Administration [FTA]) within the DOT as well as other agencies and stakeholders.

In any event, the FTA took the lead in the effort to secure mass transit systems and their nodes. It carried out a number of threat and vulnerability assessments of major transit systems, developed and disseminated guidelines and provided technical assistance to help transit agencies develop and implement security programs, and promoted training and regional collaboration. Transit agencies are specifically encouraged to: 1) establish specific integrated security programs that include emergency management plans that incorporate and update them on the basis of threat information; and 2) incorporate design criteria, an organized incident management system, and defined security responsibilities for all employees including managers who are accountable for security within their domains. Security awareness is stressed for all employees with ongoing training programs; new employees are to be checked, and to undergo security orientations. Public awareness is also emphasized and appropriate materials are to be distributed widely.

The federal nature of the American political system complicates the attempt to implement such measures. Most mass transit systems are owned and operated by state and local authorities so that responsibility for security lies with state-designated oversight agencies who are expected to follow the FTA's guidelines and requirements. The FTA designed the State Safety Oversight program as one in which the FTA, other federal agencies, states, and rail transit agencies collaborate to ensure the safety and security of rail transit systems. The FTA also requires states to designate an agency to oversee the safety and security of rail transit agencies that receive federal funding. The FTA has also used research and development funds to develop guidance for security, designed to reduce the vulnerability of transit systems to acts of terrorism. This guidance provided recommendations intended to help operators deter and minimize attacks against their facilities, riders, and employees by incorporating security features into the infrastructure.

The federal structure has also complicated the funding issue. From 2004 to 2009, the Administration requested a relatively small amount of funding for rail and mass transit security. Over four years, from fiscal years 2003 through 2006, the DHS distributed only about US$387 million for rail and mass transit security grants. The President's budget for fiscal year 2007, allocated a mere US$37.2 million in the TSA budget for non-aviation transportation security.[30] Though the amounts spent by the federal government have increased significantly to US$136 million in 2013, this is still a small amount given the nature of the problem. Moreover, expenditures on aviation security – US$5.3 billion – continue to far outstrip the amounts spent by the DHS on surface transportation.[31]

One factor that complicates decisions on how much money should be allocated is the issue of who should pay for intermodal surface security. Traditionally mass transit has been funded by state and local governments. The federal government has played a relatively minor role in providing funds for transit agencies as compared to the other entities. Now many argue that providing security from terrorist attacks is a federal responsibility and such security measures should be considered as part of national defense. On the other hand, opponents ask why all taxpayers should bear the cost of providing security improvements to a relatively small number of transit agencies, all of which are located in large metropolitan areas. Since local governments have always financed mass transit, they should bear the costs of securing their systems as well, especially since heightened security provides positive benefits to the community.[32]

Still, various measures have been taken in an effort to strengthen the security of all aspects of surface transportation. An important step in this direction was the Surface Transportation Security Priority Assessment conducted in 2010 which, with input from a variety of stakeholders, came up with a number of recommendations that 'provide a comprehensive framework for the continued improvement of surface transportation security and identify discrete areas of focus to guide the decisions and actions of security partners . . .'.[33] As part of that effort it summarized what had already been achieved in four priority areas involving the four subsectors of surface transportation, the first of which dealt with mass transit and passenger rail. The first area, personnel, included hiring another 350 officers (100 Surface Transportation Security Inspectors, nine with canine teams, 16 with four Mobile Explosives Detection Screening Teams, and 238 with 53 Anti-Terrorism Teams). The second area, better tools, included 13 intermodal security training and exercises, and developing an Information Sharing and Analysis Center, conducting corporate security reviews, and carrying out inspections. The third area, technology, involved providing additional transportation screening technology, some of which '*may have a applications in surface transportation security*' (my emphasis), and improving data bases used relating to travelers, workers, and commercial drivers' License/Hazardous Materials Endorsement, conducting blast analyses at all underwater passenger rail tunnels, and addressing critical vulnerabilities in some structures.[34] Of course, the vaunted increase in personnel so carefully specified in the official report yields a figure that is totally dwarfed by the labor force dealing with airport security – over 50 000 people.

Many of these measures were taken in response to criticisms that had been raised by the GAO regarding the way that the DHS had been dealing with surface security. For example, the increase in personnel allocated to surface transportation clearly relates to the charge that though the TSA had significantly increased the number of its inspectors, it still had not achieved an appropriate balance between aviation and surface transportation security. Moreover the DHS's efforts to establish a risk management approach and evaluate the effectiveness of its strategies reflected the GAO's long-standing view that this area certainly needed additional work.[35]

In response to such long-standing concerns, the Assessment came up with 20 major recommendations, the first of which, perhaps not surprisingly, called for designating 'a lead agency to coordinate periodic modal and cross-modal security risk analyses'. Other recommendations included more effective activities with regard to grants, education and training, information sharing, the federal role, data issues, threat assessments, and credentials.[36] Subsequently, the DHS administrator testified that all the recommendations were being implemented and that it had carried out Transportation Sector Security Risk Assessments (TSSRA) in order to evaluate the impact of over 200 attack scenarios on mass transit and passenger rail. Its Transportation Security Inspectors had also carried out Baseline Assessments for Security Engagement (BASE) to evaluate the security level for that sector, as well as exercises under the Intermodal Security Training and Exercise Program (I-STEP) in order to assess the degree to which facilities are prepared to prevent and respond to an attack. In addition, 25 VIPR teams are operational, and funding for another 17 has been requested.[37]

These teams are modeled on those operating at airports and consist of a varying number of people that may include Transportation Security Inspectors, Behavioral Detection Officers, Transportation Security Officers and Explosives Security Specialists. Their deployment depends on agreements between the TSA and local police chiefs and security directors. Sometimes, they carry additional equipment, such as radiation detectors. They may also be accompanied by Explosives Detection Canine Teams. As in airports, they carry out random, unpredictable baggage and security checks, numbering approximately 4000 in 2010.[38]

In addition to questioning their effectiveness in guarding against attacks, a topic discussed above, critics argue that such searches violate individual liberties, though to avoid charges of racial profiling each team picks a random number, say eleven, and then searches the bags of every eleventh passenger. Though passengers are not required to submit to a search, refusing to do so means that the passenger cannot continue his/ her journey. Though this may safeguard a specific terminal, a terrorist carrying explosives would obviously refuse to be searched but there is nothing that would prevent him/her from simply leaving and mounting an attack at another station. For such reasons, Christopher Calabrese of the American Civil Liberties Union has argued that this program has no security benefits but imposes costs on civil liberties and convenience. In other words, these teams provide 'security theater'. On the other hand, many security professionals argue that the element of surprise is an important deterrent factor, and that it complicates the terrorist planning process. As one analyst noted: 'This kind of unpredictability is another tool in the toolbox to manipulate and play with their minds and cause a level of tactical deterrence.'[39]

An important element in any attempt to deal with the terrorist threat involves intelligence, and the Federal Bureau of Investigation's National Joint Terrorism Task Force (NJTTF) created the Rail Liaison Agent (RLA) Program to support security efforts. Its mission is to provide a point-of-fusion for the collection and dissemination of rail related terrorism intelligence for the Counterterrorism Division and all 56 JTTFs across the U.S.

The RLA Program was created so that each FBI field office would have a designated Special Agent to develop and/or maintain liaison contacts with rail and mass transportation operations in their jurisdiction. There are presently 110 JTTF RLAs that provide intelligence briefs and products, threat assessments, RLA contacts and several other web-based products to assist in security operations. This support is crucial since by Presidential Directives and the National Response Framework, the FBI has the responsibility for terrorism investigations. In many instances, the FBI has provided 'Secret' clearances to agency heads or designated point of contacts within each agency and/or entity to enable them to have access to real-time threat information. It is interesting to note that neither the TSA nor the DHS have adopted a similar policy with regard to any of the rail or mass transit systems that they are charged with protecting.

CONCLUSION

Terrorists will continue to try to attack the U.S. and intermodal terminals will remain attractive targets. Many positive steps have been taken since 9/11 but there is obviously room for improvement, especially with regard to such perennial issues as collaboration across modes and organizations at many levels, information sharing, training, planning, the utilization of risk assessment methodologies, balancing costs and benefits, the development and deployment of technologies, and the education and training not only of a wide range of security professionals, managers, operators, and workers but of the general public as well, for security cannot be left to the DHS and the TSA.

Though many have an important role to play in the struggle against terrorism, it is the transportation professionals who are on the front line. They bear a heavy new responsibility that they must discharge effectively. This means that they must be prepared to help develop plans and policies that are designed to prevent attacks, work to reduce the vulnerabilities of their transportation facilities, and be prepared for response and recovery should a disaster occur. That is a heavy burden but a vital one for the security of our intermodal passenger systems.

NOTES

1. I have drawn upon some of my previous work for this chapter, including 'Intermodalism: The Challenge and the Promise' in *Transportation Law Journal*, Vol. 27, Number 3, September 2000; reprinted in *Intermodal Transportation: Selected Essays* (National Center for Intermodal Transportation, 2000); 'Airport Security' in *Encyclopedia of Terrorism* (Sage, 2nd edn., 2011); and 'Transportation as a Component of Homeland Security Strategy' in P. Viotti et al. (eds.), *Terrorism and Homeland Security* (Taylor & Francis, 2008).
2. Press Release Number: BTS 46-13.ate: Monday, October 28, 2013 (hereafter PRN).
3. Loc. cit.
4. See http://www.rita.dot.gov/bts/sites/rita.dot.gov.bts/files/publications/special_reports_ and_issue_briefs/special_report/2010_12_01/html/entire.html and http://www.rita.dot. gov/bts/sites/rita.dot.gov.bts/files/publications/state_transportation_statistics/state_ transportation_statistics_2011/html/table_04_08.html
5. Loc. cit.
6. Department Of Transportation: Key Issues and Management Challenges, 2013 GAO-13-402T, March 14, 2013.
7. See http://www.tsa.gov/stakeholders/intermodal-transportation-systems
8. For this history see Szyliowicz, 'Aviation Security: Promise or Reality', in R. Howard et al. (eds.), *Homeland Security and Terrorism*, (McGraw-Hill, 2006) pp. 110ff.
9. See http://www.tsa.gov/careers/federal-security-director-fsd
10. See http://www.tsa.gov/traveler-information/advanced-imaging-technology-ait
11. 'DHS and TSA Continue to Face Challenges Developing and Acquiring Screening Technologies', GAO-13-469T, May 8, 2013.
12. Homeland Security News Wire, 'Puffer machine, RIP', May 27, 2009.
13. Loc. cit.
14. US Government Accountability Office, Aviation Security, October 2009, GAO-10-28, p. 28.
15. 'DHS and TSA Continue to Face Challenges Developing and Acquiring Screening Technologies', GAO-13-469T, May 8, 2013.
16. Joe Sharkey, 'PreCheck Meets its Goal and Prepares to Expand', *The New York Times*, November 26, 2013, p. B4.

17. See http://www.tsa.gov/traveler-information/risk-based-security-initiatives
18. Joe Sharkey, 'Don't Let that Ticket out of the Screener's Sight', *The New York Times*, August 20, 2005, C7.
19. Susan Stellin, 'Airport Screening Concerns Civil Liberties Groups', *The New York Times*, March 11, 2013.
20. Sharkey, loc. cit.
21. Brian Feldman, 'TSA's Behavior Detection Procedure is Not a Good Way to Spot Terrorists', *The Atlantic Wire*, November 14, 2013.
22. 'Aviation Security: TSA Should Limit Future Funding for Behavior Detection Activities', GAO-14-158T, November 14, 2013.
23. Statement before the Subcommittee on Transportation Security, Committee on Homeland Security, U.S. House of Representatives, November 14, 2013.
24. For details see 'Airport security', Wikipedia.
25. Brian Michael Jenkins, *Aviation Security: After Four Decades, It's Time for a Fundamental Review*, Homeland Security and Defense Center, Rand Corporation, 2012, p. 1.
26. Data is available from the American Public Transit Association's (APTA) website at http://www.apta.com/research/stats/
27. Brian Michael Jenkins in Ian Simpson, 'With Security Eyes Focused on Airlines, Terrorists Look to Rail, Experts Say', *NBC News*, available at: http://investigations. nbcnews.com/_news/2013/04/24/17899212-with-security-eyes-focused-on-airlines-terror ists-look-to-rail-experts-say
28. In this section, I have drawn upon an excellent paper, 'Passenger Rail Security in the United States' by W. Brian Schmitt, prepared for my seminar, Winter 2011.
29. GAO, 'Mass Transit Federal Action Could Help Transit Agencies Address Security Challenges' (December 2002).
30. American Public Transportation Association. Statement on President Bush's Proposed FY2007 DHS Budget (February 6, 2006).
31. Simpson, loc. cit.
32. D.R. Peterman, 'Passenger Rail Security: Overview of Issues', Congressional Research Service, July 14, 2006.
33. Surface Transportation Security Priority Assessment (STSPA), Washington, DC, 2010, p. 1.
34. Ibid., pp. 5–6.
35. GAO, April 21, 2010, 'Surface Transportation Security; TSA Has Taken Actions to Manage Risk, Improve Coordination, and Measure Performance, But Additional Actions Would Enhance Its Efforts', GAO-10-650T.
36. STSPA, pp. ii, iii.
37. Testimony of Administrator John S. Pistole, Transportation Security Administration, before the Senate Committee on Homeland Security and Governmental Affairs, 'See Something, Say Something, Do Something: Next Steps for Securing Rail and Transit', June 22, 2011.
38. 'TSA Rail, Subway Spot-checks Raise Privacy Issues', Thom Patterson, CNN, updated 10:05 AM EST, Saturday January 28, 2012.
39. Loc. cit.

15. Dutch security risk analysis for multimodal transport

Coen van Gulijk, Megan Anderson and Genserik L. L. Reniers

1. INTRODUCTION

The transport sector is considered to be an important engine for the Dutch economy. The transport sector in the Netherlands is relatively well developed and traditionally relatively large in relation to the nation's size. The two major transport hubs within the Dutch borders dominate the developments within transport security: the Port of Rotterdam and Amsterdam Airport Schiphol. These hubs invest heavily in transport security systems and were important factors in the development of a national security strategy. This chapter focuses on one area in which the Dutch were particularly inspired to take action in order to take transport security to the next level: the National Risk Assessment. In this area, the Dutch government was ahead of EU legislation and has developed elaborate security control systems on a national level. Unfortunately, much of the documentation describing these systems is only available in Dutch or is classified. This chapter unveils some of the Dutch-language documentation so that others may benefit from it.

2. BRIEF OVERVIEW OF TRANSPORT IN THE NETHERLANDS

2.1 The Transport Sector

Although the Netherlands with 16.7 million inhabitants is a relatively small country in Europe it is traditionally strong in the transport sector. Densely populated residential areas, densely industrialized areas and two major transport hubs within its borders fuel the attention on transport logistics and storage.

According to the Dutch Bureau of Statistics, the transport and storage sector had a sales volume of just over 70 billion euros in 2012. According to that same report, about 380 000 people were employed in that sector in 2010 and over 30 000 transport companies existed in 2011. In total, the sector contributed as much as 4 per cent to the gross domestic product (GDP) of the Netherlands in 2012 (Dzambo and De Ruijter, 2012).

Major international transport hubs include the Port of Rotterdam and Amsterdam Airport Schiphol. The development of these transport hubs has been on the political agenda for a long time and was an important factor for the development of laws on safety and security in the last decades.

The Dutch Bureau of Statistics actually separates the transport and storage sector into five parts: transport by land, transport by water, transport by air, storage and other transport services, and mail couriers. Transport by land contributes 25.3 billion euros; water 7.3 billion euros; air 9.9 billion euros; storage and services contributes 23 billion euros; and couriers contribute about 4.8 billion euros. Moreover, 33 per cent of inland goods transport is transported by inland maritime transport which is one of the largest rations for inland maritime transport in Europe. The road freight sector is relatively large in relation to the size of the country; this is directly linked to the major transport hubs: Port of Rotterdam and Schiphol. The total volume is about 400 million tons of which about 25 per cent is international transport; it is estimated that about 46 000 people were employed by this sector in 2013 (ABN, 2014). Goods transport over rail is relatively small in the Netherlands; a major infrastructural project called 'Betuwelijn' or Betuwe Railroad was developed to strengthen that sector but it did not change the position of the relatively small sector.

2.2 Dutch Transport Sector

The transport sector is an important one for the Netherlands. It receives much political attention and large-scale projects have been performed to optimize the transportation sector.

Two major transport hubs act as flywheels for the Dutch transport sector. The Port of Rotterdam and Amsterdam Airport Schiphol have always received a lot of political attention to ensure that these transport hubs remain important international players. In that sense these hubs pave the way for the design of security systems for transport in the Netherlands.

In addition, there were significant efforts made to ensure efficient transport over roads, rails and inland waterways. These efforts were primarily aimed at safety rather than security but the fact that these networks were created made it easy to incorporate them into an integrated security system for transport in the Netherlands. How this works is treated in section 3.

The security system is particularly well developed to ensure security in the Port of Rotterdam, Schiphol and transport networks: through the National Risk Assessment and the Alerting System. These systems were, at least in part, developed to ensure the smooth operation of the major transport hubs, but they are also used for major players in the Dutch critical infrastructure. For smaller organizations, simpler systems were developed but they are not obligatory. One of these systems is briefly discussed in section 3.4.

3.   TRANSPORT SECURITY

The Netherlands has a harmonized security policy for the country as a whole, of which the transport sector is an important part. Though the responsibilities for safe and secure transport are spread around four ministries, the security system is relatively well established. The ministries involved are the following: 1) The Ministry of Safety and Justice, which deals with the criminal courts, police and, as a general notion, deals with security threats to people; 2) The Ministry of Infrastructure and the Environment, which deals with the development and mainte- nance of the various infrastructures: roads, waterways, rail and airports; 3) The Ministry of Economic Affairs, which deals with tax evasion for the transport of goods through the Douane. This one is relatively important because many goods travel through Rotterdam in transit to other coun- tries. However, financial crimes are not considered in this chapter; 4) The Ministry of Defense is the last relevant ministry – housing the military intelligence agency, MIVD – and may be called on to assist in regular policing activities in extreme situations.

3.1   NCTV

An operational role for the security of transport and infrastructures is embedded in the Ministry of Safety and Justice by its department called NCTV. NCTV stands for 'Nationaal Coördinator Terrorismebestrijding en Veiligheid', which translates into National Coordinator for Anti-terrorism and Safety. Safety, in this case, means safety and/or security problems that threaten the Netherlands as a whole, either acute (crisis management) or through prevention (alerting system). The tasks and missions of this department are as follows (NCTV, 2014):

Mission: The NCTV helps keep the Netherlands safe and stable by identifying threats and strengthening the resilience and security of vital interests. Its ultimate purpose is to prevent and minimize social disruption.

Tasks: As reflected in its organizational model, the NCTV's core tasks are as follows:
- analyzing and reducing identified threats;
- providing surveillance and protection for persons, property, services and events, as well as for vital sectors;
- expanding and strengthening cyber security;
- making property, persons, structures and networks more resistant to threats;
- ensuring effective crisis management and crisis communication.

NCTV employs about 250 people, and has five policy departments, two of which are the National Crisis Centre (NCC) and the National Operations Coordination Centre (LOCC).

A list of critical infrastructures was created at least five years before the inception of the related European Council Directive 2008/114/EC (Luijff et al., 2003). The original list of critical infrastructures and services was 31. After some restructuring for the second national analysis of critical infrastructure, the list was as shown in Table 15.1 (MinV&J, 2010). Note that the list of critical infrastructures includes the sectors mentioned by the Council Directive but also includes sectors that are strictly national such as hospital care, dikes, and the stability of the justice process. In total, 12 critical infrastructures are identified, viz. energy, telecommunications, water, food, health, financial services, surface water, public order, law, civil administration, transport, and the chemical and nuclear industries. The names of the individual organizations are classified but there are two exceptions: the Port of Rotterdam (item 28) and Schiphol (item 17) are explicitly mentioned as products in the critical infrastructure for transport. Also, the networks for road, rail and inland waterways are explicitly mentioned (items 29 and 30). This demonstrates the central role of these major transport systems for transport security.

Individual sectors or companies are bound to the government through covenants: agreements between companies (or sector-associations) and the government.

Table 15.1   Critical infrastructures in the Netherlands

Sector		Product or service	
I	Energy	1.	Electricity
		2.	Natural gas
		3.	Oil
II	Telecommunication/ICT	4.	Provision of fixed telecommunications
		5.	Provision of mobile telecommunications
		6.	Radio communication and navigation
		7.	Broadcasting (for crisis communication)
		8.	Internet
III	Water	9.	Provision of drinking water
IV	Food	10.	Provision of food and safeguarding food-safety and security
V	Health	11.	Emergency response and hospital care
		12.	Medicines
		13.	Serums and vaccines
		14.	Nuclear medical services
VI	Financial services	15.	Payment services/payment structures (private)
		16.	Government financial assignment
VII	Surface water	17.	Water quality
		18.	Dikes and water quantity
VIII	Public order and safety	19.	Maintaining public order
		20.	Maintaining public safety
IX	Law and order	21.	Administration of justice and detention
		22.	Maintaining legal order
X	Civil administration	23.	Diplomatic communications
		24.	Informing the public
		25.	Armed forces
		26.	Decision making by public services
XI	Transport	27.	Mainport Schiphol
		28.	Mainport Rotterdam
		29.	Main-roads for road and waterways
		30.	Rail roads
XII	Chemical and nuclear industry	31.	Production and storage/processing of chemical and nuclear substances

Source: MinV&J, 2010.

3.2 Setting Frameworks for Security Plans of an ECI (Article 5 of Council Directive 2008/114/EC)

Export Credit Insurance (ECI) companies and sectors have to perform a number of tasks to ensure their security. Annex II of the Council Directive 2008/114/EC describes them as follows:

> The OSP will identify critical infrastructure assets and which security solutions exist or are being implemented for their protection. The ECI OSP procedure will cover at least:
>
> 1. identification of important assets;
> 2. conducting a risk analysis based on major threat scenarios, vulnerability of each asset, and potential impact; and
> 3. identification, selection and prioritization of counter-measures and procedures with a distinction between:
>
>   – permanent security measures, which identify indispensable security investments and means which are relevant to be employed at all times. This heading will include information concerning general measures such as technical measures (including installation of detection, access control, protection and prevention means); organizational measures (including procedures for alerts and crisis management); control and verification measures; communication; awareness raising and training; and security of information systems,
>
>   – graduated security measures, which can be activated according to varying risk and threat levels.

The objective of this exercise is that ECIs perform security risk analyses and, when necessary, install security management systems. In the Dutch case, however, the government itself performs an extensive security risk analysis called National Risk Assessment (NRA).

The objective of the NRA is that risks that threaten the Netherlands as a whole are assessed and, if deemed necessary, countermeasures are installed or enforced. The Ministry of Safety and Justice has defined five vital interests that have to be protected (MinV&J, 2014):

1. territorial safety;
2. economic safety;
3. ecological safety;
4. physical safety; and
5. social and political stability.

Although the different items of consideration within the list above read 'safety' (translation from Dutch), they should be seen as 'safety and security', since they concern security for an important part, besides safety. The information about what is meant exactly is not available in the public domain but the explanation on public websites is as follows. Territorial safety deals with large-scale territorial threats to the Netherlands such as military occupation or large-scale flooding. Economic safety deals with problems such as disruptions of the internet, financial systems and power-failures. Ecological safety deals with pollution and extreme weather such as drought. Physical safety deals with pandemic illnesses, multiple-death catastrophes, injury and accidental deaths. Social and political stability deals with law and order and civil administration. A more elaborate explanation was published by Van Tuyll in 2013.

Note that the scope of the vital interests is wider than the critical infra-structures list in Table 15.1 but some elements are the same. Threats to the vital interests are analysed in the NRA.

The NRA is an extensive risk analysis method based on multi-criterion risk analysis that analyses threats to the vital interests of the Netherlands. Dozens of institutions in the Netherlands are involved in this annual exercise, the core partners forming the 'Network of analysts for national safety': RIVM (National Institute for Public Health, part of the Ministry of Health, Welfare and Sport), AIVD (General Intelligence and Security Service of the Netherlands, part of the Ministry of Safety and Justice), TNO (Dutch organization for applied research), WODC (Research and documentation centre for crime research, part of the Ministry of Safety and Justice), Clingendael (Netherlands Institute of International Relations), and ISS/Erasmus (the Institute of Social Studies at Erasmus University). The amount of money spent on the NRA is not published publicly but a large consortium is involved in this activity. One of the parties involved as a partner is the vital sectors; these are the companies in the ECI sectors as listed in Table 15.1. Note that their influence on the overall process is relatively low.

The NRA reports to the Dutch public through annual reports called the National Risk Assessment (Mennen, 2013). This document lists the threats, scenarios under consideration, impact-scores based on the threat analysis, and a risk diagram. The risk diagram shows the scenarios that were considered as part of the analysis (for instance, there were 41 scenarios in 2012) and their relative risk scores in a matrix. Many of these scenarios have an indirect impact on multimodal security for the transport of goods, for instance cyber espionage, and for influencing public order. However some scenarios are directly linked to multimodal transport security: viz. blizzards, glazed frost, autumn storms, disruption of satellite systems, disruption of electricity systems, criminalization of ECI companies, wildfires, shipping accidents and rail accidents. These are ten out of a total of 41 scenarios that were considered in 2012, so, in that sense, multimodal transport security was well represented in the NRA. This is partly due to the fact that economic safety, the second vital interest of the Netherlands, is strongly linked to the transport sector.

3.3   Mechanism Security Controls ECI: ATb

The results of the NRA help to prioritize security activities in the Netherlands and help to decide which sectors require additional attention. However, they do not provide day-to-day information flow about security measures for transport security. This task is also delegated to the NCTV (see section 3.1 above). The NCTV uses the NRA as a background for its security analysis and combines it with day-to-day intelligence information from, among other sources, the intelligence services AIVD and MIVD. What the NCTV does with that information exactly is classified but it finds its way to the ATb or 'alerting system'.

The alert system is a system of procedures and technical tools with which to warn vital industries and ECIs in transport about the threat of a terrorist attack and for taking appropriate action. If the intelligence observed increased terrorist threats in a particular sector or a part of the business sectors, relevant government agencies and operational services are informed by the ATb system. The ECI sectors or ECI companies themselves are connected to the ATb system through covenants. Some of these ECIs join out of their own free will but some ECI companies were obliged to join. ECIs that are connected to the ATb system have to develop security plans for different security threats and create a multi-level security plan. Multi-level means that several plans are in place for different threat levels. This ensures that the already prepared plans for additional security measures can be activated immediately when required. Again, the exact procedures and affiliated ECI companies and sectors are classified but it is mentioned on the website (NCTV, 2014) that:

> The decision to up- or -down an alert level for a sector in ATb has to be taken by the Minister of Security and Justice, as coordinating minister for counter-terrorism. The promulgation of an alert level is accompanied by information on the nature of the threat, so that measures can then be focused.

The same website mentions 15 sectors that are connected to the ATb network, viz. drinking water, airports, seaports, rail transport, mass transit, tunnels and flood defenses, the oil industry, the chemical industry, natural gas, telecoms, the nuclear industry, the financial sector, festivals and other public events, and hotels. Note that, again, this is not the same list as the vital sectors (Table 15.1) but it does resemble it closely. Also note that the focus on transport security is relatively strong: ports, airports and trains are among the top priorities.

The ATb system works with security threat levels. The threat levels are published in a quarterly report on terrorism threats to the Netherlands called DTN ('Threat level for terrorism in the Netherlands') that informs the Netherlands about the current threat level. These levels are: minimal, limited, substantial, and critical. The reports are published each quarter of the year but are sometimes published ahead of schedule when the need arises. To date, 35 DTN reports have appeared. These DTN reports are important for multimodal transport security because ECI companies have to adjust their security measures accordingly. That is to say, when an ECI company that is connected to ATb is alerted, it is supposed to upgrade its security measures to a higher level as agreed in the covenant that was agreed upon between the ECI and the NCTV through covenants.

3.4   Security for Companies Not Connected to ATb: VRKI

Companies that are not connected to the ATb are relatively free to choose how to organize their security. In theory, any commercial advisor could design a security system for a transport company. However, a relatively straightforward method for security analysis was developed in the Netherlands and is used relatively often in the sector: VRKI (CCV, 2012). VRKI stands for Improved Security Risk Classification, and it is aimed towards small and medium enterprises that store goods. When the procedure is followed a certificate is awarded that insurers accept as proof of good practice.

The VRKI method is described in a 17-page report that describes a method for assessing the 'attractiveness' for theft crime in relation to goods that companies store. The attractiveness level is subsequently linked to security measures that have to be installed for a certificate. The attractiveness level (or threat level) is expressed in risk classes 1 to 4. The risk classes are defined in a 4 x 5 table that cross-references the relative attractiveness of products and the total monetary value of the stocked products, as seen in Table 15.2. Goods in storage may have different attractiveness levels: computers and electronics are typically 'very high', flowers and porcelain are typical 'low'.

Depending on the risk score (1 through 4) different security measures are prescribed. The security measures are divided into four distinct parts: organizational measures; construction measures; electronic measures; and

Table 15.2   VRKI risk scoring table

Value below	7500 €	75 000 €	150 000 €	300 000 €	Over 300 000 €
Low	1	1	1	1	2
Medium	1	2	2	2	3
High	2	2	2	3	4
Very high	2	3	4	4	4

reaction speed: OBER. For example, when a risk score of 1 is scored, a security plan, a construction that provides at least three minutes delay time for a break-in, and an alarm system are required. It is beyond the scope of this chapter to describe the security prescriptions in detail; suffice to say that each higher level demands more stringent security measures.

VRKI is not a prescribed method by any Ministry but is endorsed by insurers which makes the VRKI method attractive for companies. However, a company may choose any security expertise to secure the goods that it stores and transports if it is outside the ATb system.

3.5   Discussion

The Dutch system to assess security risks for transport is an elaborate one. Many aspects of EU Directive 2008/114/EC are present in the Dutch system but the Dutch system predates that directive by at least five years. The Dutch system is also more elaborate than Directive 2008/114/EC, it does not only cover critical infrastructures on a European level but also includes national networks. Also, the starting point differs; the objective is not just to ensure the enduring operation of critical infrastructures but it is actually part of a plan to protect the critical interests of the nation as a whole.

The nexus in the system is a national risk analysis where the probability and consequence of predetermined scenarios are assessed for all critical infrastructures and their affiliated companies. The exact procedures for the assessment are cloaked in a veil of secrecy but the way in which the various elements of the analysis combine is relatively straightforward: first a context is established, then risks are identified, risks are assessed, risks are dealt with if the situation calls for it, and there is an alert system which informs the stakeholders when the risk level rises. The marvel of it is in the scale of the operation, which is classified. Nevertheless, at least dozens of relevant parties are involved in the process so in that sense it is a huge effort.

Much of the coordination and execution of the process on a national level is NCTV. The NCTV is a part of the Ministry of Security and Justice but, again, much of its work is shrouded in secrecy for obvious reasons.

For companies which were not identified as ECIs or European Critical Infrastructures the rules for security arrangements in the transport sector are less stringent. In fact, these organizations are largely free to choose how they make security arrangements. The VRKI system is relatively attractive to them because insurers may choose to lower costs for the transport organizations.

4. MULTIMODAL HUBS' SECURITY ARRANGEMENTS

While Dutch seaports and airports are embedded in an all-hazards national security framework, these are further nested within broader supranational arrangements, and above local regulations and frameworks. This section provides an overview of the layers of arrangements governing safety and security in the two largest sea- and airports in the Netherlands: the Port of Rotterdam and Amsterdam Airport Schiphol.

4.1 Port of Rotterdam Security

Security in the Port of Rotterdam is mainly governed by the International Ship and Port Facility Security Code (ISPS Code). Developed in 2002 by the International Maritime Organization (IMO) and incorporated into a European Regulation on 1 July 2004, the ISPS Code provides a comprehensive set of measures to enhance the security of ships and port facilities. Three security levels are stipulated by the Code, which is set by the government in accordance with the risk levels of security incidents.

Ocean-going vessels and companies operating a terminal or a loading/ unloading wharf in the Port of Rotterdam are required to develop a security plan based on a risk analysis. Security plans are subsequently evaluated by a team of experts from the police, customs, and Rotterdam Port Authority. It is then presented to the Mayor of Rotterdam for approval. The ISPS Code applies only to passenger ships which sail international sea lanes, mobile drilling rigs, and all terminals at which the aforementioned vessels moor. These terminals are referred to as 'Port Facilities', of which the Port of Rotterdam has 170.

Security in the Port of Rotterdam entails three phases: 1) ships and terminals; 2) port area; and 3) supply chain. Phase one ensures that terminal operators and shipping lines each complete a Port Facility Security Plan (PFSP) with the help of the Port Facility Toolkit, an online web-application that provides online assistance in completing risk analyses and the PFSP. Phase two expands risk analysis and planning to the entire port area to develop an overarching Port Security Plan. The same ISPS methodology is used (i.e. Risk Analysis, Port Security Plan, Security Levels). Phase three involves authorities and companies worldwide under various frameworks and mechanisms. These include the Customs-Trade Partnership Against Terrorism (C-TPAT), the Container Security Initiative (CSI), the 24-hour Manifest Rule, customs x-ray scanners and radiation detection gates. Phase 3 complements phases 1 and 2, providing incentives for all relevant actors to cooperate in the establishment of secure and efficient lanes.

4.2   Schiphol Airport Security

As in the case of security at the Port of Rotterdam, Schiphol Airport security is embedded among layers of supranational, national and local security arrangements. Through Regulation (EC) No 300/2008 the European Parliament and Council have established common rules to protect civil aviation against unlawful interference within the EU. The provisions apply to all airports located in an EU country that are not used exclusively for military purposes. In the Netherlands, in addition to Schiphol Airport, these include Rotterdam, Maastricht, Enschede, Eindhoven and Groningen Airports.

Detailed measures provide the requirements and procedures for the implementation of the common basic standards for protecting civil aviation. These cover: airport security; demarcated areas of airports; aircraft security; passengers and cabin baggage; hold baggage; cargo and mail; air carrier mail and air carrier materials; in-flight and airport supplies; in-flight security measures; staff recruitment and training; security equipment.

According to Regulation (EC) No 300/2008, countries must designate a single appropriate authority to be responsible for the implementation of the common basic standards. In the Netherlands the Civil Aviation Security Department is responsible for ensuring the security of civil aviation, with the Minister of Justice responsible for establishing the standard for civil aviation security (NCTV, 2014). Industry actors (e.g. airlines, airports) are responsible for implementing security measures, under the supervision of the Royal Military and Border Police, which acts on behalf of the Minister of Justice (NCTV, 2014).

The Civil Aviation Security Department is also responsible for drafting and updating national and international aviation security policy and legislation, approving airport and airline security plans, researching new

Table 15.3   Organizations as part of the Amsterdam Airport Security Apparatus

Name	Acronym	Role
Private Security Companies		
Group 4 Securicor	G4S	Guarding/screening
Trigion		Guarding/screening
Securitas		Guarding/screening
International Security and Counter-Terrorism Academy	ISCA	Training (security awareness)
Pro-Check International	PCI	Security technologies, training
ICTS Europe	ICTS	Training (profiling)
Other Security Actors		
Airlines		Security check aircrafts
National Police		Patrolling
Customs		Screening goods
Royal Constabulary (Military Police)		Border control, oversight, coordination, security infrastructure provision
Regulatory Authorities		
National Coordinator for Counterterrorism	NCC	Oversight, responsible for civil aviation security
Security and Public Safety Schiphol	BPVS	Governance platform
Ministry of Justice		Standard setting (National Civil Aviation Security Program)
European Commission	EC	Standard setting (EC Regulation No. 300/2008)

Source: Adapted from Schouten, 2014, 31.

security concepts, processes and equipment, and taking measures in the event of a threat against civil aviation (NCTV, 2014). The Department also guides the Royal Military and Border Police in its oversight tasks and with respect to armed security.

In addition to the aforementioned regulations, Schiphol security is composed of 'coordinated but widely dispersed regulations, calculative arrangements, infrastructures and technical procedures' (Mitchell, 2009, 409). These complex arrangements and networks of actors are displayed in Table 15.3.

5. MIXED RESULTS OF NATIONAL RISK ASSESSMENT STRATEGY

5.1 Nuclear Security Summit

While persistent rumors mention the success of the NRA and the safety of transport in the Netherlands, it is very hard to prove that the NRA is successful. It was suggested to the authors that the highly successful security measures of the Nuclear Security Summit on the prevention of nuclear terrorism in The Hague in 2014 were also, at least in part, due to the NRA and its associated instruments. In the absence of a public evaluation report about the Nuclear Security Summit there are some clues in the public domain that suggest the use of NRA tools.

First a few words about the Nuclear Security Summit (Fontein, 2014; NSS, 2014). The Nuclear Security Summit was held on 24–25 March 2014, in The Hague, with the aim of countering nuclear terrorism on a global scale. Fifty-eight world leaders attended the summit, including President Barack Obama, UN Secretary General Ban Ki-moon, and the King of the Netherlands. It was the largest security operation in the Netherlands in decades, with near draconic security measures that hampered transport all over the Netherlands. The measures included: closing major transport routes and highways, closing the air-space in a 100-km radius and keeping at least two jet fighter planes airborne at any given time. A huge force of 13 000 people were involved, most of whom were police but the military was involved as well. The security forces arrested 140 individuals, intercepted 10 civil unmanned aerial vehicles (UAVs) and performed numerous security checks all over the Netherlands.

Since the Ministry of Safety and Justice had a central role in the organization, the NCTV was the heart of the security coordination. This is clear from a press release of the NCTV in March 2014. In this particular press release, the NCTV thanks its partners and reports that the operation was a great success. It also specifically mentions those states with whom it had been coordinating the security efforts and providing tools analysis (NCTV3, 2014).

Schiphol Airport issued a communication in which airline operators were asked to request for landing slots due to the limited runway capacity through a website called 'Airport Coordination Netherlands' (ACN, 2014). This communication specifically mentioned that part of the Dutch airspace was closed which severely limited the runway capacity of Amsterdam Airport Schiphol. Every plane was mandated to have special permission that could only be granted through an undisclosed Dutch government-affiliated body. Though the Dutch government executed its legal power to close parts of the Dutch air-space, with which the airport had to comply, Schiphol is also an ECI that can be forced to cooperate through the covenants that bind corporations to the Dutch government on security matters. In a similar way, the covenants for railway, bus and tram operators in The Hague area were obliged to cooperate and execute plans of risk management that they were obliged to have as an ECI. It is unknown to the authors whether individual road-transportation companies were contacted in relation to the security measures for the Summit. This may not have been necessary since many roads were simply blocked – such as the A4 and the A44, two major motorways in the Netherlands.

As can be seen, it is very hard to come to a consistent conclusion about the involvement of the NCTV and the instruments for transport and infrastructure security. The document from Schiphol suggests that the covenants between NCTV and the ECIs (of which Amsterdam Airport Schiphol is one) were used to manage the individual transport security stakeholders, but even if there is no solid proof of this it is likely that the communication structures for the ATb alerting system and additional communication structures laid down for these covenants were used. However, the Nuclear Security Summit is not mentioned in the DTN documents during or around the time of the Nuclear Summit (DTN 33, 34 and 35). Also, it seems unlikely that the NRA itself was used as a tool for risk assessment since the NRA is aimed at the prioritization of security problems and the allocation of funds in the long term. For that reason, it is not fit for the task of securing a high-profile event over a short duration. It also seems unlikely that an economically-based risk analysis would justify the use of jet fighter planes to control unlikely security events because of their exorbitant costs. It is more likely that a threat-based analysis was used where all threats were covered to the best of the nation's ability.

5.2   Caveats of Secrecy

The example of the Nuclear Security Summit illustrates the major caveat for the evaluation of this method, i.e. that it is not known publicly how successful this policy for transport security really is. Vlek (2013) makes this clear in his paper on the National Risk Assessment when he writes:

> In the Netherlands so far, hardly any critical discussions about the methodology and the outcomes of the DNRA have been published. The key question for external validation is, of course: Are the Dutch [. . .] governments spending their safety money in an effective, efficient, and equitable manner, including the elaborate national and the many regional risk assessments regularly required?

This statement is still valid at the time this chapter was written. Vlek believes that the traditional concept of risk as a numeric exercise of probability multiplied by consequences may not be ideal for political decision making about risk. He suggests that an evaluation by an independent council or by the scientific community would improve the NRA in the sense that these are more suited for risk decision making. Since intermodal security is deeply ingrained in the NRA, that suggestion also holds for ECIs in the transport sector.

This chapter introduces a recommendation that is based on generic risk control principles. The authors suggest developing a broader risk control framework based on the newly developed ISO 31000 risk management process (ISO, 2009). The ISO guidelines describe the basic principles and guidelines for setting up a risk management system. An important part of this is the risk management process. The NRA mostly focuses on the development of scenarios and analysis of probability and the effects of these scenarios (Mennen, 2013). Therefore, the focus is on risk identification and risk analysis. The presentation of the risk matrix and the brief assessment of relative importance could be classified as risk evaluation. Throughout the process of risk analysis there is frequent communication and consultation but the issues of what risk treatments follow and whether there is a clear monitoring and review are completely missing from the NRA report (Mennen, 2013). This suggests that these processes are either missing or not well developed. Arguably, the multi-level security plans that ECIs are required to have and the ATb system are risk treatment instruments but their contents are, at least partly, shrouded in secrecy and therefore it is impossible to say whether those measures are sufficient and effective.

The key part that is missing in the risk control procedure and in Mennen's report is an effective instrument for monitoring and review. If a good monitoring and review process were developed, it would not be necessary to disclose security-sensitive information. This conclusion is probably true for other countries as well. Public reports can be limited to statements of parts of the system that work well and parts that require improvement. Also, some kind of metric could be developed to indicate the health of the risk management process without ever disclosing just what level of security is achieved for the transportation sector or other parts of the critical infrastructure. For that reason, the authors suggest the development of adequate monitoring and review processes for the NRA and its associated instruments such as ATb and collaborations with ECIs. Note that this recommendation is not so different from Vlek (2013) but it adds to it: a review process has to be installed. This chapter refines that statement to suggest that the review process be designed in line with generic risk management principles. The added value of this particular recommendation is that it becomes easier to publicly demonstrate the success of the vast effort to control multimodal transport and other critical infrastructures. Something that is not impossible today.

5.3   A Holistic Approach to Transport Security

The Dutch approach to multimodal transport security truly embeds transport into a broader security context. This approach is underpinned by the understanding that risks are interconnected, irrespective of organizational borders, national borders and policy fields. Actions throughout the crisis management cycle in the Netherlands all start with a proper risk assessment. Before 2011, different ministries were responsible for separate security policy areas. These responsibilities have since been consolidated and are now managed by one central organization, the Office of the National Coordinator for Security and Counterterrorism, tasked with monitoring risks and threats, protecting interests, and coordinating resistance-building measures across organizations, borders and policy fields. This holistic and integrated approach should be seen as a model by other countries struggling to establish a cohesive national security framework, since many countries are still embedded in a modal framework of regulation and oversight, etc., that affects their ability to truly deal with multimodal safety and security.

6.   CONCLUSIONS

Two major transport hubs within the borders of the Netherlands infuse the effort for transport security in the Netherlands: Amsterdam Airport Schiphol and the Port of Rotterdam. They are the crown jewels of the Dutch transport sector, which, as a whole, is a relatively large sector in relation to the size of the country. The major role of transport has sparked the political will for the improvement of infrastructure projects and infrastructure security. The system for the security of multimodal transport described in this chapter is one of those projects.

The security of multimodal transport in the Netherlands is controlled in an elaborate system where government and infrastructure partners work together. The system is a state-initiated proactive method. The method is in line with that of EU Directive 2008/114/EC but is much more elaborate. Its inception also predates the directive by at least five years which demonstrates that the Netherlands was a pioneer in developing security systems for critical infrastructures of which multimodal transport is a part.

The NCTV is the part of the Ministry of Security and Justice that is mostly responsible for the coordination of this security system. The NCTV makes sure that the NRA is timely and that threats to the infrastructures are communicated to ECIs; generally, it ensures the smooth operation of the system.

This chapter shows that the effort of ensuring safe infrastructures is significant. That is to say, it is a huge effort in which many parties partake but it is also scientifically challenging in the sense that an effective risk analysis method had to be developed that produced sensible information from intelligence, infrastructure stakeholders and the various ministries.

Unfortunately, it is not possible to assess whether the huge efforts made by the NCTV and its partners have been and are successful. This is a major caveat in an otherwise elaborate methodology. Vlek (2013) was the first to mention this, and this work corroborates that fact. Where Vlek suggested scientific and/or external review processes, we suggest that any review system is based on generic risk management principles that are laid down in ISO 31000.

As an afterthought, it is important to remember that this work is based on information that is available in the public domain. Much of the relevant information was derived from Dutch-language papers that were issued by various parts of the Ministry of Security and Justice, the Ministry of Infrastructure and the Environment, the Ministry of Economic Affairs and the Ministry of Defense. In that sense, this chapter discloses Dutch-language grey literature (that which is not controlled by commercial publishers) to a wider audience. Despite the fact that there are no clear communications concerning the exact functioning of the NRA, the data that they use, and the size of the effort of this work, provides an overview of the elaborate system that is in place for multimodal transport security in the Netherlands. We recommend that government representatives who wish to know more about this system communicate directly with NCTV; once the security clearance is out of the way it may be easier to learn more about the essence of the methods it uses.

REFERENCES

ABN (2014), Visie op Sectoren 2014, ABN-Amro Bank, Amsterdam.
CCV (2012), Verberde Risicoklassenindeling voor bedrijven, Centrum voor Criminaliteitspreventie, Document D03/376.
Dzambo, I. and De Ruijter, R. (2012), *Branchebeschrijving vervoer en opslag*, The Hague: CBS.
ISO (2009), ISO 31000 Risk management, principles and guidelines.
Luijff, E., Burger, H.H. and Klaver, M.H.A. (2003), Bescherming Vitale Infrastructuur: Quick-scan naar vitale producten en diensten (management deal), TNO report FEL-03-C001, The Hague.

Mennen, M.G. (2013), Nationale Risico-beoordeling 2012, RIVM, Report E/609042/13.

MinV&J (2010), 2e inhoudelijke analyse bescherming kritieke infrastructuur, Minstry of Justice, Report 22-02-2010.

Mitchell, T. (2009), 'Carbon democracy', *Economy and Society*, **38** (3), 399–432.

Schouten, P. (2014), 'Security as controversy: Reassembling security at Amsterdam Airport', *Security Dialogue*, **45** (1), 23–42. DOI: 10.1177/0967010613515014.

Van Tuyll, M. (2013), 'Dealing with future risks in the Netherlands', *Biosecurity and Bioterrorism: Biodefense Strategy, Practice, and Science*, **11**, Suppl. 1. Mary Ann Liebert, Inc.

Vlek, C. (2013), 'How solid is the Dutch (and British) national risk assessment? Overview and decision-theoretic evaluation', *Risk Analysis*, **33** (6), 948–971.

Electronic Sources

ACN (2014), available at: http://www.slotcoordination.nl/page.asp?tc=nss2014, (accessed July 2014).

Fontein, J. (2014), Elf dingen die u nog niet wist over de nucleare top in Den Haag, Volkskrant of March 23rd 2014, available at: http://www.volkskrant. nl/vk/nl/30400/Nucleaire-top-Den-Haag/article/detail/3620062/2014/03/21/Elf-dingen-die-u-nog-niet-wist-over-de-nucleaire-top-in-Den-Haag.dhtml (accessed May 2014).

MinV&J (2014), available at: https://www.nctv.nl/onderwerpen/nv/ (accessed May 2014).

NCTV (2014), available at: https://english.nctv.nl/themes/Counterterrorism/ Security_and_civil_aviation/ (accessed 6 October 2014).

NCTV3 (2014), available at: https://www.nctv.nl/Images/nieuwsbrief-ncc-maart-2014_tcm126-548797.htm (accessed June 2014).

NSS (2014), available at: https://www.nss2014.com/en/nss-2014 (accessed May 2014).

16. Multimodal passenger transportation security in Israel

Yair Wiseman and Yahel Giat

1. INTRODUCTION

For much of its existence, Israel has been the target of numerous terroristic organizations, which in their attempt to achieve political gains and recognition have attacked practically every form of public transportation resulting in thousands of civilian deaths and many more wounded (Rubin, 1994; Beres, 1995).

These attacks have sought to exploit the vulnerabilities of civic transportation. While aviation security has drawn most of the international attention, Israel has to deal with a more common, albeit less noticeable, problem – the problem of public and private road traffic. Although more people die in car accidents than in terror attacks on transportation, the Israeli government has put much effort into preventing terror attacks; sometimes even more than the efforts to prevent car accidents, even though Israel Defense Forces (IDF) are also involved in car accident analysis and prevention (Grinberg and Wiseman, 2007, 2010, 2013). For example, in 2013, 309 people died in many transportation accidents, whereas there were only a few terrorist attacks on transportation means and only two casualties.

In this chapter we discuss the many dimensions of the problem of transportation security in Israel and how Israel has come to deal with these threats of terroristic attacks. Special attention is given to Israel's security issues and their solutions in the interface between the different modes of transportation, for example when passengers transfer between train and bus or when buses cross security posts between the Judea and Samaria region and the rest of Israel.

This chapter is organized as follows: section 2 gives the background to the security of transportation in Israel. Section 3 reviews the security measurement of the main transportation means and infrastructures. Section 4 describes how Israel confronts the threats to transportation. Finally, the last section concludes the chapter.

2.   BACKGROUND

Of all the issues involved in transportation security, aviation security has drawn most of the attention of public awareness. Airplanes are particularly vulnerable vehicles for terrorist attacks. There is a pressure difference between the atmosphere outside of the fuselage and the aircraft interior; therefore even a small mass of explosive is able to blow up an entire plane, thus making this type of attack very attractive to terrorists. As a result, countries have come to deal with aviation security in various ways as discussed in Dempsey (2003), and with the September 11, 2001 attacks being a major drive in boosting those security measures Israel too has adopted many measures to safeguard its aviation system. However, one aspect of its approach deserves more attention – from the moment a plane takes off, the security forces on the ground are detached and their ability to lend a hand in the case of an emergency does not exist. Thus planes can not only serve as a protected shelter for hijackers but also as a convenient transportation mean to get to various hostile destinations.

Another development in transportation security concerns the rail industry. The world is well beyond the classical western train hijacking and rail security nowadays must deal with various threats and is a developed field as reported by Riley (2004) and Peterman (2005). The security of other ground transportation is described in Uschan (2006).

Intermodal hubs – airports, railroad and bus stations – are frequently attractive for terror groups. The key transportation hubs in Israel are:

● Aviation: Ben Gurion Airport and Eilat Airport.
● Rail: Tel Aviv Central Station and Haifa Central Station.
● Bus: the bus system is decentralized, with each small- to medium-sized town having its own central bus station. The major metropolitan areas have each a major central bus station as well as neighborhood 'mini' bus stations.

Most transportation hubs are in enclosed areas and are therefore relatively easy to monitor. However, some of the smaller central bus stations are open in nature and are simply a cluster of stations along a city block, with open access. Low passenger density reduces the risk posed by these stations or hubs.

The security of transportation in Israel is regulated by several authorities:

● The Department of Security and Transportation Security in Israel's Transport Ministry.
● The Israeli Police.

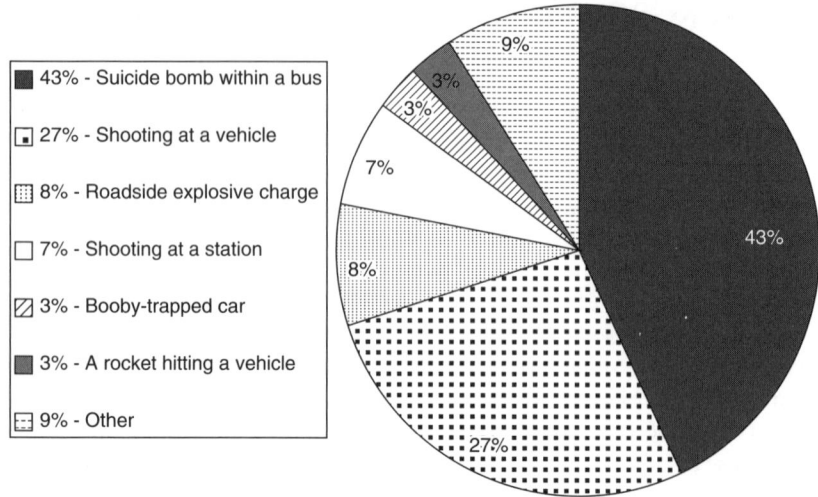

43% - Suicide bomb within a bus

27% - Shooting at a vehicle

8% - Roadside explosive charge

7% - Shooting at a station

3% - Booby-trapped car

3% - A rocket hitting a vehicle

9% - Other

Figure 16.1   Terrorist incidents by transport mode

- Israel's General Security Service.
- IDF's Home Front Command.

The number of authorities hampers security in a number of ways. Further, the various authorities tend to blame each other for the faults and usually demand that other authorities pay the expense of the security measures (Ginter and Shefer, 2007).

Unfortunately, there is no coherent regulation process for security measurements. Actually, when there is a major terror attack, the authorities set an ad hoc meeting and decide how to improve the security measures. When there is a quiet period, no new regulation is initiated.

In the first decade of the 21st century, the total number of terror incidences involving transportation was 1178. The distribution of historical terrorist incidents by type is outlined in Figure 16.1.

2.1   Attacks on Israeli Ground Transportation

Road traffic in general and passenger buses in particular were the target of attacks even before the inception of the State of Israel, and have been targeted dozens of times since. Some of these attacks have had a significant impact on security operations. These incidences have involved the hijacking of private and commercial vehicles, extended chases with shots fired, and related explosions (Shay, 2005; Marcus and Zilberdik, 2011).

Security equipment and procedures were gradually installed and implemented, mostly as a result of these attacks. Some of these measures include fences blocking access between passengers and drivers in many of the public buses, with the aim of preventing a potential terrorist from interfering with the driver's view and control of the vehicle (Emerson, 2003). In addition, the front seats in each bus are reserved for security forces personnel and increased attention has been paid to efforts to raise passenger alertness. Since attacks typically involve either a suicide bomber or explosive devices placed by terrorists, the awareness and alertness of citizens is the most important tool against these attacks. The second layer of security is security personnel randomly boarding buses to examine them for unattended bags or suspicious passengers. Any person who wants to enter a central bus station has to go through a security check and their bags must be examined. However, despite these procedures the system is flawed as passengers who board buses at regular bus stops are not examined. Such a loophole in the system allowed a Hamas suicide bomber to board a bus packed with 50 passengers and detonate a bomb that killed nine people and injured thirty-eight.

Buses are clearly the target of choice for attacks for many of the reasons discussed below in section 3. There have been three notable attacks against train stations. The first involved a suicide bomber who was able to pass the security check and enter the train station. The other two notable terroristic events relating to rail transportation happened within less than two months of each other in the summer of 2002. In both cases, explosives laid on the tracks were remotely activated (Anti-Defamation League, 2004). Fortunately, these incidents resulted in only a few injuries and, with the heightening of security measures to protect rail lines, it seems that terrorists have abandoned this form of attack.

Bearing this in mind, and the fact that many of the terroristic attacks in Israel are executed with the active help of Arab Israelis, the Israeli security procedures allow race as a parameter to be considered. Therefore, while any Israeli will have their bag checked briefly before entering a central bus station, Arab Israelis are typically subject to a more thorough search of their bag. This profiling has been approved by the court system. In order to minimize negative effects on the innocent Arab population, security personnel are trained to be as professional and cordial as possible.

3. SECURITY OF TRANSPORTATION MEANS AND INFRASTRUCTURES

3.1 Aviation Security Issues

An aircraft is a very vulnerable object (Wiseman, 2013a, 2013b, 2014); therefore terrorists have targeted it on occasion. They have carried out merciless attacks against civil aviation targets to shock world opinion. These activities have been sponsored by a number of Arab countries, which provided the terrorists with a variety of measures including training camps, diplomatic means, and forged documentation. These countries allow the hijacked planes to land in their territory and grant protection to the hijackers after the dubious missions have been accomplished.

Israel's aviation activity is very concentrated with its biggest airport handling more than 98 percent of international travel (by passengers and by planes). In total, Israel has seven active civilian airports. Most of the domestic travel is between the center of Israel (Ben Gurion and Tel Aviv Airports) and Eilat (more than 95 percent of which is passenger traffic). There is one other major international airport servicing Eilat (Ovda Airport). Three more airports have only residual international travel (Eilat, Tel Aviv and Haifa Airports). Table 16.1 presents statistics from 2012 for the five largest airports (Israel Airport Authority, 2013).

Israel security regulation centers attention on the human factor. Israeli security officers interrogate passengers with the objective of finding their ethnic group. No Jewish person has ever carried out a terror attack on a plane, but there have been a small number of Arabs who have, and so by looking at the name or physical appearance of the passenger the security officer focuses on Arabs and Muslims. In the international airport, each and every passenger (including non-Arab passengers) is questioned as to why they are visiting Israel, in addition to some other questions about their trip. The idea is that these questions might be nerve-racking for terrorists

Table 16.1   Aviation traffic for the five largest airports during 2012

	Planes (international)	Passengers (international)	Planes (domestic)	Passengers (domestic)
Ben Gurion	89737	12400479	8087	733513
Eilat	122	1259	18116	1447110
Ovda	1029	118826		
Tel Aviv	1709	7008	25084	728879
Haifa	1947	11283	10090	66750

and a potential terrorist might provide incoherent answers. In addition, passengers leaving Israel are inspected against a computerized list. The list is compiled by the Israeli Ministry of Interior, the Israeli police, and also includes data from Interpol. The purpose of the list is to make it easier to spot suspicious passengers.

While various civil rights groups have pleaded with Israel to stop its ethnic group targeting, Israel insists that it is inevitable as it is impractical to subject every passenger to a high level of scrutiny (Tucker, 2008). The reason for its scrutiny system is explained quite bluntly by Rafi Sela (a security officer at Ben Gurion International Airport):

> The Arabs are going through a much tighter investigation-interrogation because the threat they pose is larger than an Israeli who served in the army who is going on vacation. How many blond, blue-eyed ladies have brought down planes in the last 20 years? They were all fanatic Muslims. So, if you are a Muslim, we have to find out if you are a fanatic or not. (McGregor, 2010)

This policy is routinely criticized because it leads to the humiliation of many innocent people. As a result, over the years technological security procedures have been put in place to minimize these unfortunate incidents and security personnel are trained to be as professional and cordial as possible (Israel Supreme Court, 2012).

Recently, Israel asked the U.S. to postpone its new security regulations for the inspection of cargo arriving from Israeli airports. It is possible that the new regulations will increase the cost of the merchandise and threaten to hurt exports between the two countries. Director General of the Ministry of Transport, Uzi Yitzchaki sent a letter to the U.S. Transportation Security Administration (TSA) to delay the new security procedures by six months.

The subjects of the debate are El Al's dedicated cargo flights direct to the U.S. and the combined cargo and passenger flights of commercial American airlines like United Continental Airlines and Delta. Disagreements between the Ministry of Transport, the General Security Service of Israel, and the airport terminals regarding who should finance the additional expenditure involved in implementing the new U.S. regulation hinders its actual implementation.

3.2 Rail Security

In the past decade Israel's passenger train system has experienced tremendous growth, more than doubling its passenger volume. As of 2013 Israel's rail systems comprise 1100 km with 47 passenger stations and 30 freight stations. In 2011 the train system carried 40 million passengers and shipped more than 6.2 million tons. Approximately 340 passenger trains travel in the system daily, along with approximately 80 freight trains (Israel Railways, 2013).

Despite this growth, the railroad layout of the train system is quite basic, with a long single north–south line and a few short west–east lines branching off it. Since trains are clearly a more 'attractive' target than buses, the security protocols are much stricter and in fact the train system is viewed as a 'closed system' in the sense that no passenger should be able to access it without having to pass through security checks. This approach is fairly easy to implement, as there are few train stations (a total of 47).

Rail tracks are not monitored, but since an attempt to put a demolition charge on a rail track, the Israeli Parliament passed this amendment to the railways law in 2011 (Israeli Parliament [Knesset], 2011):

> A person who does one of these without an authority – is liable to one year in prison:
> (1) Puts or throws on a railway wood, stone or any material or another thing;
> (2) Picks up, removes, loosens or displaces rail, the railway sleeper or any material or other thing belonging to railways;
> (3) Turns, moves, opens or diverts a switch or any other machine belonging to railways;
> (4) Activates, shows, hides, removes or turns a light signaling device on or near a railway;
> (5) Does anything else that interferes with its activities or endangers the safety of a passenger or any other person in the railway.

Due to the limited coverage of the passenger rail system in Israel many passengers must combine train travel with bus travel. It seems as though there is not enough coordination between the two security systems. For example, passengers between bus and train stations may leave a secure zone only to have to pass a redundant security check. In our opinion there is much room for improvement in this aspect.

3.3   Scheduled Bus System

Until the end of the 1990s only two major bus companies operated in Israel. Egged, the largest of the two, was (and still is) one of the largest bus companies in the world with more than 3000 buses operating 25 267 daily routes covering 720 073 km per day (Dun & Bradstreet Israel, 2013). In the 1990s the government decided to reform the transportation system and encouraged the entry of more bus companies into the public system. Today, there are about 18 different official public bus companies with many more operating in the private sector. Buses on scheduled routes cover a distance of more than 500 million km annually (Israel Central Bureau of Statistics, 2013a).

Whereas the security approach to aviation and rail transportation systems is to sterilize them, this approach is not applicable to the bus system due to its geographic spread. The bus system is decentralized, with each small- to medium-sized town having its own central bus station. The major metropolitan areas have a major central bus station as well as neighborhood 'mini' bus stations. Most transportation hubs are in enclosed areas and are therefore relatively easy to monitor. However, some of the smaller central bus stations are open in nature and are simply a cluster of stations along a city block, with open access. As passenger density in this location is fairly low, the risk posed by these stations is fairly small. Nevertheless, as mentioned above, terrorists use these accessible stations to board buses which eventually take them into the more central bus stations. To counter these efforts, bus drivers and passengers alike are expected to be alert to any suspicious behavior and especially baggage left behind. This civic behavior has helped avert numerous attacks.

Due to the different nature of the transportation modes, each has its own security system. Except for the light rail (in Jerusalem) there is no single ticket service between rail and bus. Therefore, even for proximate bus and rail stations transferring passengers need to pass through the security and ticketing systems of each of the transportation systems.

3.4   Road Blockages

Israel has an undersized road system. As a matter of fact, the paved road system contains only 10 489 km (6 518 miles) of urban road, 6582 km (4090 miles) of non-urban roads and 1626 km (1010 miles) of access roads. Total paved roads are just 18 697 km (11 618 miles) (Israel Central Bureau of Statistics, 2013b); however, even such an undersized road system cannot be completely protected.

One remarkable phenomenon of the roads of Judea and Samaria is the coexistence of Jewish Israelis and Muslim Arabs. This daily meeting of these two populations, who are otherwise usually physically separated, seldom creates any notable story. However, these meetings are opportunities to see the human condition at its best and at its worst, with the latter requiring special attention from security forces (Seager, 2000).

The way in which Israel deals with these problems is multi-leveled.

First, Israelis are not permitted to drive in A or B areas (Area A is an area where the Palestinian Authority has civil and security control, whereas in Area B the Palestinian Authority has civic authority and Israel has security control). Moreover, it is considered a felony for Israeli citizens to enter the A areas (only enforced against Jewish citizens, as Arab citizens are de facto allowed to enter these areas).

Second, to allow for the mobility of Jewish residents in these areas, Israel has invested heavily in the construction of 'circumventing' roads; that is, roads that do not go through the Arab cities, but rather surround them so that Jewish traffic is permitted only in C areas (defined as areas where Israel has civil and security control). It should be stressed that these 'circumventing' roads are typically open to both the Israeli and the Arab populations. The only security advantage they afford to Israelis is the fact that they do not need to enter Arab cities. Therefore, Jews driving on these roads are not immune to the danger of passing car shoot-outs.

Third, as a means to prevent Jews from entering those areas they are not allowed to enter, roadblocks are placed in central junctions. These road-blocks have a double purpose – the first of which is to prevent the entry of Jewish people and the second is to control the Arab population especially in light of intelligence information with regard to possible security threats. On at least one occasion, soldiers crossed such a roadblock but were not stopped by the soldiers manning it, with terrible consequences. This could happen because unless there is specific intelligence about a terroristic activity, soldiers are instructed to allow traffic to flow with as little interference as possible.

The final level of security is the mobile or temporary roadblock. These roadblocks are designed to deter terroristic activity by creating uncertainty and surprise. Usually, the delay to Arab drivers is minimal unless specific intelligence about terroristic activities is available.

3.5 Shootings From Cars

Drive-by shooting also occurs from cars. Such cases have induced the Ministry of Defense to modify all the public transportation vehicles that go through Arab populated areas into bulletproof vehicles. The Israeli government also subsidizes travel fares for public transportation with the aim of inducing more Jewish citizens to leave behind their unprotected private cars and to use the bulletproof public transportation buses.

3.6 Hitchhikers

Until the Oslo Accords it was common practice in Israel to hitchhike. This practice has been all but eliminated in Israel.

The IDF specifically prohibits soldiers from hitchhiking, thus practically eliminating this form of transportation. There are still some groups who do hitchhike, most notably Orthodox Jews, and indeed there are many attempts by terrorists to kidnap such a soldier or civilian in order to either murder him or use him as a bargaining chip for the release of jailed convicted terrorists (Paine, 1995).

3.7 The Use of Ambulances

Since Israel admits hundreds of non-Israeli Arab patients to its hospitals for humanitarian reasons every year, the need to address the use of ambulances by terrorists is critical (Kendall, 2001). The most commonly used solution is that the Red Crescent ambulance transports the patient to a security checkpoint in which an Israeli Mogen David ambulance is waiting to continue the transfer to the Israeli hospital. Unfortunately, this solution is possible only in certain cases – where the need for the extra ambulance is known upfront. Sadly, when the Red Crescent ambulance itself needs to go through security it must be examined thoroughly despite the resulting delay. In October 2004 a plan to use an ambulance full of explosives as a bomb was thwarted, with the arrest of the plotters. This, and intelligence about planned 'unconventional' use of ambulances, instigated a temporary policy, which lasted for a few weeks, of prohibiting the passage of Red Crescent ambulances inside the Green Line.

3.8 Multimodal Transportation Hubs

Most transportation hubs in Israel are located in major cities and comprise train stations and central bus stations. The bus station is either an open space (e.g. Tel Aviv) or inside a big structure, which would also include a shopping center (e.g. Haifa). Typically, the bus station and the train station are separate entities and usually each has its own security procedures. In some locations there are passages (boardwalks or tunnels) connecting the two and allowing passengers to avoid redundant security checks. In addition to the rail and bus modes, there are taxi stations near these hubs. However, these taxi stations do not share any security functions with the rail and bus stations. Entering these hubs entails, as a minimum, passing through metal detectors and an examination of luggage and handbags. It should be noted that Israeli travelers are accustomed to these procedures as they are common practice also when entering schools and shopping malls.

Except for the rail–bus hubs, there is only one other noticeable multimodal hub in Israel. This is Ben Gurion Airport, which is also accessed by trains, buses, taxis, and other private vehicles. Security checks of passengers in this hub begin outside the airport, which has only two public access roads, and are repeated, more thoroughly, at the entrance to each terminal. A more detailed, albeit somewhat outdated, description of the security procedures in the airport is given in Tucker (2008). By layering and repeating the security checks, security officers lessen the chance of a terrorist slipping in the terminal through switching between transportation modes. For example, trying to enter the terminal by train requires passing through the security check in the original train station and the security check when entering the airport terminal. If a person boards a bus in a small rural station (with no security checks), he/she will still be inspected at the entrance of the airport and then again, more thoroughly, when entering the terminal. In addition to these specific inspections, plainclothes security officials continually scan the crowds for any suspicious travelers.

4.   SECURITY BY ATTACKS AND STRIKES

In Israel the number of terror attacks on transportation means has steadily decreased during the last decade, as can be seen in Figure 16.2.

Considering the decline in the number of attacks one might be led to believe that the procedures taken by the Israeli government and its defensive attitude are effective and successful. However, this is only a partial picture and does not provide a complete understanding of what has really happened. The terrorists' motivation to act did not decline and while this

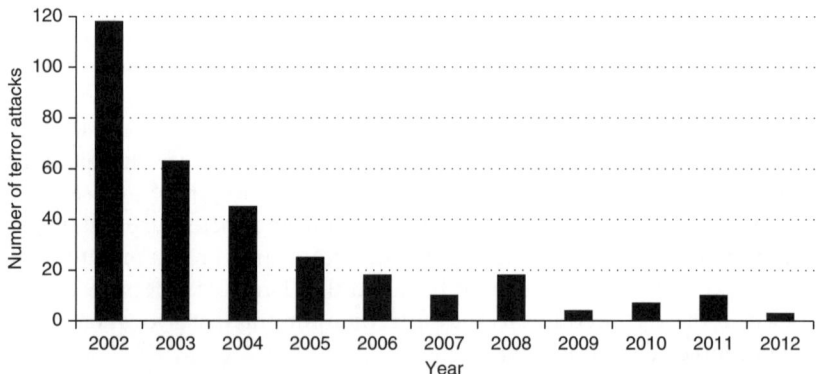

Source: Israel Ministry of Foreign Affairs, 2014b.

Figure 16.2   Number of terror attacks on transportation means from 2002 to 2012

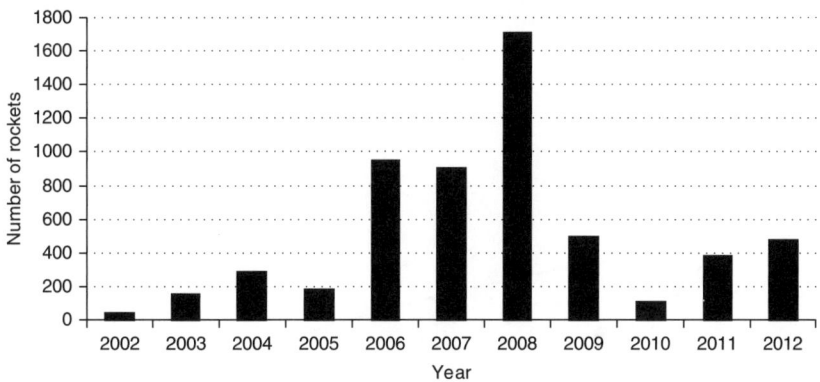

Source: Israel Ministry of Foreign Affairs, 2007, 2014a.

Figure 16.3   Number of rockets fired at Israel from 2002 to 2012

motivation did not translate into suicide bombings, it is manifested in the increasing number of rockets fired into Israel.

Figure 16.3 shows the number of rockets which hit Israel during the same period. It can be seen clearly that from 2002 to 2009 the terror efforts of the Arab militant groups changed. The terror assaults on transportation means were replaced by the terror assaults of rockets firing at Israeli cities.

The war Oferet Yezuka (Cast Lead) began on December 27, 2008 and ended on January 18, 2009. During this war Israel Defense Forces entered Gaza. Israel captured and killed 1166 Arabs, most of whom were terror activists. This strike at the terror groups in Gaza was substantial, but not incurable and the heads of these terror groups are still alive and free. As a result of the war, the level of terror was significantly reduced both in transportation means and in all the other terror issues including rocket firing. This can be also seen in Figures 16.2 and 16.3.

A statistical analysis of the relationship between rockets and terror attacks is very revealing. Until 2008, the correlation between the two is negative at −0.65. This is a very high correlation (in absolute terms) and signifies the trade-off effect between the two. Indeed, operation Oferet Yetzuka succeeded (at least temporarily) in reducing both dimensions of terror, but without continued pressure on the infrastructure and the leadership of the terror this effect will fade (Kurth, 2009). Figure 16.4 demonstrates this trade-off effect. In this figure we plot the number of rockets fired at Israel in each year against the number of attacks on transportation means during the same year. We then plot the quadratic approximation of

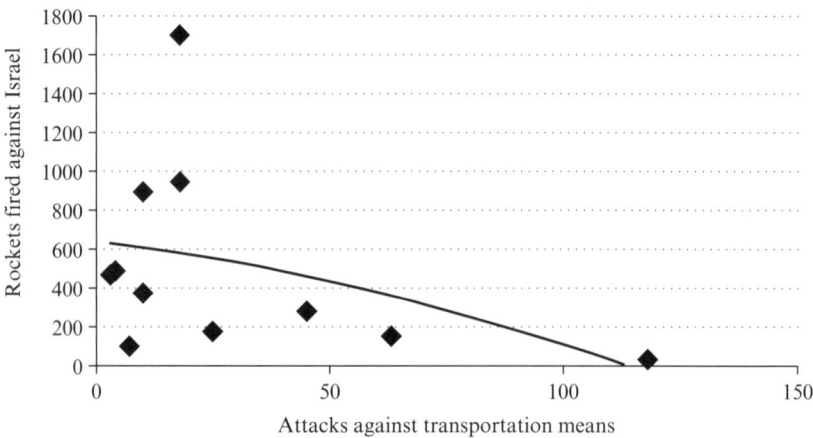

Figure 16.4   Number of rockets fired at Israel in each year and number of terroristic attacks carried out against transportation means during the same year

this scatter plot. The resulting trend line provides a stark picture of how the reduction of attacks on transportation means results in an increase of rocket attacks.

5.   CONCLUSIONS

Israel has experienced many terror attacks in the past. These terror attacks have pushed Israel to implement various security measures in transportation infrastructures and means. Although more people die in car accidents than in terror attacks on transportation, the terror attacks have a higher psychological effect (Galili-Weisstub and Benarroch, 2005). Thus the Israeli government has adopted many policies to prevent terror attacks; sometimes expending even more effort than that aimed at preventing car accidents. Though these policies have proven quite effective, Israelis continue to live under the threat of terrorist attacks.

REFERENCES

Anti-Defamation League (2004), 'Major Terrorist Attacks in Israel', available at: http://archive.adl.org/israel/israel_attacks.asp (accessed 1 February, 2014).
Beres, L. R. (1995), 'Attrition, Annihilation and the End of Israel: A Strategic

and Jurisprudential View', *University of Detroit Mercy Law Review*, **73** (3), 479–498.

Dempsey, P. S. (2003), 'Aviation Security: The Role of Law in the War Against Terrorism', *Columbia Journal of Transnational Law*, **41** (3), 649–733.

Dun & Bradstreet Israel (2013), 'Egged Transportation Cooperative Society Ltd.', available at: http://duns100.dundb.co.il/ts.cgi?tsscript=comp_heb&duns=600008114 (accessed 1 February, 2014).

Emerson, S. (2003), *American Jihad: The Terrorists Living Among Us*, New York: The Free Press.

Galili-Weisstub, E. and Benarroch, F. (2005), 'The Immediate Psychological Consequences of Terror Attacks in Children', *Journal of Aggression, Maltreatment & Trauma*, **9** (3–4), 323–334.

Ginter, D. and Shefer, H. (2007), 'Tomorrow: No Public Transport Security', available at: http://www.nrg.co.il/online/1/ART1/677/738.html (accessed 1 February, 2014).

Grinberg, I. and Wiseman, Y. (2007), 'Scalable Parallel Collision Detection Simulation', Proc. Signal and Image Processing (SIP-2007), Honolulu, Hawaii, USA, 380–385.

Grinberg, I. and Wiseman, Y. (2010), 'Scalable Parallel Simulator for Vehicular Collision Detection', Proc. IEEE Conference on Vehicular Electronics and Safety (IEEE ICVES-2010), Qingdao, ShanDong, China, 116–121.

Grinberg, I. and Wiseman, Y. (2013), 'Scalable Parallel Simulator for Vehicular Collision Detection', *International Journal of Vehicle Systems Modelling and Testing*, **8** (2), 119–144.

Israel Airport Authority (2013), 'Passenger and Aircraft Traffic', available at: http://www.iaa.gov.il/Rashat/he-IL/Rashot/AbouttheAuthority/Statistics/ (accessed 1 February, 2014).

Israel Central Bureau of Statistics (2013a), 'Roads by Length and Area', available at: http://www.cbs.gov.il/shnaton64/st24_10.pdf (accessed 1 February, 2014).

Israel Central Bureau of Statistics (2013b), 'Transport – Physical Data', available at: http://www.cbs.gov.il/reader/shnaton/templ_shnaton.html?num_tab=st24_01x&CYear=2013 (accessed 1 February, 2014).

Israel Ministry of Foreign Affairs (2007), 'Rocket Threat From the Gaza Strip, 2000–2007', available at: http://www.mfa.gov.il/mfa/foreignpolicy/terrorism/palestinian/pages/rocket%20threat%20from%20the%20gaza%20strip%202000--2007.aspx (accessed 1 February, 2014).

Israel Ministry of Foreign Affairs (2014a), 'Rocket Fire from Gaza and Palestinian Ceasefire Violations after Operation Cast Lead (Jan 2009)', available at: http://mfa.gov.il/MFA/ForeignPolicy/Terrorism/Pages/Palestinian_ceasefire_violations_since_end_Operation_Cast_Lead.aspx (accessed 1 February, 2014).

Israel Ministry of Foreign Affairs (2014b), 'Victims of Palestinian Violence and Terrorism Since September 2000', available at: http://www.mfa.gov.il/mfa/foreignpolicy/terrorism/palestinian/pages/victims%20of%20palestinian%20violence%20and%20terrorism%20sinc.aspx (accessed 1 February, 2014).

Israel Railways (2013), 'Israel Railways Statistics', available at: http://www.rail.co.il/HE/About/Pages/statistics.aspx (accessed 1 February, 2014).

Israel Supreme Court (2012), 'Bagatz' Decision 4797/07, available at: http://elyon2.court.gov.il/files/07/970/047/N35/07047970.N35.htm (accessed 1 February, 2014).

Israeli Parliament (Knesset) (2011), 'Israel Railways Ordinance', available at: http://www.nevo.co.il/Law_word/law01/260_002.doc (accessed 1 February, 2014).

Kendall, J. N. (2001), 'Israeli Counter-Terrorism: Targeted Killings under International Law', *N.C. Law Review*, **80**, 1069–1088.

Kurth, C. A. (2009), *How Terrorism Ends: Understanding the Decline and Demise of Terrorist Campaigns*, Princeton, NJ: Princeton University Press.

Marcus, I. and Zilberdik, N. J. (2011, September), 'Palestinian Authority Glorification of Terrorists and Payment of Salaries to Terrorists and British Funding', Palestinian Media Watch.

McGregor, G. (2010), 'Looking Passengers in Eye Best Airport Security, Israeli Expert Says', Canwest News Service, Canada.

Paine, R. (1995, January), 'Signal Values and Politics: The Puzzle of the Israeli-Palestinian Prisoner Exchange, May 1985', *Anthropological Forum*, **7** (2), 245–258.

Peterman, D. R. (2005, May), 'Passenger Rail Security: Overview of Issues', Library of Congress, Washington, DC, USA: Congressional Research Service.

Riley, K. J. (2004), 'Terrorism and rail security', RAND Corporation, Santa Monica, California, CT-224.

Rubin, B. (1994), *Revolution until Victory?: The Politics and History of the PLO*, Boston, MA: Harvard University Press.

Seager, M. (2000), 'I'll have nightmares for the rest of my life', available at: http://rotter.net/israel/mark.htm (accessed 1 February, 2014).

Shay, S. (2005), *The Axis of Evil: Iran, Hizballah, and the Palestinian Terror*, New Jersey: Transaction Publishers, Rutgers – The State University.

Tucker, J. (2008), 'Strategies for Countering Terrorism – Lessons from the Israeli Experience', *Coin Central, The Counter Insurgency Journal*, available at: http://coincentral.wordpress.com/2008/06/04/strategies-for-countering-terrorism-lessons-from-the-israeli-experience/ (accessed 1 February, 2014).

Uschan, M. V. (2006), *Suicide Bombings in Israel and Palestinian Terrorism*, Milwaukee, WI: World Almanac Library, Gareth Stevens Publishing.

Wiseman, Y. (2013a), 'Camera That Takes Pictures of Aircraft and Ground Vehicle Tires Can Save Lives', *Journal of Electronic Imaging*, **22** (4), 041104.

Wiseman, Y. (2013b), 'Fuselage Damage Locator System', *Advanced Science and Technology Letters*, **37**, 1–4.

Wiseman, Y. (2014), 'Device for Detection of Fuselage Defective Parts', *Information Journal*, Tokyo, Japan, **17** (9(A)), 4189–4194.

17. Multimodal passenger transportation security in Indian cities

Jay B. Kshirsagar and Pawan Kumar

1. INTRODUCTION

Multimodal passenger transport exists in many Indian cities due to the availability of multiple choice modes such as metro, bus, bus rapid transit (BRT), suburban rail, etc. Indian cities have largely road-systems except for a few cities such as Chennai, Mumbai, Kolkata, etc. which traditionally have been dependent on suburban rail. at present, many million-plus cities are adopting new modes such as Monorail (Delhi), BRT (Naya Raipur), rapid metro rail (Gurgaon), personal rapid transit (Amritsar), etc. to meet travel demand. However, all these new modes may be operationalized without proper integration with existing transport modes operated by various agencies. In this context, passenger security is an area of concern for planning agencies and operators alike.

The National Urban Transport Policy 2006, formulated by the Ministry of Urban Development, Government of India, has a broad objective to ensure safe, affordable, quick, comfortable, reliable and sustainable access for the growing number of city residents to jobs, education, recreation and such other needs. One of the methods to achieve the objective is to establish quality focused multimodal public transport which needs to be well integrated to provide seamless travel across modes (Government of India, 2006). In fact, multimodal public transport is an integrated system and therefore the need for passenger safety and security at each stage of planning, designing and operation is of paramount importance. Generally, multimodal passenger transport with world-class infrastructure and facilities is spread over the length and breadth of the city in which a significant degree of public ownership and controling power exists. Therefore, any lapse in passenger safety and security demeans the image of the government and creates doubts for the common man (Kumar et al., 2011). The slow evacuation procedure of the Delhi Metro (11 June 2013) in which

1791 passengers were stuck in a train inside a tunnel for over one-and-half hours is an example that reduces confidence in the security measures provided by the transport authority concerned. Moreover, passenger safety and security is associated with the protection of networks, safe transport infrastructure, emergency response, as well as with the government's programs and policies. Therefore, multimodal passenger security needs an integrated approach.

2. PASSENGER SECURITY CONCERNS IN MILLION-PLUS CITIES

According to the Census of India (2011), there are 53 cities with a population of one million or above which are known as million-plus cities. These cities are major urban centers with populations of 160.7 million, which is equal to 42.6 percent of the total urban population. Among the million-plus cities, there are seven mega cities with populations of 4-million plus. Table 17.1 depicts the population and status of cities and the share of public transport in mega cities and selected million-plus cities in the country.

Public transport service in mega cities and in most of the million-plus cities is below the desired level. Generally, the share of public transport is based on the population size of the city. The recommended share of public transport is 50-plus percent (3 million), 70-plus percent (6 million) and 75-plus percent (9 million), but 85 percent with a mass transit system (Government of India, 1996). In this context, most of the cities have a declining share of public transport and an increasing share of personalized modes, and therefore congestion, pollution, accidents, traffic jams, increased fuel consumption, additional journey time, delays, loss of man hours, etc. are common. Multiple agencies are responsible for planning, designing, constructing, operating, administrating and maintaining the modes in multiple jurisdictions through multiple disciplines, which leads to a disaggregated transport system. In this context, providing security for different commuters in both government and private vehicles, across different age groups, by gender, and within a limited budget allocation and power, is a challenging task.

The operation of the metro in various cities has upgraded the image and brand of public transport. The metro is one of the most capital intensive constituent modes of a multimodal transport system. There is a high demand for security and emergency services designed to make metro passengers feel safe and secure. The Delhi Metro is managed by Central Industrial Security Force (CISF) with state-of-the-art systems for

Table 17.1 Share of public transport in mega cities and selected million-plus cities in India, 2007

S.N.	City	State	Population 2011 census	Status of the cities	Modal share						
					Walk	Cycle	Two wheelers	Public transport	Car	IPT	Total in %
i.	Mumbai	Maharashtra	18 414 288	Mega and capital city	27	6	7	45	8	7	100
ii.	Delhi	Delhi	16 314 838	Mega and capital city	20	12	5	43	14	6	100
iii.	Kolkata	West Bengal	14 112 536	Mega and capital city	19	11	4	54	8	4	100
iv.	Chennai	Tamil Nadu	8 696 010	Mega and capital city	22	9	20	31	10	8	100
v.	Bengaluru	Karnataka	8 499 399	Mega and capital city	26	7	17	35	8	7	100
vi.	Hyderabad	Andhra Pradesh	7 749 334	Mega and capital city	22	9	19	35	9	7	100
vii.	Ahmedabad	Gujarat	6 240 201	Mega city	22	14	25	16	17	6	100
viii.	Jaipur	Rajasthan	3 073 350	Million-plus and capital city	26	13	26	22	8	4	100
ix.	Raipur	Chhattisgarh	1 122 555	Million-plus and capital city	35	28	25	0	9	4	100
x.	Chandigarh	Chandigarh	1 025 682	Million-plus and capital city	23	18	10	18	28	3	100

Sources: Census of India (2011); Wilbur Smith Associates and Ministry of Urban Development, Government of India (2008).

monitoring ingress and egress of passengers through the screening of passengers, x-ray detection systems, door frame metal detectors, hand-held metal detectors, etc. Sometimes, transit security programs, safety-and-security weeks etc. are organized to create awareness among stakeholders. However, security measures with more emphasis on improved preventive action and mitigation measures are required for the smooth, safe and secure movement of the commuters.

Passenger security is associated with transport infrastructure planning. Delhi falls in Seismic Zone IV. All elevated structures of the Delhi Metro have certification under the Bureau of Indian Standards (BIS)-1983, the Indian Road Congress, and the Indian Institute of Technology Kanpur–Research Designs and Standards Organization (IITK–RDSO) guidelines, and similarly underground structures follow Japanese guidelines. The 'Global Assessment Report' released by the United Nations International Strategy for Disaster Reduction (UNISDR) on 3 June 2013 estimated loss of revenue at over Rs 4100 crore (410 million, or approximately US$620 million) if a disaster had struck the Delhi Metro in 2012 (*The Times of India*, 2013b). Therefore, the consideration of disaster threats in advocacy planning and infrastructure planning are necessary in order to reduce risk for both commuters and operators/owners.

Passenger security is the function of both the software and hardware of the whole transport system. The failure of either or both can cause panic, havoc and devastating situations. Sometimes, communication breakdowns between coaches – caused by software failure, delays in rectifying problems, poor responses from operation control centers, and slow evacuation procedures – cause commuters' confidence levels in security measures to fall. It really needs a scientific and well-defined preparation strategy to respond better in cases of the evacuation of passengers who are stuck in metro coaches in the underground tunnels (*The Times of India*, 2013a). Security measures such as emergency assistance, the presence of security personnel, assistance booths, rescue plans, emergency sirens/buttons, etc. are important in order to be able to help commuters.

After every mishap, public transport authorities and city administrations promise to take bold steps to provide safe travel to each and every commuter. In the Ghatkopar bus blast of 28 July 2003, a bomb was planted under a seat on the Brihanmumbai Electric Supply and Transport Undertaking (BEST) bus. BEST sealed the space under all seats and blocked the open space near the entrance of double decker buses as a preventive measure. After a serial train blast in Mumbai on 11 July 2006, the Western Railway removed all luggage racks from suburban trains (as the space might be used to plant bombs), but these were put back because of commuters' demands. After the Delhi blasts on 13 September 2008, the railways removed all dustbins from major public places but again these were reinstated (Aklekar, 2008). However, these are the steps taken in piecemeal to reduce the vulnerability to threats and attacks. Preventive measures such as closed-circuit television (CCTV) cameras, emergency control rooms, random security checks, door frame metal detectors, sand pit posts at bus stops and metro/railway stations, etc. are necessary to reduce vulnerability and threats.

The National Urban Transport Policy (NUTP) 2006 is under revision, and the proposed modifications concern the special attention given to the issue of security for women, security against terrorism, security against vandalism, etc. In all State Transport Undertakings (STUs) and Special Purpose Vehicles (SPVs) operating public transit in all cities, only police-verified drivers and conductors should be deployed on buses for the safety and security of women and commuters. All buses should be fitted with a global positioning system (GPS) and CCTV cameras and they should be connected to a centralized control room for continuous monitoring. Similarly, intermediate public transport (IPT) modes also need to be fitted with a GPS tracking system and connected to an emergency alarm system. Further, at micro level, it should be ensured that the street design being adopted in the city will have provision for proper street lighting, avoiding dead ends or dreary, dark spaces, etc. (Institute of Urban Transport, 2013).

3.   CURRENT PRACTICES

In the Delhi Metro a separate coach is provided for women. Initially, female security personnel were also deployed. This helps to make 'metro travel' an attractive mode choice, by removing security fears as well as actual threats among commuters – particularly women, and young and school-age girls. These various provisions such as female security personnel, and a helpline number for women, make metro journeys more secure. However, CCTV on and around station areas, ticket counters, platforms, parking areas, etc. is used as a tool to aid security, reduce crime and improve services. It also enhances benefits in perceived security and helping passengers enjoy their travel experience. Delhi Metro Rail Corporation has traveled the extra mile in order to provide increased security to its female commuters, as discussed in Table 17.2.

In a survey conducted by the Delhi Metro Rail Corporation (DMRC), commuters were asked to rate their security and safety, and the alertness, frisking and behavior of the security personnel and their duties in the Delhi Metro. The survey was conducted for 18 days between 3–21 July 2013 and a sample size of 11 000 commuters was analyzed across various

Table 17.2　Security measures for women in Delhi Metro

S.N.	Security measures	Actions
i.	Reserved coach	• The first coach in the direction of train travel is reserved for women. A reserved coach especially for women commuters provides an easy, comfortable and secure journey.
ii.	Helpline numbers	• Helpline numbers of four different agencies (Delhi Metro Rail Corporation, Central Industrial Security Force, Delhi Police and the Government of Delhi) are provided for female commuters to use if they are in distress/need help or assistance during a journey.
iii.	Emergency talk	• Commuters can talk to the train operator directly by pressing a button provided in each coach and conveying the details of the emergency/assistance required during a journey.
iv.	Penalty/fine	• Entry of any unauthorized male in the women's coach is a punishable offence and a penalty of Rs 250 is levied.
v.	Monitoring inside coach	• CCTV cameras have been placed at stations, on platforms and inside the coach for the monitoring of theft and anti-social activities.
vi.	Zero tolerance	• Zero tolerance of any activities by drunkards or nuisance creation inside the women's coach. Such activities have a fine of Rs 200 and/or other penalty actions.

Source:　Delhi Metro.

Metro stations. The findings of the survey revealed that 97 percent of commuters rated the security and safety of the Delhi Metro as satisfactory, whereas 2 percent of commuters thought that improvement was required. With regard to the behavior of CISF personnel, whose public interface is largely with regard to frisking commuters and scanning their baggage, the survey stated that 25 percent of commuters rated it as good and satisfactory, 34 percent rated it very good, and 28 percent reported it to be excellent. About 95 percent of the commuters said 'yes' in answer to a question about the alertness of CISF security staff, and, of these, 80 percent rated the level of the security alertness of personnel between excellent and good. However, 5 percent felt that further improvement was required. The commuters were also asked to share their experiences about frisking. Approximately 89 percent of metro commuters were satisfied with the time taken in frisking. However, 10 percent of commuters felt the time taken in frisking required improvement. Further, 3.2 percent of commuters felt that frisking carried out by CISF staff required improvement (Delhi Metro Rail Corporation, 2013).

To fine-tune security services, new frisking booths for female commuters are being procured by the Delhi Metro, and female CISF constables will use them to frisk female passengers. The frisking booths are part of enhanced measures to make Metro commuters feel comfortable and secure (*The Hindu*, 2014c).

In most Indian cities, development around transport hubs such as railway stations, bus stops, interchanges nodes, etc. is characterized by a high intensity of development on account of mixed land uses. Mixed land use ensures that streets and urban spaces are vibrant and interactive throughout the day, thereby addressing further the security concerns of the populace. The Delhi Development Authority (DDA) undertook a comprehensive review of the Master Plan for Delhi 2021 in February 2007 as a result of which transit-oriented development (TOD) is being advocated (Delhi Development Authority, 2007). Commuter security in the transit environment is affected by surrounding land uses, by the spatial distribution of transit stations/bus stops, by lighting, and by potential hiding places surrounding the stops/stations and their visibility from the street and neighborhood areas. TOD promotes mixed land uses and compact development which ensures a higher degree of safety and security for commuters.

To provide freedom from being 'teased, touched and threatened', the Delhi Transport Corporation (DTC) has provided 'Ladies Special Buses'. These provide safe and secure travel for female commuters. The drivers and conductors are under strict instructions to take the bus to the nearest police station in the case of any untoward incident. Further, the responsibility of reporting an incident has been placed on the bus staff instead of the victim (*The Hindu*, 2014a). To further increase confidence among female commuters and empower women in public transport, the DTC has also appointed 300 female conductors – which is a bold step to regaining the image of bus transport as a safe and secure mode of public transport for all strata of society, and particularly for women and children.

Many incidents reveal that women, school-age girls and children are at risk from molestation and sexual violence in public places like bus stops, even in broad daylight, reflecting serious public law and order problems in cities. Recently, the United States of America and Japan announced support for the U.N.'s Women's Safe City Programme in Delhi which aims to prevent sexual violence in public spaces through alliances with women's communities, local government, civic societies, etc. Such initiatives strengthen the commitment of the government to building a safe and secure city for women and girls to live free from violence and to exercise their rights and freedom in an inclusive city (*The Hindu*, 2014d).

Delhi's police force has launched a mobile application 'Himmat', to increase women's safety. The user has to register with the Delhi Police website and submit the numbers of at least two members of their family or friends. The application allows women to send a distress call to the police control room and to their relatives in case of any emergency (*The Hindustan Times*, 2015).

4.   ISSUES IN PASSENGER SECURITY

A public transport system is vulnerable to terrorist attacks which cause large-scale destruction due to the high concentration of passengers. In the recent past, the Mumbai train attack (12 March 1993), the Brahmaputra mail train attack (30 December 1996), the Nagaland bus attack (30 December 2000), the Samjhauta express train bomb (18 February 2007), among others, are examples of terrorist attacks on both bus and rail-based transport. Sometimes, terrorist attacks on public transport take place during an election period. The Modinagar bus bomb blast, which occurred on 27 April 1996 during an election period, killed 15 people.

According to a Mineta Transportation Institute Report on 'Explosives and Incendiaries used in Terrorist Attacks on Public Surface Transportation: A Preliminary Empirical Examination', India stands out as a country where average fatalities per attack (FPA) and injuries per attack (IPA) are 5.3 and 17.6 respectively, based on data available as on 20 February 2010. Similarly, levels of average fatalities per device (FPD) and injuries per device (IPD) – where either explosives or incendiaries were used – are 4.9 and 18.9 respectively. The statistics also analyzed modes and found that the FPA and IPA values of bus bomb attacks were 3.0 and 14.5 respectively, compared to FPA and IPA values of train bomb attacks of 8.0 and 27.5 respectively (MTI, 2010). Thus, the risks of security lapses in rail transport are higher than in bus transport.

The security of passengers inside the vehicles (bus/metro) is not a serious issue but commuters making access trips to bus stops/transit stations are more vulnerable. The risk of death per trip for a bus user is very high on an access trip. In fact, the actual statistics may be much higher as many cases are neither reported nor recorded properly. There is no segregation of non-motorized and motorized transport in cities. Separate lanes may help to make access/dispersal trips to and from metro stations and bus stops more safe and secure.

The transport system becomes more efficient and effective when feeder modes such as cars, mini-buses, two wheelers and sustainable low-cost modes such as bicycles, cycle rickshaws and pedestrians are safe. The wearing of helmets for all men and women driving or riding pillion on two wheelers makes their travel safe and secure. Pedestrian behavior and a poorly-designed built environment along the transport corridors have an adverse impact on mobility. Pedestrian traffic is always high and is continuous particularly during peak hours in the morning and evening. Similarly, the pedestrian flow is mixed in terms of age, gender, purpose, length, etc. In fact, the design components of pedestrian facilities, their locations, and increased awareness about the use of pelican signals and how to abide by the rules of the road are the main issues for providing better security.

The route, frequency, and occupancy of public transport and the surrounding land uses has a direct impact on the commuter's perception of security. The land uses around bus stops/BRT stops/mass rapid transit (MRT) stations, and longer wait-times at night, induce feelings of fear of crime, particularly for women, children and senior citizens. Generally, mixed land uses along the transit corridor ensure more movement, commercial activities and watchful eyes and, hence, may lead to a possible reduction in crimes. However, fear of crime when using public transport significantly influences the travel pattern. Compared to daily commuters, occasional commuters are more fearful during access and dispersal trips and while waiting at bus stops in remote and isolated localities. Thus, the environment both outside and inside transit areas affects commuter security. Further, help from fellow passengers, the personal determination to protect someone in danger, requires high moral courage and freedom from fear of police harassment and legal problems.

The spatial distribution of the road network and having to use public transport on those routes which pass through slums and squatter settlements creates a sense of insecurity in commuters' minds, which affects their use of the system. Often, public transport routes pass through inner-cities or very congested parts of cities where the threat of pickpocketing, molestation, and sexual abuse, etc., is higher. This demands cost-effective measures to reduce crime and increase commuter usage.

Data on the various elements of transit define its commuter usage in both peak and off-peak hours. Nowadays, security is one of the major determinants for women commuters in selecting the metro, bus or suburban rail as a mode. The number of transit crimes on a particular mode/

route affects commuters' attitude towards its security measures. The collection, compilation, analysis and dispersal of transit crimes data in a timely and hassle-free manner changes commuters' perception of security. Such an approach is a good start to creating awareness and developing confidence among commuters.

For operators, transport system attributes such as routes, journey times, fares, etc., are more important than the comfort levels of the journey and passenger security. This may be due to the huge gap between the demand and supply of public transport on a particular route. Thus, assessment of actual travel demand, fleet size, route rationalization, corridor length, etc., is necessary alongside on-vehicle passenger surveys. Finally, the safety and security of passenger travel are key issues for enhancing revenue and heightening brand awareness for operators.

Differences in age and gender produce different perspectives on transit security. Women, teenagers, schoolgirls, children, etc., perceive the threat or risk of danger as horrific and terrible. Generally, women prefer not to take the bus after dark, as it is perceived as being less safe than the metro. Therefore, the presence of security personnel is always desirable. In terms of last-mile connectivity, e-rickshaws (a battery-operated three wheeler with four seats) are seen as a safe way to commute even after dark. At the very least, passengers are able to travel with other passengers at an affordable price compared to auto-rickshaw, and they are visible. Thus, shared vehicles with a lower seating capacity (four or five seats) at an affordable price may be considered to be the safest mode of transport for some commuters, especially for women.

Multimodal transport is open, accessible, and spread throughout the city. A high-density population, increased vehicle ownership, more personalized vehicles on the road during peak hours, etc., all put extra stress on the transport infrastructure. The increasing number of passengers on the Delhi Metro (peaking at 2 362 249 on 1 July 2015) demands a greater number of security personnel at entry/exit gates, checkpoints, on platforms, etc. In Delhi, 21 percent of the state is taken up by transport modes. Due to its large geographical area and high-density population, this creates a significant physical challenge in terms of handling any anti-social attack, e.g. on the movement of passengers. Moreover, securing the safety of passenger trains is a complex and difficult task. Over 13 million passengers pass through railway stations every day. It is a challenging task for both India's Railway Protection Force – mandated to protect trains – and the state government-controled Government Reserve Police to search all luggage and frisk all passengers. On-train robbery rates have risen from 382 (in 2003) to 1096 (in 2013) and murder rates have risen from 246 (in 2003) to 270 (in 2013). This suggests that all kinds of criminals, not just terrorists, have a free run of trains (*The Hindu*, 2014e). However, rail passengers are much safer than road commuters. It is also true that transport authorities are more concerned about safety than security. Similarly, financial challenges such as a lack of funds for security improvements, emergency planning and preparedness, resource mobilization, etc., are additional constraints.

Many commuters do not behave like rule-abiding citizens. The announcements made in the Delhi Metro say not to sit on the floor, that eating on trains is prohibited, and that men are not allowed in the women-only coaches, etc. Despite this, these and other rules are broken by educated men and women every day. According to the records of the CISF – which is responsible for the Delhi Metro security – around 90 percent of the 400-plus pickpocketing cases on the metro during 2013 involved female perpetrators (*The Hindu*, 2014b). Such activities took place on busy routes connecting railway stations, inter-state bus terminals, central business districts, market places, etc., and are dealt with under Indian Penal Codes. On occasion, non-functioning baggage scanners at the entry gates of railway stations cause turmoil, and if checking has to be done manually passengers sometimes lose patience and fights break out over the delay in boarding their trains. In fact, co-operation with police personnel is an issue of civic responsibility and duty.

5. CONCLUDING REMARKS

Passenger security is associated with the proper application of an intelligent transport system (ITS) in the movement of vehicles, particularly during emergency/crisis situations. The communication systems and their connectivity with the central control unit play a crucial role in making a more efficient, secure and user-friendly transport system. The modern bus fleet with ITS applications, real-time information and a proper connection with the control room 24/7 can enhance commuters' sense of security. The installation of a simple alarm in a bus increases passengers' sense of personal security during a journey and draws the attention of the neighborhood/surrounding areas in a critical situation. However, the use – and misuse – of the alarm depends totally on passengers' perception of danger and assessment of risk before pressing the button for any outside help or assistance.

Passenger security demands public transport oriented to both a physical and digital infrastructure – with, for example, low-floor air-conditioned buses, operation through a vehicle tracking system, use of a global positioning system, etc. – to improve the sense of security. Interchange nodes are places of transfer, movement and waiting which require both general and specific security measures. The various transport authorities, police and city administrations need to co-ordinate and co-operate to record and monitor day-to-day incidents/complaints related to theft, lost and found property, robberies, and emergency responses, etc.

The sense of security experienced by commuters varies at different times for different modes. During peak hours, commuters give 'less travel time' priority over comfort, convenience, security, etc., and accordingly choose the mode to perform the journey in that way. Generally, the metro offers a better service, and greater comfort and security, and therefore commuters prefer to travel that way even when they feel physically uncomfortable due to overcrowding, jostling, the lack of seats, the inconvenience of carrying luggage, etc. But, on the other hand, fewer security measures are required inside the bus. The presence of a driver, conductor, ticket checkers and co-passengers inside the bus change the passengers' sense of security. Also, bus routes which pass through residential, commercial, and institutional areas can reduce commuters' feelings of fear.

The use of surveillance technology in transit is not just for the detection of crimes but also to improve services provided by the authorities. Nowadays, multimodal transport systems have been well accepted at a regional level as they cover the inner city, the hinterland and the surrounding areas of neighboring states. Thus, it is important to have video recording in local trains running between two or more major cities in the region. This feature can help to detect prohibited materials inside the coach and monitor suspicious activities. Aside from the use of the latest technology, institutional integration of various transport agencies with government departments, police and security forces is always necessary. Further, there is a need to initiate a 'Security Program in Public Transport', with political and financial support, in order to energize existing public transport users to carry on using the system and to attract personal vehicle users to view public transport – particularly bus travel – as safe and secure. However, financially such a transport security program should support the cost of security measures and the consequences of security failures.

Passenger security as an integral part of multimodal transport system is the overriding need. The required ratio of security personnel per thousand passengers depends on the operation of the mode, the corridor length, the line density, etc., but a sufficient number of such personnel reinforces the commuter's sense of security. The cost of both security personnel and the installation of a security system is always less than the construction and operation of a multimodal transport system and, therefore, the supply of skilled security personnel who could be trained as experts to perform duties in both normal and crisis situations should be prioritized. Improved security provides a direct benefit to commuters, security personnel and transport staff on duty; and indirect benefits would include a reduction in the risk of physical and mental harm, lower monetary loss for medical expenses and productivity during recovery, and physiological and psychological relief for the families of victims.

Generally, emergency management plans for transit routes and plans for the evacuation of transit commuters are prepared well, but planning to make commuters feel safe and secure when accessing and leaving bus stops and transit stations to and from relevant destinations is avoided. Security in transit planning needs not only to consider those factors which affect transit usage but must also include the reduction of vulnerability, violence, and crimes, etc., and moreover must also include preparedness and speed of response during critical situations. Further, designing a transit infra-structure to resist natural disasters/terrorist attacks, bomb explosions, etc., is important. A security cum mobility plan based on threat and vulner-ability analysis and reduction has a direct relationship in the mind of com-muters with the perception of public transport as a safe and secure mode for day-to-day activities.

Transit corridor planning in terms of the location of bus stops, spacing of transit stations, network accessibility, non-motorized connectivity, etc., in different land use zones requires a comprehensive understanding of sustainability and an inclusive approach for safe and secure mobility at city level. Therefore, various land use zones should sustain the growth of various activities and ensure the security of passengers along the transit corridor. Mixed land uses and diversified commercial activities during the evening/at night attract city residents, who act as a watchdog for commut-ers coming and going to the stations/stops. The presence of such activi-ties reduces crimes, threats, etc., and increases personal security. Further, transit corridors should not include negative spaces such as long stretches of vacant plots, wine shops, nightclubs, bars, etc., which may increase passengers' feelings of vulnerability and insecurity. Therefore, security in transit planning needs to consider the physical layout of rights of way and the design of streets and surrounding areas to create vibrant, dynamic, alive and multi-functional urban spaces for pleasant, enjoyable, safe, and secure mobility.

Safe transport infrastructure systems – particularly underground/elevated metro corridors, interchange hubs, etc. – are designed by assessing all the possible range of potential man-made disasters and terrorist attacks, and the stresses they would impose on the transport system, and by evalu-ating a wide range of possible solutions. The contemporary design of a transport infrastructure requires it to withstand extreme conditions due to earthquakes, storms, bomb explosions, etc. Through the use of various software, a mock experimental study based on the effects of explosions in stations (elevated/underground), the assessments made and the resultant findings, can be used in the design of transport infrastructure and effective emergency planning.

Further, the planning of safe routes, regular inspections of railways tracks, the use of state-of-the-art technology to sense any explosives and incendiary devices, the presence of security personnel, and a strong communication network, etc., are prerequisites. In addition, agencies responsible for the operation and maintenance of transport security, and allied areas such as the police, the fire brigade, transport authorities, and the city administration and intelligence bureau, should have closer technical co-operation and scientific co-ordination in the prevention and detection of threats and immediate actions for rescue and relief. It is also imperative to raise awareness among commuters to spot threats, to respond in a timely way to the relevant security personnel/agencies, and to be vigilant, etc., in order to help protect property and infrastructure from terrorist threats, and to save precious human lives.

REFERENCES

Aklekar, Rajendra (2008), 'Integrated transport security need of hour', available at: www.hindustantimes.com/storypage/storypage.aspx (accessed 7 February 2009).
Census of India (2011), 'Provisional population totals: urban agglomerations and cities', Ministry of Home Affairs, Government of India, New Delhi.
Delhi Development Authority (2007), 'Master plan of Delhi for 2021', Ministry of Urban Development (Delhi Division), New Delhi.
Delhi Metro Rail Corporation (2013), 'Safety, security in Delhi Metro satisfactory: survey', available at: www.post.jagran.com/safety-security-in-delhi-metro-satisfactory-survey-1378368099 (accessed 25 October 2013).
Government of India (1996), 'Urban development project formulation and implementation guidelines', Ministry of Urban Affairs and Employment, New Delhi.
Government of India (2006), 'National urban transport policy', Ministry of Urban Development, New Delhi.
Institute of Urban Transport (2013), 'Proposed modifications in national urban transport policy 2006', Draft Version, July 2013.
Kumar, P., Kulkarni, S.Y., Parida, M. (2011), 'Security perceptions of Delhi commuters at metro-bus interchange in multimodal perspective', *International Journal of Transportation Security*, **4** (4), December, 295–307.
MTI (2010), 'Explosives and incendiaries used in terrorist attacks on public surface transportation: a preliminary empirical examination', MTI Report 09-02, Mineta Transportation Institute, San Jose, California.
The Hindu (2014a), Delhi Edition, 13 March 2014.
The Hindu (2014b), Delhi Edition, 13 April 2014.
The Hindu (2014c), Delhi Edition, 21 April 2014.
The Hindu (2014d), Delhi Edition, 27 April 2014.
The Hindu (2014e), Delhi Edition, 2 May 2014.

The Hindustan Times (2015), Delhi Edition, 16 February 2015.
The Times of India (2013a), Delhi Edition, 13 June 2013.
The Times of India (2013b), Delhi Edition, 25 June 2013.
Wilbur Smith Associates and Ministry of Urban Development (2008), 'Traffic and transportation policies and strategies in urban areas in India', New Delhi.

18. Multimodal passenger transportation security in Brazil

Dawna L. Rhoades

INTRODUCTION

As one of the rapidly growing developing nations in the so-called BRIC group, Brazil is often overshadowed by the more populous India and China. Yet, Brazil ranks fifth in the world in both population and land-mass (CIA Factbook, 2013). Further, it faces far fewer strategic international security threats than the other BRICS; it currently has no border conflicts like the Indian–Pakistani 'war' with its neighbors, nor is it facing any internal insurgencies like the Chechnyan threat to Russia or the Maoist threat in Nepal and northeast India. None of Brazil's near neighbors is a nuclear threat or likely to be in the foreseeable future. It is also rich in natural resources (Stuenkel, 2010). In a time of rising fuel prices, Brazil is virtually energy independent, exporting roughly as much oil as it imports and continuing to increase its production of ethanol made from sugar cane (Reel, 2006). Recent offshore oil finds could make Brazil the fourth-largest oil producing nation in the world by 2020 (Romero, 2011). In short, Brazil is well-positioned to be a key player in its region and the world in the twenty-first century. Brazil will host the World Cup competition in 2014 and the Summer Olympic Games in 2016. An estimated six million passengers are expected to arrive at Brazil's airports for the World Cup which will be spread over 12 cities. Millions are expected for the 2016 Olympics, not least as this is the first time the event will be hosted by a South American country (Gregoire, 2011).

These upcoming events present both challenge and motivation to Brazil. Security and transportation infrastructure represent key concerns as Brazil faces these events. While the overall transportation system itself is large, as befits a nation of Brazil's size, the quality of this infrastructure is relatively poor (Williams, 2011). After a brief overview of the geographic and demographic landscape of Brazil, this chapter will explore the current passenger transportation system with particular emphasis on transportation mode and usage. Then, the regulatory and security framework governing the country and transportation will be examined. Finally, security challenges and the actions to address them will be explored.

OVERVIEW

This section presents a general overview of Brazil, starting with a brief look at the geography and population. The geography of Brazil affects the design and accessibility of transportation. Further, it has significant implications for the safety and security of the system. Likewise, demographic issues are also closely linked to the demand for and design of transportation systems.

Diversity: Geography and Population

Brazil is the fifth-largest nation in the world in terms of landmass (Table 18.1) and shares a border with Argentina and Uruguay to the south, Bolivia, Paraguay, and Peru to the west, and Colombia, Venezuela, Guyana, French Guiana, and Suriname to the north. Its Atlantic coastline is 7491 kilometers with a continental shelf (and exclusive economic zone) of 200 nautical miles. There are 55 600 kilometers of internal water, including the all-important Amazon River system and basin (CIA Factbook, 2013). Much of the north is covered in rolling lowlands with tropical rainforests in the Amazon region. The Amazon starts in the mountains of Peru and flows eastward for approximately 6400 kilometers (4000 miles) before it empties into the Atlantic at Belem, Brazil. The Amazon basin covers an area of approximately 650 million hectares (2.5 million square miles) and contains over two-thirds of all the freshwater on earth. There are no

Table 18.1   Geography and population

Total area	8 514 877 sq km
Land	8 459 417
Water	55 460
Population	201 009 622
Birth rate	14.97 per 1000
Death rate	6.51 per 1000
Median age	30.3
Life expectancy	73.02
Urban population	87%

Source: CIA Factbook (2013).

bridges over the Amazon River itself. Almost 60 percent of the rainforest is contained in Brazil (Amazon Center for Environmental Education and Research, 2013). The river has roughly 1100 tributaries. The Rio Negro is the largest tributary and will be the first river of the Amazon system to have a bridge located near the city of Manaus. The bridge is part of a larger effort to develop the Amazon region (Carrington, 2010).

Brazil is ranked fifth in the world in terms of total population with a 2013 estimated population of 201 million (CIA Factbook, 2013). The largest cities include Sao Paulo with 11.3 million residents, Rio de Janeiro with 6.3 million residents, Salvador with 2.7 million residents, and Brasilia with 2.5 million residents (World Population Review, 2013). Eighty-seven percent of the population is classified as urban, a slightly higher percentage than the US which is 82 percent. Like most developing nations, the demographic pyramid of Brazil has a large base reflecting a relatively young population and a birth rate that is slightly double that of the death rate; however, the fertility rate declined rapidly in the 1960s to an estimated 2013 rate of 1.81 children per female. Brazil's population growth rate is now 132nd in the world at 0.83 percent (CIA Factbook, 2013). Brazil's average population density is relatively low at 23 people per square kilometer (the US population density is 34 people per square kilometer); however, the majority of the population is concentrated along the coast with the interior Amazon basin being much more sparsely settled (Brazilian Institute of Geography and Statistics, 2013). In fact, it is estimated that the Amazon region is home to only about 25 million Brazilians (Carrington, 2010). This means that in this region there is less than one person per square mile or hectare. This low interior density has implications for development, transportation systems, and security. Access to the interior from the coast is achieved primarily through air or road. Much of the air travel involves non-commercial, general aviation aircraft and airports. Only about 16 percent of the roads in Brazil are paved, with most of the unpaved roads in the Amazon region (Table 18.2). Increasing access to this region has implications for economic development in Brazil as well as the environment in this sensitive natural area.

Transportation

In size, Brazil has one of the largest transportation networks in the world (Table 18.2); however, the UN World Tourism Organization has ranked the quality of its transport network 95th out of 130 (Williams, 2011). In terms of sheer numbers, Brazil ranks second behind the US in designated airports; however, note that the vast majority of the runways are unpaved and likely to serve only small general aviation aircraft rather than scheduled

Table 18.2   Brazilian transportation system

Mode	Size/number	Ranking in world
Airports		2nd
Paved runways	713	
Unpaved runways	3392	
Air passenger departures	884755	
General Aviation aircraft	13094	3rd
Corporate	1700	
Highway km		
Federal	62351	
Total paved	212798	
Total unpaved	1368166	4th
Cars per 1000	178	
Railway	28538	10th
Ports	219	
Waterways km	50000	3rd

Source: CIA Factbook (2013).

large commercial aircraft (LCA). The scheduled LCA market in Brazil has almost tripled in the last decade with additional demand expected for the 2014 World Cup and the 2016 Summer Olympics (Sibaja, 2012). As of 2012, 17 of the 20 top airports in Brazil were operating at full capacity, thus making airport expansion a top priority ahead of the 2014 and 2016 events (Fischer, 2012). This demand is in addition to the overall trend of an increase in air travel. Table 18.3 presents the seven largest airports by passenger volume while Table 18.4 lists the five main Brazilian airlines with the number of passengers, total fleet, and network as of 2012.

Table 18.3   Brazil's largest airports

City	Airport	Passengers (000s)
Rio de Janeiro		17713
Belo Horizonte	Tancredo Neves International	10505
Brasilia		15901
Sao Paulo	Guarulhos International	32477
Sao Paulo	Congonhas	16703
Sao Paulo	Viracopos International	8931
Salvador	Dois de Julho International	9068

Source: FlightGlobal.

Table 18.4   Brazilian airlines

Airlines	City base	Passengers	Fleet	Destinations
Avianca	Rio Santos	3553	35	17
Azul	Sao Paulo	10035	78	25
GOL	Sao Paulo	39164	109	41
TAM	Sao Paulo	37700	163	43
TRIP	Sao Paulo	5688	44	25

Source: FlightGlobal.

In addition to the commercial aviation sector, the general aviation (GA) sector which includes all non-military and non-scheduled passenger and cargo flights has been active in Brazil for many years. According to the Brazilian Association for General Aviation (2011), Brazil had 10315 general aviation aircraft registered in 1996 and over 19765 in 2009. The majority of these aircraft are propeller, piston engine aircraft. It is estimated that commercial aviation serves 130 destinations across Brazil while GA serves over 3500 or roughly 75 percent of the country (Agence France-Presse, 2012). Many of the destinations are in the less developed interior where unbridged river systems and unpaved roads make small aircraft GA a very viable option. The largest category of GA after private aircraft is air taxi. This category includes both fixed wing and rotor aircraft. These aircraft are available for hire on a single or annual time/hour-share basis. The six busiest GA aerodromes are located in the metropolitan areas adjacent to Sao Paulo, Rio de Janeiro, Curitiba, Goiania, and Belo Horizonte: Campo de Marte, Jacarepagua, Bacacheri, Pampulha, Congongas, and Santa Genoveva Campo de Marte in Sao Paulo posted 120000 aircraft movements in 2011, while Jacarepagua in Rio de Janeiro posted 94000 (Brazilian Association for General Aviation, 2011). The GA sector is expected to grow 9.5 percent in 2013 with business aviation leading the way (Hilderbrand, 2013).

Brazil's road network ranks 4th in the world in total size; however, as already noted, only approximately 16 percent of the roads and highways are paved. Most of these unpaved roads lie in the interior Amazon basin, a fact that for better or for worse has impeded the development of this region. It is estimated that unpaved road travel is up to 35 percent more expensive due to added travel time and vehicle damage. Within the cities, traffic congestion also creates costs in terms of lost time and pollution. Sao Paulo is considered to have some of the worst congestion problems in the world (Gregoire, 2011). There are currently 64.8 million vehicles

Table 18.5   Brazil's main inland waterway

Inland waterway	Length (km)
Parana-Tiete	1660
Amazonas-Madeira	4164
Tapajos	1046
Capim	372
Tocantins-Araguaia	3040
Sao Francisco	1371
Paraguai	1323
Jacui-Taquari/Lagoa dos Patos	670

Source: Perrupato, Marcelo (2011), 'Logistic infrastructure scenario in Brazil', available at: http://www.transportes.gov.br/public/arquivo/arq1318615138.pdf.

registered in Brazil, with motorcars representing 61 percent of the total and motorized 2- and 3-wheel vehicles representing 22 percent (World Health Organization, 2013). Currently almost 85 percent of the population and goods travel by road and highway (Embassy of Brazil in Wellington, 2013).

In total size, Brazil's waterway network ranks 3rd in the world with 60 000 kilometers, although only 13 000 kilometers are currently used (World Wide Inland Navigation Network, 2013). Table 18.5 lists the top inland waterways in Brazil. In many of the interior areas of Brazil, water transport by boat or ferry may be the only means of travel (see public transport below). The second phase of Brazil's Growth Acceleration Program (PAC2) has targeted the waterway sector for additional investment. Much of this spending, however, is targeted on the construction of waterways and terminals for freight shipment as only about 13 percent of freight in Brazil travels by boat (Pires and Oliveira, 2011).

Public Transport

New efforts by the Brazilian government are attempting to address the availability of public transport. Currently, eight cities in Brazil have metro systems including Sao Paulo, Rio de Janeiro, and Belo Horizonte (Gray, 2013). Table 18.6 lists the major light rail metro systems. Almost all of these systems are targeted for expansion as part of the overall effort to improve the transportation infrastructure. Interstate passenger rail service is very limited. Sao Paulo, the largest city in Brazil, currently does not have any rail connections to other cities. A proposed high speed rail system would link Sao Paulo and Rio de Janeiro, a journey of almost 2000 kilometers, allowing passengers to complete the full journey in less

Table 18.6   Brazil's existing rail metro systems

Metro	Existing lines/km	Pax/day
Sao Paulo	4/62.3	3 500 000
CPTM VLT	6/260.8	2 150 000
Maceio Diesel VLT	1/32.1	6 000
Salvador Surface Rail	1/17	12 000
Salvador (Metro)	1/6	200 000
Fortaleza	1/17	190 000
Fortaleza Diesel VLT	1/21	8 000
Brasilia	1/40.3	120 000
Belo Horizonte	1/2	170 000
Recife CBTU	2/39.7	220 000
Recife VLT	2/26.1	6 000
Rio de Janeiro	2/35.6	550 000
Rio de Janeiro Supervia	5/225	500 000
Natal Diesel VLT	2/56.2	7 000
Porto Alegre VLT	1/33.8	160 000

Source: Perrupato, Marcelo (2011), 'Logistic infrastructure scenario in Brazil', available at: http://www.transportes.gov.br/public/arquivo/arq1318615138.pdf.

than two hours. Given the topography, including a 660-meter rise in elevation and Brazil's extensive river system, the line is estimated to require 130 kilometers of bridges and tunnels. The current target date for completion is 2016 (Gregoire, 2011). At the present time, only three of the bordering countries can be reached by rail (Argentina, Uruguay, and Bolivia). Bus services exist at the federal, state, and local level with international service to all the bordering nations (Williams, 2011). Half of all motorized urban travel in Brazil occurs on public transport, the vast majority by bus (Gregoire, 2011). Since interstate rail service is rare in Brazil, buses are the main form of public transport. There are often a number of different lines serving the same route and Brazilian bus companies are considered some of the best in Latin America. The so-called semi-cama (bed) service features reclining (although not fully) seats and bathrooms for long-distance travel (Green Toad Bus, 2013).

While Brazil has a large number of coastal ports, these are mostly used for freight (Angloinfo Brazil, 2013). There are cruise options for either round-the-horn cruises that stop in Brazil, Amazon cruises, or All-Brazil coastal cruises. In 2011, 800 000 tourists participated in cruising involving a Brazilian port; however, the lack of port infrastructure led to reductions in 2012. In anticipation of a World Cup increase, Brazil is building six new terminals (MercoPress, 2011). Internally, the river system is used for passenger transport in certain areas. For example, in the State of Para in northern Brazil, almost 250 000 passengers a year travel by water from the city of Santarem to neighboring cities. After almost 50 years without water transport service, the Porto-Guaiba line is expected to serve 2000 passengers daily (Pires and Oliveira, 2011).

REGULATORY AND POLICY FRAMEWORK

Like many Latin American countries, Brazil experienced economic and political instability in the 1960s and 1970s. During the 1990s, President Collor created an economic plan with five goals: reduce inflation, liberalize trade, deregulate assets, privatize sectors of the economy, and reconcile with the international financial community. The current Brazilian President, Dilma Rousseff, has frequently articulated a policy of strong government activism in areas vital to economic development – banking, oil, industry, energy, and transportation. A former energy minister, she helped create the legislative framework for the exploration of offshore oil. She is also called 'the mother of the PAC' or the Program for Accelerated Growth (PAC). The first PAC (2007–2010) devoted R\$503.9 billion to a series of projects. The monies were divided into three main areas: logistics (roads, airports, and ports), energy, and social and urban. The largest share of the spending was targeted toward energy (R\$274.8 billion). Transportation is budgeted to receive R\$1088.5 trillion with the bulk of this investment occurring after 2014 (Moraes, 2010).

Given the need to accelerate infrastructure development ahead of the 2014 and 2016 world events, the government must deal with the issue of speed. In order to address this and other challenges in the transportation sector, the government has announced a new agency to centralize policy, the Logistical Planning Company (EPL). EPL is tasked with directing investment into the infrastructure projects targeted by PAC. The president of the newly created EPL, Bernardo Figueiredo, estimates the logistical deficit in Brazil to be US\$250 billion (Moraes, 2010).

Regulation

Oversight of day-to-day transport is the function of the Ministry of Transport (MoT). The MoT is responsible for regulation of most of the transport sector, including agencies overseeing land (highway and rail) and water. Water usage is actually controled by two agencies, the National Water Transport Agency (ANTAQ) and the National Water

Agency (ANA). There is also a National Department of Transportation Infrastructure which is responsible for research and planning. The aviation sector is regulated by the Agencia Nacional de Aviacao Civil (ANAC). ANAC has a five member board which includes the president. There is a Department of Airport Infrastructure that oversees planning, safety, security, and airport fiscalization. Infraero is the government-controled agency that oversees the design, construction, operation, and management of 67 airports and 81 navigation support stations (Moraes, 2010). The Air Force Department of Air Space Control (DECEA) is responsible for air-space control. The Center for the Investigation and Prevention of Aviation Accidents (CENIPA) which is charged with the investigation and prevention of aviation accidents is also subordinate to the Air Force.

SECURITY STRUCTURE

Brazil adopted the federal structure of government with authority distributed at the national, state, and local level. At the national level, the Federal Police investigate crimes of national significance such as the illegal drug and arms trade, terrorism, and human trafficking. The Federal Police include the head of immigration. Other federal security forces include: 1) the Federal Highway Police Department (DPRF); 2) the Federal Railway Police Department (DPFF); and 3) the National Public Safety Force (FNSP). The DPRF patrol highways for crime and theft, inspect for dangerous cargo, and serve as a border patrol. The DPFF serve the same function for the rail system. The FNSP came into being because of early distrust of the Brazilian military and concern about their deployment to help in emergency crisis situations. Brazil has 26 states, each with a civilian police force as well as a military police force. The FNSP has been compared to a UN peacekeeping force while the state military police have been compared to the US National Guard. Local (city) administrations also have Municipal Guards. On public security issues, they play only a secondary role and some state Municipal Guards are not an armed force. From the above overview, it is clear that the prior history of military rule in Brazil has impacted the security structure. The creation of the Safety Force and the separation of military and civilian forces is a clear indication of public concerns; however, it raises serious concerns about the coordination of forces and their effectiveness in maintaining security. One possible solution would be to unify all civilian federal forces, but this potentially only improves efficiency at the federal level while leaving state-level issues unresolved. At the state level, there are also concerns about the separate civilian and military police forces. Critics of the civilian force argue over its corruption and inefficiency while critics of the military force cite previous examples of civil rights abuses (Vergueiro, 2010).

SECURITY CHALLENGES

At the strategic international level, Stuenkel (2010) cites the primary strategic challenges for Brazil as drug-trafficking, arms smuggling, guerilla activity, and illegal mining and logging in the Amazon region. Domestically, Brazil's challenges are crime and infrastructure development. All of these challenges have implications for the transport sector.

Border and Interior Security

The Brazilian borders in the Amazon region are five times longer than the US–Mexico border and involve ten different countries. Almost 6000 miles of Brazil's border are formed by rivers that flow into Brazil from other countries through the dense rainforest. Across these poorly-controled rainforest borders flow drugs, illegal goods and people, and guerillas from neighboring states (Winter, 2012). Drug and arms smuggling are part of the larger crime challenge for Brazil. Efforts are under way to improve Brazilian border defense through the purchase and use of unmanned aerial vehicles (UAVs) for border patrol (Schoon, 2014). While UAVs make a great deal of sense for patroling this region, there are a number of concerns relating to their integration into the national airspace of Brazil. The air traffic control (ATC) system, as noted above, is already considered antiquated and recent incidents with small, manned aircraft raise the possibility that even smaller unmanned systems could represent a safety risk unless carefully integrated into an improved ATC system.

Crime

The United States Department of State-Bureau of Diplomatic Security (Overseas Security Advisory Council) issues crime and safety reports on country issues. The 2013 report on Brazil's Rio de Janeiro area noted the following issues: 1) critical levels of crime, particularly homicide; 2) street robberies; 3) high levels of vehicle accident and death; 4) bus system violence; and 5) robbery of motorists at stoplights as well as carjacking (US Department of State, 2013a). The 2013 OSAC report on Brasilia has noted that the highest crime rates are occurring at public transportation hubs and tourist areas (US Department of State, 2013b). As part of the

Brazilian bid for the Olympics, the government promised to reduce violent crime (Associated Press, 2013). One of the key initiatives to reduce crime is the Favela Pacification Program which is designed to increase police presence on the streets of Brazil (US Department of State, 2013a). In Rio de Janeiro, the Pacifying Police Units have been cited as the main reason for the decline in violent crime (Ribeiro, 2012). Other measures include increased use of cameras and drones for surveillance and the use of military police for special events (Associated Press, 2013). During the recent visit of Pope Francis for World Youth Day, a number of issues surfaced including gridlock due to traffic and bad weather, crowd control, and a security scare (Prada and Boadle, 2013). Given that transportation hubs are a main target of crime, it is likely that they will be some of the first areas to receive camera surveillance.

Infrastructure

According to a report issued by the Institute for Applied Economic Research, Brazilian infrastructure is suffering from a lack of both public and private investment made worse by economic growth rates above international averages. This lack of investment affects all areas of transport including roads, ports and waterways, railways, and airports (Oliveira, 2011). The MoT has identified one of Brazil's biggest problems to be an unbalanced transportation mix, one that relies too heavily on road and air travel rather than rail and water transport, the latter being more efficient in terms of energy consumption (Gregoire, 2011). Hence, the government has taken a number of actions to improve and expand the transportation infrastructure, shift the mix of transport modes, and improve its safety and security. While safety/security and infrastructure are clearly linked, they will initially be addressed separately.

The Brazilian government launched the first PAC in January 2007 to restart public investment and encourage private sector involvement. In the first phase of PAC, the program concluded work on 6377 kilometers of road and 909 kilometers of railway, only approximately 15 percent of its roadway goal and 36 percent of its goal for the rail system. The government announced Phase 2 of PAC in March 2011, but critics fear that it too will fall short of its goals (Oliveira, 2011). On 15 August 2012, President Rousseff announced plans to privatize the road and railway system to boost investment. The first phase of road concessions included federal highways in three states: Rio de Janeiro, Sao Paulo, and Rio Grande do Sul. The second phase added four more states while an additional five states were added in the third phase. Public–private railway projects under PAC include north-south railway and west-east integration railway projects as well as plans for a high-speed rail from Rio de Janeiro to Sao Paulo to Campinas.

In February 2012, a decision was made to grant 20-year concessions for the three main airports in Sao Paulo and Brasilia (Infosurhoy, 2012). In December 2012, the Brazilian government released a plan to construct eight new mega-airports and 800 new regional airports. The goal, according to Brazilian President Dilma Rousseff, is to have an airport within 60 kilometers of any city with 100 000 or more people (Hilderbrand, 2013).

The Brazilian government is committed to infrastructure development in the Amazon region as well. The new bridge over the Rio Negro is part of a much larger development plan that includes the re-paving of almost 900 kilometers of highway into Manaus, a new road south to Porto Vehlo, and a 600-kilometer gas pipeline designed to power a new electricity power plant for the region (Carrington, 2010).

CONCLUSION

The last two decades have brought tremendous change to Brazil. Economic growth and the demographic and social changes that come with it have placed increasing pressure on the transportation sector. In terms of transportation safety and security, there are actually two Brazils. The coastal cities have reasonably developed public transportation, although there is a lack of transport linkage between cities other than by air and road. The key security challenges in coastal Brazil are crime and drug-related activity. Transportation is vital to the movement of illegal cargos and passenger transportation hubs represent areas of crime opportunity as they provide a high concentration of crime targets. The Favela Pacification Program represents one way to deal with crime hot spots as it targets such areas for additional police presence. Other means of dealing with this issue include the non-human presence of surveillance technology and the design or redesign of public areas.

If the concentration of human activity in coastal Brazil creates a certain set of challenges in this area, then the Brazilian interior which is dominated by the Amazon basin represents the opposite problem, that is, sparsely populated, undeveloped areas with limited access and even more limited control. This is where Brazil struggles with controling activity across its borders – smuggling (drugs, weapons, goods such as derived from illegal mining or logging) and criminal/insurgent activity aimed at or involving neighboring countries. This is where aerial surveillance can assist with a special emphasis on unmanned systems; however, integrating unmanned systems into a national airspace is not simple, as even developed nations have discovered. This area of Brazil has a high concentration of general aviation traffic. Much of this traffic flies using Visual Flight Rules (VFR) rather than Instrument Flight Rules (IFR). Small, unmanned systems would certainly represent a safety risk and require additional equipage to aircraft, such as GPS. Even general aviation pilots/owners in developed nations such as the US have resisted calls to mandate GPS or Automated Dependent Surveillance-Broadcast (ADS-B) technology into their aircraft due to costs. Safety and security on the ground also present challenges. This region contains the bulk of the unpaved roads and airports. These are a source of safety concern. Further, security can be problematic. On the roadways, there is limited monitoring, human or technological. At some airports, there may be little more than a grassy field and a windsock. Clearly, this interior Brazil presents many transportation security concerns. It also represents a difficult set of trade-offs for Brazil and the world. The more developed the infrastructure becomes, the more access the outside has to this sensitive, ecological region. There will be more tourists, more industrial development, and more permanent settlement. While economic growth and transportation development have the potential to raise standards of living in the region and in Brazil overall, they will have a generally negative impact on the fragile Amazon basin.

REFERENCES

Agence France-Presse (2012), 'Brazil's general aviation sector booming despite global woes', *Hurriyet Daily News*, available at: http://www.hurriyetdailynews.com/brazils-general-aviation-sector-booming-despite-global-woes.aspx?pageID=238&nID=28131&NewsCatID=344 (accessed 7 August 2013).

Amazon Center for Environmental Education and Research (2013), 'The Amazon basin: amazing facts and figures', available at: http://www.wcupa.edu/aceer/amigos/cd/rainforest.htm (accessed 6 August 2013).

Angloinfo Brazil (2013), 'Transport in Brazil', available at: http://brazil.angloinfo.com/transport/ (accessed 6 August 2013).

Associated Press (2013), 'Security concerns dog Brazil in World Cup anticipation', Fox News Latino, available at: http://latino.foxnews.com/latino/sports2012.06/13/security-concerns-dog-brazil-in-world-cup-anticipation (accessed 15 April 2015).

Brazilian Association for General Aviation (2011), '2nd Yearbook of Brazilian General Aviation', available at: http://www.abag.org.br/anuario_aviacao/documents/2ndYearbookofBrazillianGeneralAviation.pdf (accessed 8 August 2013).

Brazilian Institute of Geography and Statistics (2013), 'Population', available at: http://www.ibge.gov.br/english/#sub_populacao (accessed 6 August 2013).

Carrington, Damian (2010), 'First Amazon bridge to open world's greatest rainforest to development', *The Guardian*, available at: http://www.theguardian.com/

environment/2010/jul/29/manaus-bridge-amazon-rainforest (accessed 7 August 2013).
CIA Factbook (2013), 'The World Factbook: Brazil', available at: https://www.cia. gov/library/publications/the-world-factbook/geos/br.html (accessed 6 August 2013).
Embassy of Brazil in Wellington (2013), 'Transportation', available at: http://www. brazil.org.nz/page/transportation.aspx (accessed 6 August 2013).
Fischer, E. (2012), 'Brazil's airport expansions: ready for takeoff?', airport-technology.com, available at: http://www.airport-technology.com/features/ featurebrazil-airport-expansion-ready-for-take-off (accessed 15 April 2015).
Gray, D. (2013), 'Brazil faces infrastructure shortfalls', *The Rio Times*, 1 October, available at: http://riotimesonline.com/page/5/?s=Doug+Gray (accessed 29 September 2015).
Green Toad Bus (2013), 'Green Toad: Brazil bus travel', available at: http://www. greentoadbus.com/en/Bus-travel-in-brazil-196 (accessed 15 April 2015).
Gregoire, James (2011), 'Transport infrastructure in Brazil and the consequences of development failure', NEXUS Infrastructure, available at: http://www.nexus-infrastructure.com (accessed 15 April 2015).
Hilderbrand, Van P. (2013), 'Strong economic growth has Brazil's business aviation market booming', Association of Corporate Counsel, available at: http://www. lexology.com/library/detail.aspx?g=03cfb47d-d6d9-4087-a482-ce0d19078578 (accessed 7 August 2013).
Infosurhoy (2012), 'Brazil unveils transport bids to boost economy', available at: http://infosurhoy.com/cocoon/saii/xhtml/en_GB/features/saii/news-briefs/2012/08/16/newsbrief-03 (accessed 15 April 2015).
MercoPress (2011), 'Brazilian cruise industry expects sharp slowdown because of limited port capacity', available at: http://en.mercopress.com/2011/07/21/ brazilian-cruise-industry-expects-sharp-slowdown-because-of-limited-port-capacity (accessed 15 April 2015).
Moraes, T. (2010), 'Brazil Infrastructure', available at: http://www.gwu.edu/~clai/ working_papers/Moraes_Thais_11-10.pdf (accessed 15 April 2015).
Oliveira, Nelza (2011), 'Brazil overcoming historical lack of infrastructure investment', Infosurhoy, available at: http://infosurhoy.com/cocoon/saii/xhtml/en_GB/ features/saii/features/economy/2011/01/06/feature-03 (accessed 7 August 2013).
Pires, Christine and Oliveira, Nelza (2011), 'Brazil: waterways gain prominence in 2011', Infosurhoy, available at: http://infosurhoy.com/cocoon/saii/xhtml/en_GB/ features/saii/features/economy/2011/03/01/feature-03 (accessed 6 August 2013).
Prada, Paulo and Boadle, Anthony (2013), 'Pope's Brazil visit raises red flags for World Cup, Olympics', Reuters, available at: http://in.reuters.com/assets/ rpint?aid=INDEE96R07J20130728 (accessed 2 August 2013).
Reel, Monte (2006), 'Brazil's road to energy independence', *Washington Post*, available at: http://www.washingtonpost.com/wp-dyn/content/article/2006/08/19/ AR2006081900842.html (accessed 6 August 2013).
Ribeiro, Flavia (2012), 'Rio+20: a security force of 20,000', Infosurhoy, available at: http://infosurhoy.com/cocoon/saii/xhtml/en_GB/features/saii/features/ main/2012/05/31/feature-02 (accessed 15 April 2015).
Romero, Simon (2011), 'Special Report: energy; offshore oil helps Brazil lead boom', *The New York Times*, available at: http://query.nytimes.com/gst/fullpage. html?res=9B0CE1D91439F937A25753C1A9679D8B63 (accessed 6 August 2013).

Schoon, Robert (2014), 'Brazil increases drone power as Spain transfers UAV tech to South America giant', *Latin Post*, available at: http://www.latinpost.com/articles/7299/20140213/brazil-increases-drone-power-as-spain-transfers-uav-tech-to-the-south-american-giant.htm (accessed 15 April 2015).

Sibaja, Marco (2012), 'Brazil air travel triples since 2002 – pressure to prepare for the 2014 World Cup and 2016 Olympics', available at: http://dilemma-x.net/2012/01/26/brazil-air-travel-triples-since-2002-pressure-to-prepare-for-the-2014-world-cup-and-2016-olympics/ (accessed 6 August 2013).

Stuenkel, O. (2010), 'Strategic international threats surrounding Brazil', KAS International Reports, available at: http://www.gppi.net/fileadmin/gppi/Stuenkel_KAS_Report_2010_.pdf (accessed 15 April 2015).

US Department of State (2013a), 'Brazil 2013 Crime and Safety report: Rio de Janeiro', OSAC, available at: https://www.osac.gov/Pages/ContentReportDetails.aspx?cid=13966 (accessed 7 August 2013).

US Department of State (2013b), 'Brazil 2013 Crime and Safety report: Brasilia', OSAC, available at: https://www.osac.gov/Pages/ContentReportDetails.aspx?cid=13966 (accessed 7 August 2013).

Vergueiro (2010), 'Brazilian Security Structure', available at: https://www.fas.org/irp/world/brazil/fabrverg.pdf (accessed 15 April 2015).

Williams, Nathan E. (2011), 'Brazil faces infrastructure race', *The Rio Times*, http://riotimesonline.com/brazil-news/rio-business/brazil-faces-2014-infrastructure-race/ (accessed 6 August 2013).

Winter, Brian (2012), 'Special Report: Brazil's gringo problem: its borders', available at: http://www.reuters.com/article/2012/04/13/us-brazil-borders-idUSBRE83C0KB20120413 (accessed 15 April 2015).

World Health Organization (2013), 'Number of Registered Vehicles Data by Country', available at: APPS.WHO.INT/GHO/DATA/NODE.MAIN.A995 (accessed 29 September 2015).

World Population Review (2013), 'Population of Brazil 2013', available at: http://worldpopulationreview.com/population-of-brazil/ (accessed 7 August 2013).

World Wide Inland Navigation Network (2013), 'South America: Brazil', available at: http://www.wwinn.org/brazil-inland-waterways (accessed 15 April 2015).

19. Conclusions

Genserik L. L. Reniers, Dawna L. Rhoades, Joseph S. Szyliowicz and Luca Zamparini

The goal of this book has been to provide a theoretical and practical review of the safety and security issues associated with transports of freight and/ or passengers via road, rail, water or air, or so-called multimodal transportation. As has been noted in the Introduction and by Nieuwenhuis (Chapter 2), the first challenge is to define the concept of intermodalism and to distinguish between multimodal and intermodal transportation. Multimodal transportation literally means the use of more than one mode of transport for the movement of people or goods from an origin to a destination. The term intermodal, on the other hand, refers to a very different analytical concept; intermodal suggests a level of integration, coordination, and efficiency that may well be missing from a simple multimodal journey. Though 'intermodalism' captures the essence of the process, what the process actually involves remains unclear as is evident if we consider some of the ways in which the term has been defined.

For example, consider the following popular definition: 'the coordinated passage of goods and people by way of two or more of the primary modes of transport (sea, air, rail, road) from origin to destination as defined by the passenger or the shipper and consignee, with a single travel directive bill of lading or ticket and a single price covering the entire trip' (Alt et al., 1997, p. 36ff.). This definition captures the integration dimension well but it fails to include other critical elements – choice and inclusiveness – that many consider to be integral dimensions. Thus, intermodalism has also been defined more broadly as: 'a system that is both safe and efficient and productive and flexible in responding to the needs for good movements and . . . offer(s) people choices and flexibility in their personal movements. This system must also be "international, intelligent and inclusive"' (Jeff, 1998, p. 13). Yet many would argue that even this definition is inadequate because it does not recognize explicitly the externalities of a transportation system. It is obviously possible to develop an integrated system that is safe, efficient, flexible, intelligent, international and inclusive but which continues to pollute the environment and waste energy. Nor does it consider the critical elements of safety and security, elements that are essential in today's world.

Accordingly, it is necessary to expand the definition to include such factors as safety, efficiency, cost-effectiveness and long-term sustainability. Thus, we suggest the following definition: An intermodal system is one in which the individual modes are linked, governed, and managed in a manner that creates a seamless and sustainable transportation system. Such a system should be economically efficient, environmentally sound, safe and secure, and ethically based.

We are convinced that this view of 'intermodal transportation' is truly the 'destination' that is required if we are ever to create a safe and secure global system of transportation that serves the needs of people everywhere.

Given this perspective, it is clear that we believe that if stakeholders approach the transportation system as separate modes which happen to be connected in a current origin–destination itinerary, then it will be difficult if not impossible to achieve an adequate level of safety and security because it is at the nexus of the different modes that the issue of safety and security is most acute. Only through coordination and information exchange at all steps of the transportation journey, can systems that foster safety and security be developed. Because the transportation system is global in nature, this coordination and communication must take place not only between the different modes of transport and the parties involved in these personal or firm journeys, but also between the various national governments over which the journeys will take place. Disagreements over the various roles, responsibilities and requirements continue to create friction in the transportation system itself and require attention.

The editors faced a second decision point early in the planning for this volume: Can we adequately cover multimodal transport for both passenger and freight transportation in a single volume? After serious debate, the decision was made to combine both areas in a single volume, although this necessarily limited the coverage of both areas. A comprehensive coverage of the topic would have required multiple volumes in a series. Further, the reality is that passenger travel in many countries has continued to shift to road transport and many overall trips include only this form of transport. Two examples of this unbalanced passenger system can be found in Chapter 14 on the United States and Chapter 18 on Brazil. Both countries have transportation systems that emphasize road transport over all other forms of travel. In the case of Brazil, this emphasis on road transport occurs even when the infrastructure is seriously inadequate. Still, the stated goal of the national policies reviewed across this volume is to develop a more balanced, sustainable (safe and secure) passenger transport system. Whether the actual policies proposed and implemented in these countries will achieve this goal is a matter for the reader to decide, although most of the authors in this volume have assumed that the actions reviewed are moving in a positive direction.

For freight transport, there is no question that intermodalism is the rule rather than the exception with containerized traffic representing the bulk of the tonnage shipped. Globalization, communications, container and related technologies, just-in-time processes, and cost pressures have led to increasingly long and complex supply chains that invariably include a variety of transportation modes. Seven years on from the events of the Global Financial Crisis of 2008/2009 the levels of trade and the sense of a system bursting at the seams have not yet returned, but global supply chains continue to present challenges to safety and security. The complexity of these networks and the growing number of parties involved in them has added to the vulnerability of these supply chains.

Part I began this volume with a review of the challenges posed by complex multimodal supply chains. Nieuwenhuis (Chapter 2) explored the links and parties involved in a typical supply chain from the Far East to Europe, setting the stage for Zamparini (Chapter 3) to discuss economic models, including cost and benefit calculations, affecting firm choices in transport. Having examined the challenges and the basic economics, Vilko, Lättilä, and Hallikas (Chapter 4) added the assessment of vulnerabilities into consideration of supply chain design. Depré, Reniers and Zamparini (Chapter 5) further looked at ways to insure against certain risks involved in multimodal transports. Likewise, Part III set the stage for discussions on passenger transport viewing the challenges (Chapter 12 by Bak and Burnewicz) and economic models and policy issues (Chapter 13 by Zamparini). Again, these chapters are intended to be a starting point in understanding intermodal safety and security issues. It is clear from these chapters that there is no one best approach nor any simple answer that ensures a high degree of safety and security with a low level of investment. The unique circumstances of each supply chain (links from origin to destination, parties and commodities involved) make simple answers unworkable. Each contribution to this volume has attempted to raise key country issues for consideration and outline ways that they are or can be resolved. It is therefore important to analyze these measures and approaches in order to identify their strengths and weaknesses. By taking a practical look at national efforts to create and implement approaches and policies that are designed to increase the safety and security of their transportation system in the era of global trade and global terrorism, we are able to evaluate the contemporary levels of security that have been achieved and identify promising approaches that deserve careful consideration by all.

The countries in this volume represent developed and developing nations in each key region of the world. Though they reflect a great deal of diversity in culture, economic development, and political structure, it is clear that many face similar problems.

The example of Rail Baltica (Chapter 8 by Hilmola) shows the benefits of targeted investment on safety and security in transportation systems. Since safety and security improvements are increasingly linked to high technology investments, it is instructive to compare this example to those presented in Chapters 9 through 11. All of these examples deal with developing nations which face two challenges – less developed infrastructure and less money for development. These problems are acute in Africa (Chapter 9), but clearly still present in the more developed BRIC nations of China and Brazil. In Chapter 10, the authors note that small-scale theft and pilferage of cargo is rampant in China while halfway around the world, Brazil (Chapter 11) is struggling with a reputation as one of the most dangerous countries in the world for crimes involving cargo. Its geography, drug trafficking, corruption, and conflicting federal, civilian and military policing hamper coordination of transportation safety and security. In both countries, there are issues of ineffective policing in the face of well-trained and organized criminal organizations. However, though each country confronts a similar security issue, the many differences between them clearly call for different approaches to enhancing cargo security. In China, which does not confront the same administrative problems, increased technological surveillance may well provide an effective solution. Brazil, for its part, will clearly need to focus more on corruption since there are estimates that 80 percent of the crimes may involve company insiders. Still, while in one case there appears to be an urgent need to adopt policies and programs that minimize corruption, attention must also be paid to the adoption of other measures including the deployment of modern technologies since achieving intermodal passenger and freight security requires the implementation of a range of policies in many sectors.

This is the perspective that has been adopted by the US which has been a driving force in freight security and has adopted a number of strategic and tactical measures in its efforts to enhance passenger security as well. Chapter 14 discusses these measures which include the development and implementation of a strategic plan that focuses on the security of modal interactions. Though these measures have significantly increased passenger security, many perennial issues, that all states confront, require continuing attention. These include achieving effective and comprehensive collaboration among modes and organizations in the public and private sectors, including information sharing, the education and training of professionals at all levels, and the appropriate use of technology. Chapter 15 introduces an excellent example of efforts in the Netherlands to develop a truly comprehensive approach to intermodal transportation issues in accordance with EU Directive 2008/114/EC. The cornerstone of Dutch national security policy is a nationwide threat assessment called National Risk Assessment (NRA). Together with the NRA, large-scale well-elaborated intelligence is used to inform critical infrastructures, and thereby deal with the security of (among others) multimodal transport. A national coordinator for anti-terrorism and safety organism is responsible for proactively (through taking preventive measures) and reactively (via crisis management and emergency planning) handling security issues. The approach is driven by the fact that risks are interconnected and are not characterized with organizational borders, national borders, and policy fields. The Dutch example can provide a blueprint for countries inside and outside of the EU. Chapter 16 on Israel describes a multi-leveled approach to safety and security that has evolved over decades of threat in this nation. Israel has long been recognized by the level of security that operates throughout its system and this is particularly evident in its transportation networks. However, the system relies on 'solutions' that might not be acceptable or workable in a country such as India (Chapter 17). The explicit use of ethnic profiling might be politically unacceptable in any country with a large, multi-ethnic population. Further, efforts to separate travelers and limit access to certain neighborhoods could prove problematic. As a developing nation, India also has limited resources to invest in the hardware and software (GPS, CCTV) that could increase surveillance and reduce threats.

Profiling as a technique to improve security has received a great deal of attention and criticism in many countries including the US where diversity, civil liberties, and freedom from government actions have been considered cornerstones of political discourse and development for most of its history (Chapter 6). Of course, this did not prevent the development of watch lists based on 'behavioral factors' not explicitly linked to race, religion, or ethnicity.

After reading through this volume, it will be clear that experts in many nations have converged on some key elements of a safer, more secure system of multimodal transportation; however, several other facts will also become clear. In a world of multimodal transport governments by and large are still frozen in a regulatory world of single modalities: road, rail, water, air. Governments still make policy and promulgate regulations largely as if the different modes of transport were unconnected. High-level White Papers may discuss plans to correct this situation and coordinate regulation and oversight, but bureaucratic inertia and jurisdictional disputes hamper changes. Thus, while safety and security challenges are most pressing at the hubs and nodes where transport modes and cargos meet, it is clear that policy, oversight, and regulations remain weak. In a rapidly changing world, governments remain one of the slowest parts of the system. Changing the stovepipe structure of transportation regulation in ways that allow for the type of interconnected regulation, oversight, and information sharing necessary to improve the overall system remains an unmet goal over a decade on from the events of 9/11. It is also true that while other modes of transport have advocacy groups that represent their interests to governments and work to create processes and systems that 'work' for their members, there is no such group for multimodal transportation similar to the International Air Transport Association (IATA) or the International Maritime Organization (IMO). Although these organizations are trade associations which have a political agenda to advocate for policies and regulations that foster and protect their members, they have also been the source of a number of coordinating policies over the years that have added to the safety and security of their respective systems. For example, IATA was instrumental in the creation of standards for ticketing, interlining, carry-on size, and devising methods for payment, etc. Through their connection with the intergovernmental International Civil Aviation Organization (ICAO), they have worked on the various annexes to the ICAO Convention. These 18 annexes cover everything from personnel licensing through safe transport of dangerous goods. Whether such an intermodal trade association is necessary or desirable is a matter of debate, but it would certainly provide a way of organizing this group of stakeholders and allow them to counter other groups that might be presenting policies and proposals that they perceive as harming their interests.

While Van Gulijk, Anderson and Reniers (Chapter 15) provided an example of comprehensive transportation safety and security planning, even when governments attempt to create such plans, the classic Total Quality Management problem occurs, that is, the weakness is not in the planning nor in the doing, but in the checking (monitoring), and acting (revising for continuous improvement). The finding that public and private institutions across the board tend to be weakest in the monitoring and continuous improvement area would not surprise either academics or practitioners. Of course, there is a further complication in these efforts, namely secrecy. There are clearly valid reasons why governments and firms do not want to reveal the flaws and weaknesses in their systems to potential thieves, pirates, and terrorists. This limits the ability of researchers and other members of the public in our efforts to judge the efficiency and effectiveness of policies and programs. At its most extreme, we may be left to conclude that if no incidences have occurred (become public), then the system is working. There are obvious flaws with this assumption and the very nature of political processes tend to highlight success and downplay failure, unless you are the opposition party.

Clearly, the groups intent on challenging intermodal transportation safety and security continue to evolve their targets and tactics, but the global community has also developed a host of countermeasures, including a number of advanced hardware and software solutions. As this volume has demonstrated, there continues to be wide variation in the application of some of these solutions. Other 'answers' to security solutions have been driven by the major trading nations, notably the US. While we have not seen any physical attacks on the scale of 9/11, Madrid 2004 or London 2005, we cannot conclude that we have overcome the issues that threaten intermodal freight and passenger security and safety. We still have few answers in the case of Malaysia Airlines Flight 370, but what we do know seems to indicate that intragovernmental and intergovernmental conflicts in roles and resources contributed to the situation. It is essential that all of the parties in the global transportation network come together to create the seamless and sustainable transportation system that we have suggested should be our goal.

REFERENCES

Alt, R., P. Forster and J. King (1997), 'The great reversal; information and transportation infrastructure in the intermodal vision', in *National Conference on Intermodal Transportation Research Framework*, Washington, DC, p. 34.

Jeff, G. (1998), 'Welcoming remarks', in *Intermodal Education and Training*, Washington, DC: National Academy Press, p. 13.

Index

310 *Multimodal transport security*